Ethical Journalism in a Populist Age

The Democratically Engaged Journalist

STEPHEN J. A. WARD

ROWMAN & LITTLEFIELD
Lanham • Boulder • New York • London

Executive Editor: Elizabeth Swayze
Assistant Editor: Megan Manzano
Senior Marketing Manager: Kim Lyons

Credits and acknowledgments for material borrowed from other sources, and reproduced with permission, appear on the appropriate page within the text.

Published by Rowman & Littlefield
An imprint of The Rowman & Littlefield Publishing Group, Inc.
4501 Forbes Boulevard, Suite 200, Lanham, Maryland 20706
www.rowman.com

Unit A, Whitacre Mews, 26-34 Stannary Street, London SE11 4AB, United Kingdom

British Library Cataloguing in Publication Information Available

Library of Congress Cataloging-in-Publication Data Available

ISBN 978-1-5381-1071-3 (cloth : alk. paper)
ISBN 978-1-5381-1072-0 (pbk. : alk. paper)
ISBN 978-1-5381-1073-7 (electronic)

♾™ The paper used in this publication meets the minimum requirements of American National Standard for Information Sciences—Permanence of Paper for Printed Library Materials, ANSI/NISO Z39.48-1992.

Printed in the United States of America

To the ethical journalists who toil in the fields of journalism, upholding their integrity and their public purpose, in a media world seemingly gone mad.

Contents

Acknowledgments

I owe a debt of gratitude to my spouse and musical muse, Nadia Francavilla, for patiently supporting my writing of this book over the dead of a Canadian winter, as my mind abided in the luxurious realm of ideas. I thank poet Robert Shiplett and artist Stephen Scott for welcoming me to my new home in Fredericton, with weekly discourses on politics, media, and art over a glass of wine.

I

JOURNALISM IN A TOXIC PUBLIC SPHERE

Polluted Spheres,
Eroding Democracies

What is the city but the people?

—*William Shakespeare, Coriolanus*

A POLLUTED PUBLIC SPHERE

Democracy Eroding

This book explains how journalists can protect and advance egalitarian, dialogic democracy, locally and globally. Rescuing democracy will require that journalists reconceive their role in society. It will require the articulation of new ethical norms and practices. It will require concrete action. Journalists, in collaboration with other democratic agencies, need to join common cause to detox a polluted public sphere.

This book is a work in journalism ethics, defined as the norms that should guide the social practice of journalism. It presumes that democracy is in serious trouble, and journalists can—and must—do something about it. It also presumes that, of all the problems that beset journalism, its troubled relationship to democracy is crucial. Journalism should be a democratic craft, antagonistic to undemocratic forces of any type. While journalism can (and does) exist without democracy, no form of democracy worth having can exist without a journalism dedicated to democratic principles.

Democracy is a problem for several reasons. The *practice* of democracy, as a working system of government that seeks to be plural and egalitarian, is in deep trouble. The pillars of egalitarian democracy are shaken every day by intolerant voices advancing racism or xenophobia or representing some form of economic or class privilege. The *ideal* of democracy—a place where citizens deliberate impartially and factually on the common good—fails to guide politics. In the United States and many other countries, we witness the erosion of democratic communities bound by norms of tolerance, compromise, dialogue, and objective facts. Citizens who disagree with extreme populists or intolerant majorities are dismissed as unpatriotic citizens.

Three large factors have created, in large part, this current turmoil: (1) the rise of a global public sphere; (2) the rise of extremism populism, and its infiltration of mainstream politics; and (3) the rise of information technologies that can be used to spread misinformation, division, and hatred. Despite the creative media unleashed by the digital revolution, the public sphere is corrupted in its capacity to discern truth from falsity, sincere reporters from manipulative voices, experts from ideologues, facts from uninformed assertion. The channels of information that inform democratic citizens—the very lifeblood of democracy—are polluted by false information, conspiracy theories, ideological extremism, and manipulative groups. Not *all* of the public sphere is polluted. But so much of it is corrupted that new and strenuous efforts are needed to detox the sphere.

Extremism

At the center of the book's focus is extremism in thought, word, and deed, especially in the domain of politics. Extremism leads to groups using the latest in communication technology to create a populist political media that disturbs and biases how the public understands issues and how they make political decisions. The more that extreme messages are circulated in our digital, global media, the greater likelihood that citizens, often frustrated by more moderate politics, may adopt more extreme beliefs and "solutions" to complex problems.

To call anything "extreme" is to say that an object has some feature to a high or intense degree, such as extremely hot or extremely inflammable. *Extreme* is a relative term. Saying something is extreme makes sense if we agree on what constitutes moderation in this case. I say my kitchen oven, when turned on "high" for its self-cleaning process, is extremely hot, relative to lower temperatures. But my oven is barely warm compared to the heat of the earth's core. Similarly, people can be extremely irritable or extremely violent compared with more placid, nonviolent people. It all depends on your frame of reference.

The frame of reference is important in politics when we talk about extreme beliefs and groups. Depending on the context, some people may think my strong support for free speech an extreme viewpoint. An association of atheists may be regarded by conservative Christians as promoting an extreme, even dangerous, belief, but more-liberal Christians may disagree. We may say that "X is more extreme in his views about when to use nuclear weapons than Y, who is a moderate, stressing restraint." One might define moderate views statistically as the mean between weak and extreme forms of a belief, or what is "normal" from a quantitative perspective. But such methods are not always reliable. In a country that is enthralled with a young, extreme distractor who promises to rid a country of Jews and other miscreants, the mean for political beliefs will be extreme.

The frame of reference for this book is the principles of one form of moderate democracy: egalitarian, dialogic democracy. I will define this form of democracy later. Examples of its principles are the right of all citizens to vote, equality before the law, and respect for all groups. This political framework is moderate relative to what? Relative to other views of democracy and the principles of nondemocratic systems. What makes moderate democracy moderate is its inclusive, tolerant attitude toward all groups in society and its opposition to measures that would discriminate against any of them. It is also moderate in its attitude toward foreigners, new immigrants, and other countries. As I discuss later, moderate democracy does not view its nation as superior, nor does it adopt a xenophobic, aggressive stance toward other nations or cultures. Moderate democracy is not tribalism.

From the perspective of moderate democracy, we can identify three forms of extremism in political speech, where "speech" covers beliefs, communications, and conduct. The primary object of attack is social groups based on race, ethnicity, religion, or other features. In each case, the extremism ranges from strong speech to extreme speech to hate speech in two ways:

Extreme in content: There is a continuum where the content of political speech is increasingly extreme in terms of intensity and cruelty. Strong speech is the expressions of people with firm, negative opinions about other people, other races, or other religions. People may say that blacks, Catholics, the Irish, or Jews are not to be trusted or have immoral characters, such as being prone to crime, drunkenness, or unpatriotic loyalties (e.g., to a pope). This bias may be expressed indirectly, such as by opposing further immigration of refugees as a way of excluding people of certain nationalities or religions. Extreme speech turns these views "up a notch" in strength. Extremists do not simply suggest that certain groups are inferior, but state it publicly and repeatedly. They malign the persons, beliefs, and/or practices of certain groups, while praising the virtues of their favored groups. They ridicule a group's beliefs, such as the Catholic belief in the transubstantiation of the host during mass. Hate speech goes even further than extreme speech. It is virulent and *sustained* attacks on the integrity of a group, usually associated with threats or violent action against the hated groups. Hate speech dehumanizes the group by comparing them to rats, dogs, or scum or uses old conspiracy theories to stereotype the group as dangerous. It declares that the group is not entitled to citizenship or participation in society.

Extreme in action: As we move along the continuum of extremism, we also notice a continuum concerning action—what extremists are prepared to do. A person who has strong opinions about groups may keep them to himself, but the person of extreme speech will be more willing to engage in media and political campaigns to support his political views and more willing to publicly insult groups. Persons of extreme or hate speech are more likely to physically attack groups. In what follows, I will take extremists on the right to be the main examples of people on the strong-extreme-hate speech continuum. There are far-left groups who display intolerant attitudes. But I focus on the right wing because, today, they are the most influential and numerous sources of extremism in society.

The Circle of Extremism

What types of people engage in extremism in politics? The most familiar examples come to mind immediately: neo-Nazi groups, members of the KKK, and so on. However, if we pay attention only to these examples, we fail to see how the continuum from strong to extreme to hate speech applies to many other groups. There are groups less obnoxious and more socially respectable. There are right-wing institutes and highly conservative think tanks that support their strong, and at times extreme, speech on issues with studies and experts. There are groups that watch the mainstream media and look for liberal biases. There is, online, every type of extreme speech possible, such as trolls who harass moderates and liberals. There are people who spread conspiracy theories; there are extremists who act as political activists and lobbyists in state capitals. There are the politicians, party leaders, and presidents of countries who are spokespersons for strong or extreme views, supported by media outlets and commentators.

Some of these groups are directly known to each other and form networks. Many are not connected. For example, the conservative Heritage Foundation in the United States would, I believe, disavow any linkage with neo-Nazis groups. Yet, in total, right-wing groups form a web of organizations that have overlapping political attitudes. They share views on the problems and solutions to issues, from the need to restrict immigration and scale down (or privatize) social programs to the need for firm, militaristic responses to foreign enemies. Over time, this form of political discourse has a cumulative effect, creating a political climate that makes strong and extreme attitudes more acceptable, and mainstream. I call this the circle of extremism. The circle can push forward ever increasing intolerant views, even if the groups have different aims and do not work in concert.

Figure 1.1 represents the circle of extremism as a number of embedded circles.

The continuum of extremism helps us to understand the types of public debate in a democracy. Figure 1.2 represents the types as belonging to zones, the main division being the difference between zones of respectful or disrespectful speech. Disrespectful means the participants have little or no tolerance for the other person's view, a penchant to misrepresent and ridicule other views, a willingness to restrict the expression of that view, and a tendency to attribute the absurdity or falsehood of the view to alleged weaknesses in the intelligence or character of the people who hold the view. Disrespectful speech does not care to listen or learn, let along seek a compromise. In the diagram, the worst forms of extreme speech are on the right.

It is not the aim of this book to explain scientifically why humans are drawn to extremism. That is a task for social psychology. But I do offer these thoughts. Extreme speech is a persistent feature of human history, rooted in tribalism, a product of evolution. Within humans, there is, and will always be, a core of emotions, feelings, and desires that await a stressful circumstance or a timely speech by a persuasive orator to turn us into intolerant, unjust,

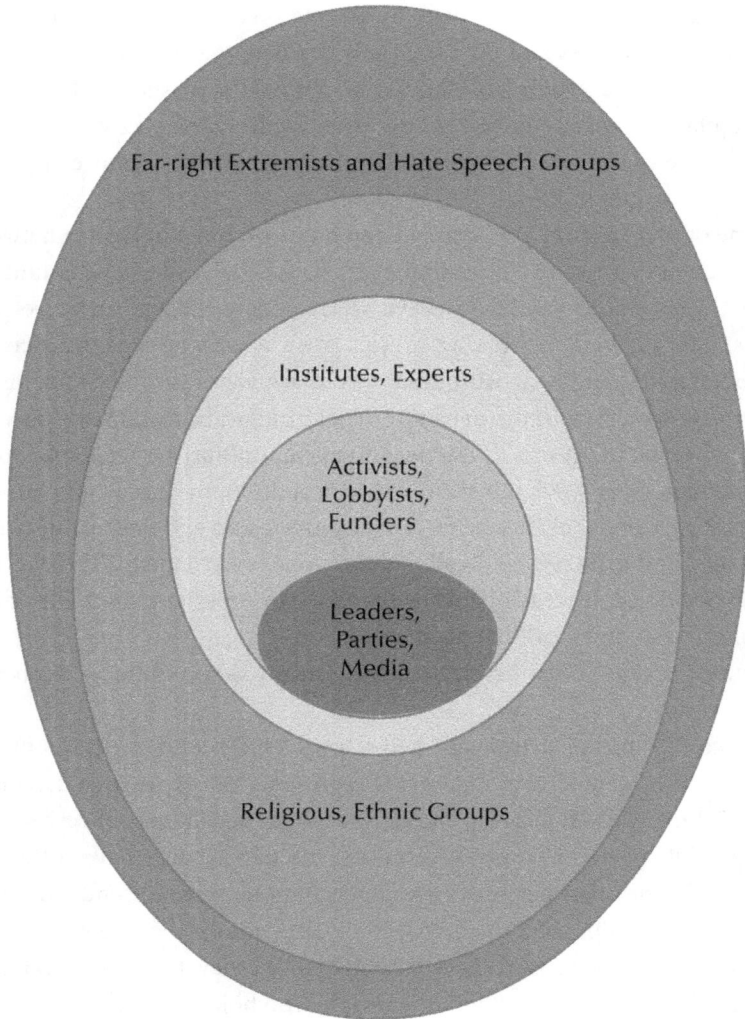

Far-right Extremists and Hate Speech Groups

Institutes, Experts

Activists,
Lobbyists,
Funders

Leaders,
Parties,
Media

Religious, Ethnic Groups

FIGURE 1.1

and unthinking members of groups. As a war reporter, I witnessed otherwise civilized peoples kill each other in brutal civil wars, attacking people who not long ago were their neighbors. If civilization is a sort of "veneer" over our rough human nature, then extreme speech is an effective means of cracking that vital veneer and probing deeper into the human psyche. For whatever

Zone of Respectful Speech		Zone of Disrespectful Speech	
⬇		⬇	
Agreement	Reasonable Disagreement	Strong or Extreme Disagreement	Hate Speech

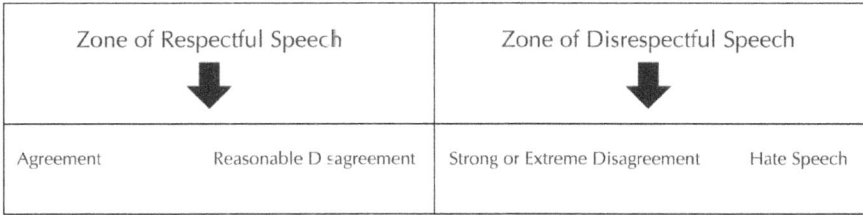

FIGURE 1.2
Forms of Public Debate

reason, human psychology changes when an individual enters a group, and some group ecologies, like that of extreme political groups, can transform people from moderates to immoderates; from people who once espoused peace, love, and charity to people who desire retribution, conflict, cruelty, and violence. This is not to return to the medieval Augustinian view of "man" as so thoroughly corrupted by sin that he is naturally and incurably bad or evil, and so needs strong authoritarian leadership. It is to say that humans consist of faculties and capacities that can be developed for good or evil. The social environment, including the speech of the community, is crucial in deciding whether we resist extremism or not.

Extremism and Populism

In the following chapters, I will have much to say about populism and extreme populism. In this introductory chapter, my aim is to alert the reader to how the rise of global media has given extreme groups new opportunities to publicize their opinions, malign innocent people, incite intolerance, scapegoat the vulnerable, and, today, have real influence in elections from the United States to France and Italy, and beyond. The extremists are skilled in combining journalism (techniques of arresting narrative and dramatic images) and populism (appeals to the people) to create what I call a powerful, extreme Net populism, which, as much as anything else, is a threat to moderate democracy.

Surveys show that what are called populist parties, when they should be called extreme populist parties, on the right and the left have enjoyed increasing electoral success in Western democracies. The average share of the vote for "populist right" parties doubled from 6.7 percent in the 1960s to 13.4 percent in the 2010s, while "populist left" parties support rose from 2.4 percent to

12.7 percent in the same period.[1] Consider only one recent example. In Italy, the March 2018 federal election, the first in five years, was watched closely as a test of extreme populism. Voters handed a majority of votes in a national election to the Five Star Movement and the League, "hard-right and populist forces that ran a campaign fueled by anti-immigrant anger."[2] The election threw cold water on the growing belief that "populists" were in retreat in Western Europe after Chancellor Angela Merkel of Germany and President Emmanuel Macron of France overcame far-right insurgencies in the past year or so. The problem here is not so much populism. As I will argue later, populism has taken good and bad forms historically. What is worrisome is the *use* of populist techniques of persuasion and rhetoric to make extremism attractive and popular in many parts of the world.

Extreme populists gain popularity when countries experience difficult social and economic conditions and democratic mechanisms are slow to respond to crises. Portraying themselves as "outsiders" to the governing establishment, the extremists become dangerous demagogues. They take advantage of deep divides, fears, hatreds, and inequalities inherent in societies that are growing increasingly polarized. They work to undermine democracy *internally*, i.e., by using the institutions and rules of democracy against itself until they, or their party, control the levers of power. Meanwhile, the values, virtues, and unwritten norms of democratic culture—tolerance, restraint, compromise, dialogue, a desire for impartiality and objective fact, and respect for political opponents—is rejected for "politics as warfare," where one's ideological and personal ends justify almost any means. All is done, cynically, in the name of the people. They are assisted in their political rise to power by news media, journalists, sympathetic civic groups, powerful businessmen and corporations, members of the military, and so on. And now these "tyrants-in-waiting," as Plato called democratic demagogues, have the immense global power of the Internet, including social media, to recruit, persuade, and disrupt.

Can It Happen in the USA?

How far will extreme populism go? What about in the United States? Could extremism undermine its democracy?

Surely, one of the world's oldest and most stable (and affluent) democratic republics, with its constitution, checks and balances, and large middle class, cannot be shaken by a swaggering demagogue who panders to people's biases and fears? I would warn against any complacency. In 2016, the country elected a swaggering demagogue who took advantage of a violent and polarized society, an "outsider" who accelerates the erosion of democratic norms. As Steven Levitsky and Daniel Ziblatt write:[3]

> If twenty-five years ago, someone had described to you a country in which candidates threatened to lock up their rivals, political opponents accused the government of stealing the election or establishing a dictatorship, and parties used their legislative majorities to impeach presidents and steal supreme court seats, you might have thought of Ecuador or Romania. You probably would not have thought of the United States.

Trump's electoral campaign and his first year or so in office used strategies of extreme populism: politicize institutions, demonize Mexicans as rapists and Muslims as terrorists, attack judges and the media, create fear and hatred, play to one's extreme electoral base, scapegoat immigrants or religious minorities, and dismiss criticism as "fake news" manufactured by your enemies. The real "decoded" meaning of "Make America Great Again" and "America First" is political tribalism, us versus them. He has filled the White House with war hawks, racist advisers, family, and cronies, while discarding staff who show the slightest disloyalty. His unending tweets and racist comments[4] erode unwritten democratic norms of decent presidential conduct.[5] A study using the *Washington Post*'s Fact Checker organization, which has been tracking Trump's false statements, found that by 2018 Trump made 1,628 false or misleading claims, about 6 per day. The study also found that the average rate of lying among university students and members of the public is about 1 per day. An "astonishing" 50 percent of Trump's lies were hurtful or disparaging of others.

Trump's odious behavior, once thought to be something we could just laugh at and dismiss, has a long-term impact on politics. It desensitizes us to lying, exaggeration, and arrogance, paving the way for similar conduct by others in the future. This is democracy by whim, not fact; by emotion, not reason; by loyalty rather than merit; by authoritarian bullying and threatening, not by dialogue or empathy. It is, by my definition, extreme.

Worries about Trump's impact on democratic institutions are growing. When in early 2018 Trump fired Andrew McCabe, former deputy director of the FBI, for supposed incompetence, it was clear that the firing was politically motivated, and worse, callous. McCabe was fired two days before he was to retire, making him ineligible for a pension. McCabe responded by saying the president was waging an "ongoing war" on the FBI, and his firing shows what happens when people who are supposed to "protect our institutions become instruments for damaging those institutions and people." John Brennan, who ran the CIA under Obama, attacked Trump: "When the full extent of your venality, moral turpitude, and political corruption becomes known, you will take your place as a disgraced demagogue in the dustbin of history."[6]

Even should Trump disappear from the scene, the extreme and right-wing forces that propelled him to the White House will not disappear. The damage of allowing a right-wing demagogue into the White House has been done. It will not easily be mended. Yet this book is not about Trump. It is about the media and populist forces that create a public sphere where leaders *like* Trump can move into the mainstream of democratic politics.

MEASURING DEMOCRACY

State of Democracy, Globally

Is my view of the public sphere and democracy too negative?

Some American scholars are worried about Trump but have a rosier view of democracy than me. For example, Levitsky and Ziblatt doubt that democracy is declining in the world. They note that the number of democracies grew in the 1980s and 1990s and peaked in about 2005. It has remained stable since then.[7] Troubled democracies grab the headlines, but for every Hungary, Turkey, and Venezuela there is a Colombia, Sri Lanka, and Tunisia, which have become more democratic over the past decade. They acknowledge problems in European democracies but say there is "little evidence in any of them of the kind of fundamental erosion of norms we have seen in the United States." Despite "fundamental erosion," they do not believe American democracy will actually fail.

Other experts are not so sanguine.

Larry Diamond, a leading authority on democracy globally, believes the world has entered a period of "democratic recession."[8] The premise of a recent book, *Authoritarianism Goes Global*, by Diamond and others is that, over the past decade, illiberal powers have grown ever stronger and bolder in the global arena. Leading authoritarian countries—including China, Iran, Russia,

Saudi Arabia, and Venezuela—have developed new tools and strategies to contain the spread of democracy and challenge liberal movements internationally. At the same time, advanced democracies are failing to respond to the authoritarian threat. Undemocratic regimes repress civil society and control cyberspace. Diamond thinks the main task is to "reform and consolidate" democratic movements in emerging democracies in recent decades, such as South Africa.[9]

The news about human rights is also worrying. Amnesty International's 2016 report on the state of human rights stated:[10]

> 2016 saw the idea of human dignity and equality, the very notion of a human family, coming under vigorous and relentless assault from powerful narratives of blame, fear, and scapegoating, propagated by those who take or cling on to power at almost any cost . . . Donald Trump's poisonous campaign rhetoric exemplifies a global trend towards angrier and more divisive politics. Across the world, leaders and politicians wagered their future power on narratives of fear and disunity, pinning blame on the "other" for the real or manufactured grievances of the electorate.

To trace the trajectory of global democracy, we can consult many institutes, media organizations, and academics. Using detailed criteria, researchers measure whether democracy, free speech, human rights, and happiness are increasing or decreasing. The studies range from the United Nations survey of human happiness, *The Economist's* annual ranking of democracies, Freedom House's tracking of free speech, the Pew Research Center's polling on democracy, the World Press Freedom Index by Reporters Without Borders, and Amnesty International's reports on human rights. In addition, there are humanitarian groups such as the Millennium Project and journals such as *Journalism of Democracy*. Researchers can consult the World Values Survey, an expansive survey of changing social and political values conducted by social scientists around the world.[11] Also, the changing values of journalism are studied by the Worlds of Journalism project.[12] Finally, there are a host of "barometers" such as the Eurobarometer surveys, the Asian Barometer, and the Gallup polls.

There is no consensus on the correct way to measure democracy. Definitions of democracy are debated, and groups use different systems of measurement. One can approach democracy as a binary term—a country either is a democracy or is not. However, most groups measure democracy as a matter of degree, placing countries on a continuum from weak to full democracy. Also, there are differences in the use of indicators. One approach is "thin" or minimalist. A minimalist approach, such as employed by Freedom House in the United States, uses a limited number of indicators, e.g., free elections and respect for civil liberties.[13] For minimalists, democracy includes (1) government based on majority rule and consent of the governed; (2) the existence of free and fair elections; (3) protection and respect for minorities and human rights; and (4) equality before the law, due process, and political pluralism.

The thin approach corresponds to Robert Dahl's influential definition of democracy as government responsiveness to people's preferences. Democracy is measured by the capacity of citizens to participate in democratic processes, such as voting, competing for offices, and competing with others over policy. Dahl lists eight "guarantees" of democracy, from freedom of expression to freedom to form associations.[14] The guarantees indicate the degree to which a democracy allows citizens to participate in the "public contestation" that is politics. Another approach to defining democracy, such as employed by *The Economist*, is called "thick" because it includes variables not included by Dahl and other minimalists, such as the norms of political culture, the capacity of the government to function effectively, and so on.

Contrary to Levitsky and Ziblatt, recent measurements of democracy have found that democracy (and free speech and human rights) is in trouble while authoritarianism is on the rise. For example, the headline for *The Economist*'s 2017 democracy index, released in January 2018, was "Democracy Continues Its Disturbing Retreat."[15] According to the index, Norway remains the most democratic. Western Europe accounted for fourteen of the nineteen full democracies. The index concluded that the 2017 study "records the worst decline in global democracy in years. Not a single region recorded an improvement in its average score since 2016, as countries grapple with increasingly divided electorates. Freedom of expression in particular is facing new challenges from both state and non-state actors." Less than 5 percent of the world's population live in a "full democracy." Nearly a third live under authoritarian rule. Overall, 89 of the 167 countries assessed in 2017 received lower scores than they had the year before.

The Pew's polling also reveals important trends. In January 2018, the center published a poll that found a "deepening anxiety" around the world about the future of democracy. "Emboldened autocrats and rising populists have shaken assumptions about the future trajectory of liberal democracy," the report stated.[16] The thirty-eight-nation poll found more than 50 percent support for representative democracy, yet it *also* found an "openness" to nondemocratic forms of government, such as rule by experts (independent of any legislature) and rule by the military. The poll called the commitment to representative democracy "shallow."

In my view, the research shows that if we simply count the *number* of democracies, then the news is not alarming. Those numbers have not changed substantially. But if we use more fine-grained metrics, there is reason for concern. For example, by dividing democracies into failed, full, or hybrid democracies, *The Economist* developed a portrait of global democracy that is decidedly less positive. Also, if we use a detailed system of indicators, we find democratic problems *within* countries. Especially worrisome is the aforementioned "openness" of people surveyed to nondemocratic governance. Finally, by focusing on the number of democracies, we fail to recognize the strengthening of authoritarian regimes.

How Does Democracy Erode?

In this book, I am interested in how democracies erode, even if they do not completely die. The hypothesis is that, increasingly, democracies do not change by violent coup d'état or by attacks from external forces; rather, they erode by a more gradual, often imperceptible, *internal* degeneration. Despite the persistence of a constitution, events erode democratic political culture until not only do the country and its politicians not *act* like a democracy, but also fewer people strongly believe in democracy. I am especially concerned about erosion in liberal egalitarian nations, such as the United States, Canada, and European countries, which are essential to maintaining democracy globally.

Historically, the question of why democracies live or die has been dominated by scholars attempting to explain how in the first half of the twentieth century democracies were replaced by extreme fascist and socialist regimes, from Madrid and Berlin to Rome and Russia. There have been two rival perspectives: One, an internalist (or intentionalist) approach, attributes the failure of these democracies to the intentions, attitudes, and decisions of leaders and leading groups. Faulty leadership and bad decisions undermine democracy in the face of undemocratic forces. The second, an externalist approach, stresses the role of socioeconomic conditions in the country. Distressing material conditions in society, not the psychology of leaders, are instrumental to the erosion of support for democracy.

An example of the intentionalist approach is Karl Bracher's 1970 classic *The German Dictatorship: Origins, Structure, and Consequences of National Socialism*, a monumental work, and the first systematic attempt to explain the rise of Hitler. Bracher rejected the idea that Hitler was the inevitable culmination of German history or the harsh terms of the Treaty of Versailles. Rather, Bracher regarded the rise of Nazism as the result of human decision making, a combination of poor judgment, weakness, and misguided hostility toward democracy. Bracher is unsparing in his critical judgment of Heinrich Brüning, conservative chancellor of the Weimar Republic from 1930 to 1932, and the aging president, Paul von Hindenburg. Another example of the internalist perspective is the work of Juan J. Linz, who in 1978 published his influential book *The Breakdown of Democratic Regimes*. While acknowledging socioeconomic influences, Linz stressed the actions of individuals.[17] What Linz was interested in were the actions of leaders trying to save democracy, and whether they were successful or not. Social and political structures, including conflicts within society, provide "opportunities and constraints" for actors.[18] But in the end, it is the actors' choices that increase or decrease the stability of a regime.

The best-known example of the external approach is the Marxist or socialist view that what happens in society at the level of ideology and politics is a reflection of the more basic material conditions and especially the inequality of society. It focuses on the underlying social and class conflicts that weaken the stability of democracies.

My approach is holistic. It avoids a dualism that says either psychological or material conditions are the drivers of democratic stability or erosion. Analytically, we can distinguish psychological and material factors, but in reality, they intertwine. I also prefer "thick" explanations of what democracy is. As I argue in chapter 4, democracy is a form of community where norms of political culture—how people act toward each other—are as important as formal institutions. Our best hope is a democratic society where both democratic culture and institutions develop together.

THE DEMOCRAT'S NIGHTMARE

From Dream to Nightmare

Putting surveys and theories of democracy aside, I want to view the trajectory of the democratic public sphere from an historical perspective. From the early 1900s to today, we have moved from what I call a democrat's dream to a democrat's nightmare.

The dream was a relatively simple, optimistic view of liberal democracy in Western nations, especially the United States. It marked the development of mass democracy and mass media in the early 1900s, followed by great economic growth after the Second World War. The dream is this: The purpose of mass news media is to accurately and objectively inform the public at large so they can be self-governing. The media will help the people form rational decisions and affirm the best policies, in a spirit of compromise and devotion to the common good. The ideal is populist and democratic. Its roots go back to the eighteenth-century Enlightenment. The ideal played a large role in the construction of an ideology for democratic mass journalism, resulting in the first major codes of journalism ethics. The ideology was this: A professional objective press would make possible, and promote, rational public judgment and debate.[19] Journalism ethics was based on the democrat's dream of a co-operating, rational public sphere.

It was, of course, a dream, an ideal. Democracy, then and now, has always been more complex and more riven with deep problems than the dream recognized. But the central assumption that the public could, and were willing to, form rational, informed, and fair judgments on issues could not be rejected without undermining the very belief in popular democracy. Unfortunately, over the following decades, developments in society and news media "ate away" at this premise of democratic ideology. In the United States and other countries, new methods of "manufacturing public consent" for political leaders, wars, and domestic policies arose, such as the machinations of the public relations expert, manipulative advertising techniques, and the drift of mainstream media to "infotainment" and whatever improved ratings. Then, with the late 1900s, two developments significantly altered the public sphere's capacity for rational debate. Radio and cable news broadcasters, like Fox News, astutely noted that they could be commercially successful if they dropped neutral reporting and engaged in partisan coverage, ranting, and "hot talk." At the same time, the new online media became overtly engaged in rumor, bias, and strong speech. This was the media's contribution to the ideological division of the public, from which America has yet to recover.[20] The idea of careful, rational discussion came to seem boring or "old hat"; others asserted that what the country needed was firm, uncompromising speech, not a search for common ground. The democrat's dream turned into today's nightmare where public discourse is a war zone.

To appreciate how nonrational or manipulative the political sphere is today, one only has to watch an undercover investigation by Channel 4 News in Britain, broadcast in early 2018, on how the firm Cambridge Analytica used citizens' personal data in elections.[21] One of the senior executives is taped as saying: "We just put information into the bloodstream of the Internet, and then watch it grow, give it a little push every now and again . . . like a remote control. It has to happen without anyone thinking, 'That's propaganda,' because the moment you think, 'That's propaganda,' the next question is, 'Who's put that out?'"

We the Global Media, Unfortunately

A crucial contributor to the nightmare was something that at first looked like a ground-shaking, positive technological achievement. It was the development of a global media based on the Internet, accessible to citizens outside of professional journalism.

Global, digital media emerged in the second half of the 1990s, but only today are we appreciating its full social and political significance. In the early days, the late 1990s and early 2000s, digital media was praised as populist, as ending the information control of elite mainstream news media. Prevailing journalistic ideals of neutrality, strict verification, and "just the facts" gave way to values of immediacy, sharing, and opining. Initially, the many voices online were described as a "democratization" of media, leading to "we the media." More information, more voices online, more "sharing"—is this not the populist ideal of participatory democracy? What could go wrong?

In recent years, this naïve enthusiasm has waned. The negative, ugly side of digital media dominates the daily headlines. It became clear that online "sharing" of information and views could be undemocratic, used by elites in government, public relations, or the military. It turned the public sphere into a raucous, sometimes dangerous, global space of trolls, hackers, conspiracy theorists, racists, unwarranted surveillance, and robotic manipulation of social media by governments.

Global media networks give citizens, political groups, and nations the capacity to do journalism in two ways. They can, regularly or randomly, do "acts of journalism" by publishing or circulating articles or commentary. Or they can use journalistic techniques to advance their ends or ideologies. Citizens now can use networks, websites, blogs, and social media to advocate or spread propaganda. They can bring together multiple forms of media—text, video, audio—to create powerful media content, touching the rationality, emotions, or biases of audiences. The vastly increased number of participants in media communication, far beyond the ranks of professional journalism, means that the people who produce your media content may not care about journalism ethics, may not care about the verification of claims. Unfortunately, we the global media can use technology to advance almost anything, from defending human rights to denying the Holocaust.

Moreover, the digital public sphere tends to underline the economic, ethnic, and ideological divisions among us, encouraging a hostile approach to online discourse. The voice of the fact-stating, fair journalist is diminished, lost in a roiling sea of opinion. Inside their ideological silos, people close their ears to inconvenient facts and close their hearts to strangers. A new tyranny of angry majorities, full of fear and tribalism, threatens.

It is nasty out there on the Internet.

The result is that we inhabit a virtual world of wall-to-wall opinion, a democracy seemingly without facts. Yet at the same time, we are inundated with a glut of information. The Data Justice Lab at Cardiff University calls this era the age of "datafication." We live in an age of massive data collection and surveillance. Firm belief in facts coexists with utter certainty of opinion. Every politician with an opinion cites his or her favorite facts. Public channels of information are saturated by the opinion of every Tom, Dick, and Mary. Citizens wonder what media reports they can trust; civic groups worry that they will not be heard in a democracy of hyper-opinion. Information is power. But *misinformation* is also power, and issues of discrimination and privacy surround the use of data. In 2017, when the BBC's Future Now project interviewed fifty experts on the great challenges of our century, many named the breakdown of trusted information.

Information Disorder, Globally

It is important to realize how *big* the misuse of digital media really is.

I attended a NATO conference on communication in a global, digital world in Riga, Latvia, in July 2017. I listened to speaker after speaker warn political agencies, military, and state officials that they must become as sophisticated and "hip" as young people and popular online voices in using new media to promote their ideas. One speaker decried: "We must stop talking to our twenty-first-century audiences in twentieth-century forms based on technology from the nineteenth century." Yet much of the conference discussion was too narrow. Speakers wanted to blame one country, Russia, for the world's political misinformation. Discussion tended to ignore the fact that we live at a time of a worldwide "war" (or arms race) for communication and propaganda supremacy. Among the means of warfare are the hacking of computers and distribution of propaganda through social media. Meanwhile, government surveillance of citizens, combined with technology to block Internet content, grows.

In recent years, media scholars have begun to grasp the enormity of the problem. They have moved beyond talking about the biased reports of individual mainstream journalists and their newsrooms. They focus on the global public sphere, where misinforming is systematic. These scholars have searched for words to do justice to the trend, calling it "information disorder"[22] or "digital deceit."[23] They talk about "digital demagogues."[24] Others call ideological global media "computational propaganda," defined as "the use of information and communication technologies to manipulate perceptions, affect cognition, and influence behavior" to manipulate the perceptions of the public and the actions of elected officials.[25]

In *Information Disorder*, Claire Wardle and Hossein Derakhshan call the public sphere "a global media environment of information disorder":

> While the historical impact of rumours and fabricated content have been well documented, we argue that contemporary social technology means that we are witnessing something new: information pollution at a global scale; a complex web of motivations for creating, disseminating and consuming these "polluted" messages; a myriad of content types and techniques for amplifying content; innumerable platforms hosting and reproducing this content; and breakneck speeds of communication between trusted peers.[26]

Wardle and Derakhshan point to the need to think more subtly about the "elements" of information disorder—the agents who create or distribute the misinformation; the types of messages and their media; and those who receive, interpret, and redistribute the message, after editing.[27] The most "successful" messages play on people's emotions, encouraging feelings of superiority, anger, or fear. These factors drive resharing among people who want to connect with their online communities and online "tribes."

In our global media sphere, false information spreads more quickly and more extensively than truthful information, a technological proof of the old adage that a lie can travel halfway around the world before the truth can get its boots on. For example, one study at the University of Wisconsin investigated the true and false news stories distributed on Twitter from 2006 to 2017.[28] The data comprise over 126,000 stories tweeted by about 3 million people more than 4.5 million times. The findings? Falsehood diffused significantly farther, faster, deeper, and more broadly than the truth in all categories of information. False news was more novel than true news, which suggests that people were more likely to share novel information.

In *Digital Deceit*, Dipayan Ghosh and Ben Scott argue that sophisticated computer algorithms to gather detailed information on people who are online is used by political parties, governments, and extreme groups to send messages to citizens through social media and other means, such as the Russian government's use of Facebook to affect elections.[29] Ghosh and Scott note that Google, Facebook, and Twitter "are at the center of a vast ecosystem of services that enable highly targeted political communications that reach millions of people with customized messages that are invisible to the broader public."[30] The methods have complex names: *microtargeting* during campaigns; *computational amplification*, e.g., using "bots" and "cyborgs" to manipulate online petitions; *behavioral data collection* (every post, click, search, and share is logged to a user profile); *search engine optimization* (using people's searches to direct them to specific content or websites); and *advances by artificial intelligence* and *filter bubbles* (when a website algorithm selects what information a user would like to see).[31] As Ghosh and Scott state: "When disinformation operators leverage this system for precision propaganda, the harm to the public interest, the political culture, and the integrity of democracy is substantial."[32]

By the time this book is published, new data-rich technologies will be invented.

Engagement, Not Neutrality

Given this context, I can restate the purpose of this book: It lays out an ethic for democratic journalism in a global public sphere where manipulative, often extreme, groups use populist rhetoric to promote their media-empowered agendas and weaken democratic systems.

Populism and disinformation have existed in our societies for a long time. Populism and demagoguery go back at least to ancient Athenian democracy. Disinformation and other dubious forms of persuasion have been a preoccupation since humans first attempted to influence each other through communication. Modern representative democracy has never been without its populist critics. Extreme, undemocratic populism has been modern democracy's "permanent shadow" and its "constant peril."[33] Yet historical reflection should not lull us into a false confidence that there is nothing new about current extreme forms of populism, that we have endured them before and we will do so again. This attitude underestimates the threat. As shown above, we face new and virulent forms of disinformation. Our goal is to protect our democracies from further degradation and to create a healthier, but never perfect, media sphere.

Disengagement is not an ethical option. We must do more than shake our heads at the "fake news" bounding across the global Internet or simply feel anxious for democracy. Journalists and citizens need to act in two ways: philosophically, to understand the worrisome phenomena; and practically, to figure out how democratic media should respond to the challenges. How respond, practically? In the United States, faced with an erratic, media-bashing president, some mainstream journalists call on reporters to remain neutral and return to basic principles such as reporting just the facts. To "double down" on the traditional norms of objective reporting. Ironically, a good number of journalists, after decades of skepticism about objectivity, want to revive a journalism of facts. Others call for a partisan, anti-Trump media.

Truly, these are confused times.

There is no going back to journalists as neutral stenographers of fact. And partisanship will not help. If journalists join the protesters, it will erode media credibility and contribute to an already partisan-soaked media sphere. It will give populists and others evidence for their mantra that the media (as a whole) is biased and the generator of fake facts. Yet a journalism of just the facts is too passive and ripe for manipulation. In a partisan public sphere, what *is* a fact is up for debate and requires active investigation. We need to undermine both of these options.

In this book, beginning in chapter 4, I argue that we should replace the idea of "journalism of fact" with the idea of an interpretive "journalism beyond facts," and we should replace the idea of neutral stenography with the idea of impartially engaged journalism for democracy. I propose we think of journalism as lying between partisan advocacy and mincing neutrality. Democratically engaged journalism must not be a neutral spectator or a channel of information that merely repeats people's alleged facts. Critical evaluation and informed interpretation motivated by a clear notion of the goal of democratic media are essential.

Some people will rightly say there must be a third way between being neutral and being partisan. There must be a view of journalism that allows journalists to be factual and yet not simply repeat the dubious "factual" assertions of leaders. Surely there is a middle or hybrid conception of good journalism that is both impartial and engaged. But many of these citizens would be hard-pressed to say *what* that ethic of objective engagement is. What are its principles and aims? How does it differ from partisan journalism? How would it work in practice? The purpose of this book is to describe, in some detail, that third way—what I call democratically engaged journalism.

CONCLUSION: STRUCTURE OF THE BOOK

I approach the topic by dividing the book into two parts. The first part explains my conception of the problems facing journalism. In chapter 2, I provide a history of populism and how journalism's history is intertwined with it. The history helps us, in chapter 3, to define populism and extreme populism and enumerate their strategies. The second part examines what journalists should do to counter extreme populism and misinformation in the global public sphere. Chapter 4 redefines journalism as democratically engaged journalism and provides journalists with a litmus test for dangerous demagogues. Chapters 5 and 6 provide practical guidelines for covering extreme populists and such issues as hate speech, extreme patriotism, fake news, and the role of journalism objectivity.

The Role of Philosophy

As the reader will notice, philosophy plays a large part in this book. Why? Because I believe that practical thought, such as providing guidelines for journalism, should be based on clear philosophical positions on the principles that guide our conduct, whether the issue be coverage of hate speech or guidelines for covering minorities. To know how we should approach such issues, and to be able to be answer critics, we need clear notions of what democracy is and what it entails; why reasoned argument is an important goal; and why we should be respectful of people (and views) with which we strongly disagree. Moreover, even where we seek to avoid philosophy, our practical beliefs and conduct imply philosophical presumptions, which we need to critique and of which we need to be conscious.

Yet my attachment to philosophy is not only because it helps us to arrive at some defensible principles—some content that helps us decide and judge. Long ago, I adopted a view of philosophy as an activity of the whole mind, not just the activity of logical reason. It is to entirely immerse oneself in a topic or issue, opening oneself up to any kind of writing and stimulation and allowing one's intuitions, common sense, and emotions to also have their say. Philosophy, as we might say, is a full-body experience.

The value of philosophy is not that it promises to give you a complete, and satisfying, worldview, and not that it banishes doubt by providing allegedly absolute insights into reality. There are few, or no, such infallible deliverances from philosophical reason. The value of philosophy is in its constant, nagging insistence—that philosophical voice within us—to avoid dogmatism and to always be ready to question and improve beliefs and practices.

My view of philosophizing is derived from two sources: American pragmatists like John Dewey and Enlightenment philosophes such as Voltaire. Dewey urges us to use philosophy practically, i.e., to help cultures address the most important social and moral problems of their day. Voltaire, in the middle of the eighteenth century, created, in his own style of writing, the image of the radical philosophe who is willing to question the unquestioned assumptions of an era. The philosophe is not someone who quietly spends his or her time systematizing abstract theories and arguing on a metaphysical plane only. The philosophe is an agent in the world; a public intellectual; an irritant to the great, conservative "weight" of our traditions and people who fear, despise, or want no truck with skeptical and evolving modes of thinking or living. Like Socrates, Voltaire sought to help individuals (and groups) through criticism, self-reflection, and a courage to voice contrary views. The "enlightenment" was overcoming the domination of authoritarian dogmatism and irrational prejudice.

Hence, philosophy is as much about adopting alternate intellectual stances and exploring new lines of thought as it is about justifying systems of thought. The "doing" of philosophy can take many forms, far beyond the traditional format of rational, logical presentations. One can do or "have" philosophical impact even where one does not intend to do so, such as the seemingly outrageous new art of a painter whose work makes us look at life differently. Over time, the experiencing of new forms of expression and new thoughts seeps through the defenses of our mind, so attached to established patterns and concepts, and alters how we view life, our lifestyles, and our ethics. Philosophizing can operate, seductively and implicitly, in literature, satire, new music, the use of wit and comedy, and so on. It can occur in the coffee shop, the wine bar, the monastery, the prison, or the workplace. Philosophy is canny, influencing us when we least expect it—even when we scornfully reject philosophy as useless twaddle. For to say why philosophy is useless is to philosophize.

Philosophy is critical public reason plus advocacy of new thought, an activity that can be applied beneficially not only to intellectual traditions but to practical traditions such as journalism.

NOTES

1. See Claes H. de Vreese, "Political Journalism in a Populist Age," https://shorensteincenter.org/political-journalism-populist-age.

2. Jason Horowitz, "Italy Election Gives Big Lift to Far Right and Populists," *The New York Times*, March 4, 2018.

3. Steven Levitsky and Daniel Ziblatt, *How Democracies Die* (New York: Crown Publishing Group, 2018), 167.

4. For a long list of Trump's racist, or near-racist, remarks, see *The New York Times'* ongoing compilation, "Donald Trump's Racism: The Definitive List," at https://www.nytimes.com/interactive/2018/01/15/opinion/leonhardt-trump-racist.html.

5. Here is a sample of his rhetoric: "People coming through the border, that are from all over, and they are bad, they are really bad. . . . You have people coming in, and I am not just saying Mexicans, I am talking about people that are from all over that are killers, and rapists." Cited in Christian Fuchs, *Digital Demagogue:*

Authoritarian Capitalism in the Age of Trump and Twitter (Chicago: Pluto Press, 2018), 1.

6. Both quotes from *New York Times*, editorial, "The Wrong People Are Criticizing Donald Trump," March 19, 2018.

7. Levitsky and Ziblatt, *How Democracies Die*, 205.

8. Larry Diamond, "Facing Up to the Democratic Recession," *Journal of Democracy*, vol. 26, no. 1 (2015): 141–155, https://www.journalofdemocracy.org/sites/default/files/Diamond-26-1_0.pdf.

9. Diamond, "Facing Up to the Democratic Recession," 142, 154.

10. Amnesty International, *Amnesty International Report 2016/17: The State of the World's Human Rights* (London: Amnesty International, 2017), 12, https://www.amnesty.org/download/Documents/POL1048002017ENGLISH.PDF.

11. At http://www.worldvaluessurvey.org/wvs.jsp.

12. At http://www.worldsofjournalism.org.

13. See www.freedomhouse.org.

14. Robert A. Dahl, *Polyarchy: Participation and Opposition* (New Haven, CT: Yale University Press, 1971), 3. The eight components are the right to vote; eligible for office; leaders can compete for votes; free and fair elections; right to form parties and associations; freedom of speech on political issues; diverse sources of information on politics that are protected by law; and government policies depend on votes and other expressions of preferences.

15. *The Economist* evaluated 167 countries on a scale of 0 to 10 based on 60 indicators (or criteria). The study divided regimes into (1) authoritarian regimes, (2) hybrid regimes, (3) flawed democracy, and (4) full democracy. The indicators fall into several categories, such as electoral process and pluralism, functioning of government, political participation, democratic political culture, and civil liberties.

16. Richard Wike, Katie Simmons, Bruce Stokes, and Janell Fetterolf, "Globally, Broad Support for Representative and Direct Democracy," Pew Research Center, October 16, 2017, http://www.pewglobal.org/2017/10/16/globally-broad-support-for-representative-and-direct-democracy/.

17. Linz's starting point was Max Weber's method for the social sciences, "methodological solipsism." It lays down the rule: Sociological explanations must start

from the actions of one, few, or many individuals. See Juan Linz, *The Breakdown of Democratic Regimes* (Baltimore: Johns Hopkins University Press, 1978), 100.

18. Linz, *The Breakdown of Democratic Regimes*, 4.

19. For the full story of the development of this ideology, see my *The Invention of Journalism Ethics* (Montreal: McGill-Queen's University Press, 2015).

20. The media did not divide the American public sphere by itself. For an accessible history of how U.S. politics was divided into intolerant, ideological camps, see Levitsky and Ziblatt, *How Democracies Die*.

21. The reporters filmed the meetings at London hotels over four months, between November 2017 and January 2018. An undercover reporter for Channel 4 News posed as a fixer for a wealthy client hoping to get candidates elected in Sri Lanka.

22. Claire Wardle and Hossein Derakhshan, *Information Disorder* (Strasbourg, France: Council of Europe, 2017), https://rm.coe.int/information-disorder-report -november-2017/1680764666.

23. Dipayan Ghosh and Ben Scott, *Digital Deceit: The Technologies behind Precision Propaganda on the Internet* (Washington: New America, 2018), https://www .newamerica.org/documents/2068/digital-deceit-final.pdf.

24. See Fuchs, *Digital Demagogue*.

25. See https://prezi.com/b_vewutjwzut/computational-propaganda/.

26. Wardle and Derakhshan, *Information Disorder*, 4.

27. Wardle and Derakhshan, *Information Disorder*, 5–6.

28. At https://uwmadison.app.box.com/v/TwitterExploit.

29. Ghosh and Scott, *Digital Deceit*.

30. Ghosh and Scott, *Digital Deceit*, 2.

31. Eli Pariser, *The Filter Bubble: What the Internet Is Hiding from You* (New York: Penguin Books, 2012).

32. Ghosh and Scott, *Digital Deceit*, 3.

33. Jan-Werner Müller, *What Is Populism?* (London: Penguin Random House, 2017), 11.

Journalism, Populism, and the Problem of Democracy

Revolutions in democracies are generally caused by the intemperance of demagogues.

—*Aristotle, Politics*[1]

The upkeep of the aristocracy has been the hard work of all civilizations.

—*Winston Churchill*[2]

Our task for this chapter is to gain an overview of the history of populism and how it intertwines with the development of journalism.

The generality of populism's core ideas creates a problem for the historian. It is possible to read into history at almost every turn some anticipation of populism. The history of ideas is populated with many candidates for the terms *populist* or *populism*. Were the ideas of Renaissance republicanism not the precursors of modern populist and democratic notions? It is sometimes difficult to judge examples: Was Chairman Mao a Chinese populist when he led a "people's army" initially comprising peasants? Was Ho Chi Minh in Vietnam a populist, Communist demagogue?

The first step is to distinguish between intellectual and practical contributions to populism. John Locke's social contract ideas were an intellectual contribution to the later emergence of populist views and democratic theory, whether or not that was Locke's intention. The American Revolution was a practical contribution—a populist revolt against British elites through war. Although ideas are important, the beating heart of populism is the *overt expressions* of populism—movements and manifestos leading to action and new political structures.

Historically, I group forms of populism into three large groups: ancient, early modern, and modern. Ancient populisms, from antiquity until the sixteenth century, belonged to the lower social classes, at times erupting in violence against princes. In Greek antiquity, populism became direct democracy.

Early modern populisms, in the seventeenth and eighteenth centuries, arose within nation-states ruled by monarchs and increasingly powerful parliaments. The context for populism was political parties, representative assemblies, a public sphere, and increasing demands for more representation and more liberties. On the political stage were new ideologies and movements, from bourgeois liberalism and conservativism to revolutionary factions. The struggle for representation and power brought forward other classes of people such as the urban proletariat and the rising middle classes of the Industrial Revolution. The eighteenth century ended with populist revolutions where new constitutions, encouraged by Enlightenment ideas, referred idealistically to all the people as citizens, presumably equal in basic rights.

Modern populism, in the nineteenth and twentieth centuries, expressed itself in an age of liberal movements to create open marketplaces of ideas and commerce, workers movements to obtain universal suffrage and other reforms, movements fueled by socialist and communist ideologies, and, eventually, attempts to make political systems more democratic. In this period, populism did not simply amount to supporting the ideals of liberalism and democracy. By the second half of the 1800s populism found a new, distinct voice. Populist movements emerged as severe critics of democracy, including criticism of elite capitalism and liberalism.

Populism became a critic of democracy, internally and externally. Internally, left-wing populist groups, such as the farmers of the American Populist Party, sought to reform democracy and end the control of the country by international financiers, big business, and other elites. Socialist populism grew as an alternative to liberal capitalism. Externally, right-wing populist movements in Germany and in other areas rejected liberal democracy and supported nationalistic government led by demagogic leaders. The result was an extreme populism, or an extreme misuse of populist ideas, by Hitler, Mussolini, Stalin, and others. Nondemocratic power was obtained by appeal to a dissatisfied or distressed populace, a manipulation of the masses. Populism as critic set the stage for populism in our time, Net populism.

The history of populism is so rich with clear, contentious, and just plain odd examples of populism and demagogues that multiple category schemes are possible. Mine is just one scheme. Nor do I claim that my scheme contains no gray areas. I doubt that any scheme can crisply assign all examples to leakproof categories.

ANCIENT POPULISM

Athenian Democracy

The pulse of populism began in Greek antiquity.

Ancient Greece invented the city-state as a law-governed polis.[3] A polis was not just a city. It was a city with a political structure—an independent state organized around an urban center. Typically, it had constitutional government. The constitutions contained the fundamental laws, as they do today. They provided a measure of equality before law, rather than the arbitrary justice of despots. Being a constitutional city-state did not mean being a democratic city-state. The political structure could be monarchic, oligarchic, or democratic. The constitution of aristocratic Sparta, with its rigid social system, communal life, and strong military, was different from the constitution of populist Athens.[4]

The politics of a constitutional polis was not the wielding of power by a strong leader or by an upper class of citizens. Politics was the art of balancing the interests of social classes to maintain political stability. Before democracy, the Greeks had experienced kings, tyrants, and oligarchs. Athens was ruled by archons (or chief magistrates) and other aristocrats who sat in an assembly called the Areopagus, governing Athens to their advantage. In 621 BC, Draco codified a set of harsh laws to the detriment of the lower classes; hence our term *draconian*. Athens was "riddled throughout with inequalities."[5] In his *Iliad*, Homer portrayed the attitudes of proud, upper-class leaders. In contrast, Hesiod, a Boeotian poet and farmer, complained about his narrow aristocratic society and its arbitrary justice.[6]

The attempt at "class balancing" began in the eighth century of the archaic period.[7] Times were changing. Greeks began trading across Asia Minor, which led them to reflect on the status quo at home. Eventually, in Athens, the feuding among aristocrats, the harsh laws, and aristocratic indifference to the lower classes caused a simmering resentment. Resentment fueled a revolt that became direct democracy. Athenians called their political system *demokratia*, a compound of *demos* (the people) and *kratos* (power or rule).[8] But they had other phrases for it, such as "equality for all under the law" and "the right of everyone to have his say."[9] These themes would be part of democratic movements for the rest of Western history.

Living at the opposite ends of the sixth century BC, Solon and Cleisthenes were leaders whose reforms—in the 590s[10] and 508–507, respectively—began the democratization of Athens. Cleisthenes, seeking leadership of Athens, turned to the people to support him against the aristocrats, winning them over with reforms. Herodotus said this appeal to the demos was a novelty at the time, since politics typically consisted of strategies among aristocrats.[11] Solon and Cleisthenes acted as mediators among social classes. They allowed aristocrats to maintain their property and way of life while shifting the center of power to the people by broadening the definition of citizens. They turned the courts over to the people and strengthened the people's assembly, the *ecclesia*.[12]

Athenian democracy is called direct because Athenians participated directly in court trials as judges and jurists and voted in the *ecclesia* on the Pnyx, a hill in Athens.[13] This assembly used a simple majority vote to approve new laws, appoint generals, banish powerful men, judge serious criminal charges, and decide on war.

Athens did not have a "government" in our sense. There was no parliament where parties sought power and elected members represented constituencies. There was no party that formed the government and brought forward financial budgets and laws. The courts played a much larger part in the life of citizens than they do today, and they were not like our courts. There were no professional judges, no professional prosecutors, and not much written law. The judges were citizens who organized the court sessions. Citizens took turns being judge or juror. People served in state positions or assembly by lot (randomly) or by election by fellow citizens. Citizens lacked a daily media to keep them abreast of politics. Books were few. For political information, people had to attend meetings or depend on the accounts of other citizens.

In 431 BC, Pericles, in his famous funeral oration, lauded the unique virtues of Athenian democracy, which had put power in the hands "not of a minority but of the whole people."[14] However, women, slaves, foreign residents, and others could not vote. The voters were adult, free males of Athenian ancestry from all classes. Scholars estimate that eligible Athenian voters amounted to 40,000 at most.[15] There were about 100,000 slaves. When you add women, children, and other denizens of Athens and surrounding Attica, you reach a total population of about 200,000, maybe 225,000. The excluded outnumbered the eligible voters. Nonetheless, the number of participating citizens, and their many duties, is impressive. With the *ecclesia* meeting about forty times a year, being a citizen was demanding. Thousands attended the *ecclesia*'s meetings on the Pnyx. A quorum of 6,000 people was needed for important votes. Citizens served in the military for continual wars against Persia, Sparta, and other powers. Court juries could range from 200 to 1,500 people. The trial of Socrates had more than 500 jurists.[16]

The political structure of Athenian democracy was not simple. In its classic form, Athenian democracy consisted of institutions and assemblies populated by men of different classes performing different civic tasks. There was the people's assembly, the Council of 500, the courts, and the magistrates who ran the political offices, such as commanding the navy.

The history of this remarkable political experiment is turbulent, subject to the changing fortunes of Athens as it came up against Sparta, Macedonia, Persia, and other military powers. Athenian democracy was hijacked by demagogues and tyrants, disrupted by an aristocratic coup, threatened by Sparta and Persia, and then undermined by Macedonian kings and Roman conquest. After Greek democracy ended, *democracy* would not become a positive word until the eighteenth century.[17] Athenian and Roman experiments that allowed the people significant control of political life seemed lost forever to ancient history.

Greek Demagogues

Direct democracy opened the door to a strong-willed, persuasive orator called the demagogue, dominating meetings on the Pnyx. Elite politicians like Pericles spoke in a manner that was moderate and dignified. It left room for folksy, immoderate orators who could connect with the crowd. In Greek, *demagogue* meant, neutrally, a leader of the people. But little was neutral about demagogues. They pandered to the people's biases and emotions and insisted on wars and other strong responses to complex problems.

The demagogue launched personal attacks and loved to scapegoat. He claimed to speak for the people.

One of the most brutal demagogues was Cleon, who became head of Athenian democracy with the death of Pericles in 429 BC. A leather tanner, Cleon came to prominence because of his opposition to Pericles' handling of the Peloponnesian War. A fierce, sometimes drunk orator with a huge voice, Cleon was not above handing out money to the people. During his demagogic reign of terror, Cleon demanded strong actions from the city-state, such as proposing to kill all men of the city of Mytilene after an unsuccessful revolt against the Athenians—and selling their wives and children as slaves. He falsely accused Pericles of the improper use of public money, leading to the latter's temporary demise. He came close to executing Aristophanes for his anti-demagogue play, *The Knights*. He pushed Athens into a disastrous war with Sparta that would damage Athenian democracy.

Cleon and other demagogues were despised by Athenian aristocrats and intellectuals such as Thucydides, Aristophanes, and Plato. This attitude was partly based on class. Yet these critics had reason to worry. All had seen, in their lifetimes, the consequences of following demagogues. Plato compared demagogues to bloodthirsty wolves, tyrants-in-waiting.[18] Aristotle thought true monarchy and true aristocracy (rule by a virtuous monarch or a virtuous elite) were theoretically the best choices but were unlikely outcomes. After comparing constitutions, Aristotle identified the best regime as a polity with a mixed government, that is, a regime that has elements of aristocracy (virtuous men), oligarchy (wealthy men), middle-class men, and democracy (members of the lower classes). The virtuous aristocracy directs the state, yet citizens get a chance to hold public office. They "rule and are ruled by turn." Aristotle thought this ideal polity would be stable for two reasons: It has the moderating influence of a large middle class, and power is monopolized by no particular class. Most people have a voice. Ideally, this mixed government would follow laws. It would not depend on the whim or wisdom of a strong leader.

Aristotle, unlike Plato, did not dismiss democracy as the worst form of government. But like Plato, Aristotle warned that democracies frequently fail, caused by the "intemperance of demagogues." The masses abandon law for the decrees of populist leaders. When democracy becomes rule by demagogues, "flatterers are held in honor" and democracy becomes a tyranny of the many.[19]

Cycle of Regimes

Central to the Greek view of politics was the idea that forms of government degenerate from good to bad over time. Kingship degenerates into tyranny, democracy into mob rule. Societies follow a pattern of degeneration from which they cannot escape without great effort.

The idea of degeneration is discussed in Plato's *Republic* and by Aristotle in his *Politics*.[20]

Later, the Greek historian Polybius, in his *Histories*, developed a theory of the cycle of regimes, as part of his account of how Rome came to control most of the known world. He viewed the growth and "utter collapse over and over again" of regimes as a natural process.[21] He argued, following Aristotle and Cicero, that the best constitution mixes elements of kingship, aristocracy, and democracy. By democracy, Polybius meant a system where the majority decide, yet the society retains traditional values, pieties to the gods, care of elders, and "obedience to the laws."[22] Each of the systems degenerates into a worse form: kingship into tyranny; aristocracy into oligarchy; and democracy into mob rule, violence, and then a despotism of the strong man. Societies pass through this six-stage cycle of constitutions.[23] The decline of democracy happens like this: Demagogues arise in a troubled democracy; they take away freedoms to impose order; and they then become despots, followed by massacres and banishments.

After the reign of Cleon, Athenians sought to protect themselves from demagogues and the cycle of regimes. In 427 BC, they passed a law allowing people to be exiled if they proposed an anti-democratic measure. In 410 BC, a decade after Cleon's death, they passed a law allowing citizens to kill, without penalty, anyone who subverts democracy or takes office after democracy has been suppressed.[24]

Why did Athenians opt for a demanding, cumbersome, direct democracy? Because democracy secured for the ordinary Athenian the best protection under law. Democracy was not based on a naïve romanticism about the goodness of the Greek folk. It was quite the opposite. Democracy was based, at least in part, on mistrust. The Greeks knew, through hard experience, that power corrupts. So they divided the levers of power among many people and made citizens daily monitors of, and participants in, political affairs.

Populist Elements of Roman Republic

As Athens was establishing direct democracy, Rome was constructing an aristocratic republic with populist elements. The republic began in 509 BC when nobles overthrew Etruscan rule. Romans called their city *res publica*, or "property of the people."[25] The republic would last until about 27 BC, when Rome was led by Emperor Octavian Augustus.

The republic comprised numerous public officers and a cascade of social classes from the consuls, senators, and soldiers to the plebs. The republic was a mixed government with a monarchic element—consuls elected annually as chief magistrates; an aristocratic element—wealthy senators for life; and a populist element—popular assemblies, plus tribunes, for the people. [26] In reality, the republic was governed by the consuls and Senate, with popular elements attempting to restrain the aristocracy. In the Senate, populist politics was played out between senators who claimed to represent the common people, the Populares, and the aristocratic senators, the Optimates. The populists—from Mark Antony to Caesar Augustus—did not argue for government by the plebs. Rather, in demagogic fashion, they used language that appealed to the people and favored populist initiatives such as a grain dole for the poor. Both Julius Caesar and Caesar Augustus used referenda to bypass the Roman Senate. The people were politically useful. With the Roman Populares we encounter a seeming paradox of populism, called "Caesarism," the popular support of strong leaders from the upper classes.[27]

However, not all populist feeling was contained within the Senate.

In the late second century BC, a populist revolution was led by two brothers, Tiberius and Gaius Gracchus. When they became tribunes in 133 and 123 BC, respectively, they attempted to pass land reform legislation that would distribute land among urban poor and military veterans. As their support grew among plebs and soldiers, the aristocrats grew fearful of losing their land. Senators gathered an ad hoc force, marched to the Forum, and clubbed to death Tiberius and 300 of his supporters. Later, in 121 BC, a mob was raised to assassinate Gaius as he carried on with reforms after his brother's death. Knowing his death was imminent, Gaius committed suicide. About 3,000 of Gaius' supporters were put to death.

The death of the brothers Gracchus did not bring stable government to the weakened republic, as new groups—urban factions, rural voters, and others—engaged in conflict for their own interests. With the assassination of Julius Caesar, the republic became mired in a prolonged civil war among powerful men, leading to the rule of Augustus. When Octavian died in AD 14, Rome was an empire and memory of the former republic was receding.[28]

The descent of the Roman republic raises the question of a cycle of regimes. Roman citizens, tired of civil strife, set aside the unstable rule of the Senate and popular assemblies for the firm hand of Augustus. About 2,000 years later, the German people would do the same, preferring Hitler to the struggling Weimar Republic.

Greek and Roman Populism

How was the Roman republic different, in political structure, from Athenian democracy?

First, the republic was not a direct democracy. The republic was an aristocratic government where the prominent controlled the ordinary people. Republicanism emphasized indirect government where the people entrusted government to representatives such as consuls and tribunes. Important political discussions did not take place in a Roman version of the *ecclesia*. They took place in the Senate. Most Roman officers of the state were not, as in Athens, chosen by lot from the population. Unlike in Athens, the consuls had wide discretionary power. Senators were senators for life. Many Senate decrees required no further approval by any other body. It was rare when a proposal came before the Roman popular assemblies that had not received Senate approval. The Roman courts were run by the two highest social classes, the senators and the knights.

Another contrasting feature was popular violence. We do not see in Athens extensive and repeated violence by (or against) the lower classes, as we see in Rome. The background to Cicero's Platonic dialogue, *The Republic*, is despair at the increasing violence among groups—from mob violence to gang warfare. By the 50s BC there were also problems of empire. Rome was too far for citizens in the provinces to attend meetings. Far-flung governors could exploit their populations. So many farmers were needed in the military that farmland went unused and created unemployment. Generals recruited the workless with promises of land and loot.

In ancient Athens, direct democracy gave a substantial percentage of citizens a sense of control over their fate. Athenian leaders, unlike their Roman counterparts, did not have to control the masses with "bread and circuses" or by "bloody acts of repression."[29]

MIDDLE AGES, RENAISSANCE, AND REFORMATION

With the end of the Roman republic, populism declined as an important political force during the Middle Ages, especially from the fifth to the tenth century. As Western civilization recovered from the collapse of the Roman Empire, the emerging political structures were anything but democratic. There were plenty of princes, emperors, monarchs, bishops, and popes to impose their will on serfs, vassals, tradesmen, peasants, farmers, and merchants. The people were not a public. They were subjects of (and subjected to) the lords and clerics. Few, if any, European governments in this long era could be called populist, democratic, or a republic. As historian Josiah Ober noted, after Athenian democracy ended, European government was domination of the people.

The medieval worldview was not conducive to populist views of society. Sovereignty resided at the top, in God's authority as king of the universe. Everyone had their place in a medieval "chain of being" from God to angels to humans to animals to material objects.[30] Divine authority grounded the authority of popes and princes, who were God's vice-regents on earth. Christian absolutism, in the form of enforced religious dogma, supported the medieval social order. Popular sovereignty, therefore, was a neglected idea. To justify a doctrine of the church or a political action through an "appeal to the people" would be idiosyncratic. It would also lack credibility. Who would claim that the (largely) uneducated medieval masses, who could not read the Bible in Latin or Greek, should judge theological and political questions? They were like children who should obey their masters.

However, it is wrong to suggest that in the Middle Ages, and then into the Renaissance, nothing of importance for the history of populism can be found—that one might as well skip to modern times.[31] As we scan the era in question, especially from the thirteenth century onward, we find the pulse of populism in writings that affirm the people as a legitimate political authority—or at least argue that the people had a right to be consulted. Thomas Aquinas's theology, a synthesis of scripture and Aristotle, corrects the negative view of man and society in St. Augustine, who regarded powerful secular rulers as necessary to constrain a "fallen" and sinful man. Rulers must be concerned for the people's welfare. Populist themes appear in new and radical works of theology and political theory, such as in the work of Bartolus of Saxoferrato (1314–1357) and Marsilius of Padua (1275–1342).[32] Both Italian jurists developed theories of popular sovereignty.

In medieval political culture, we also observe populist-friendly developments, such as the first parliaments, and increasing demands that the people be represented in courts and in government and that new taxes be approved by assemblies. Although the "people" were typically nobles, clerics, and property owners, the seeds of populist governance were planted.

Republicanism and Humanism

With the flowering of culture and learning in the Renaissance, anticipations of populism are found in the creation (and philosophical defense) of independent Italian republics and in the writings of humanists on the "powers of man." One power was the capacity (and right) of citizens in republics to govern themselves.

In the twelfth and thirteenth centuries, republic city-states arose in northern and north-central Italy—e.g., Milan, Bologna, Florence, and Siena. They rejected feudalism and asserted independence from the "two swords"—the papacy and the Holy Roman Emperor. In the republics, the idea of the people selecting their leaders gained credibility. But by the end of the thirteenth century, the republican experiment came to an end. Most cities were so riven with internal factions that they abandoned their republican constitutions to accept the "strong rule" of a single man or *signore*, the head of a powerful family. Citizens exchanged liberty for civil peace by despotism.

Yet efforts to justify the independence of republics, and to resist the *signore*, led to defenses of liberty and republicanism, and eventually to civic humanism. Alamanno Rinuccini writes, in his *Dialogue on Liberty* of 1479, that liberty is a property of a strong mind that refuses to obey others "unless his commands are just and legitimate and serve a useful purpose."[33] The humanists undermined authoritarianism by rejecting the Augustinian view of society. Petrarch takes up Cicero's idea that the goal of education is worldly virtue. Petrarch, in *On His Own Ignorance*, says the vital task of philosophy is not only instruction in the virtues but to incite the performance of virtuous acts.[34] Later, Coluccio Salutati and Leonardo Bruni would argue that all knowledge must be useful—a theme of Francis Bacon. Humanists extolled the dignity of man, the most famous example of which is Pico della Mirandola's *Oration on the Dignity of Man* in 1484. They express a confidence in man. Humanists sought to create "a desirable type of human being."[35]

Reformation: Revolts and the Right to Resist

During the Renaissance and Reformation, there was a growing circle of rebellions against monarchs and emperors, from the German peasant war and the Dutch revolt against the Spanish empire to the English Civil War.

In Germany, peasants rose up against princes, popes, Catholic clergy, and patricians. Insurrections such as the German Peasants' War (1524–1525) and the Munster Rebellion (1534–1535) began in southern Germany and spread to Alsace, Austria, and parts of Switzerland. Supported by Anabaptist clergy, the revolts were class warfare: the tyranny of princes, clergy, and patrician families over struggling serfs, farmers, and peasants. The armies of nobles, in suppressing the unrest, slaughtered more than 100,000 poorly armed peasants and farmers. It would be Europe's largest popular uprising prior to the French Revolution of 1789. A major text of the period, "The Twelve Articles of the Peasants," is one of the earliest European declarations of human rights.

Similar populist revolts occurred a century later during the English Civil War. Christopher Hill, in *The World Turned Upside Down*, documents how, in the middle of the seventeenth century, the lower classes joined the New Model Army and wealthy merchants to defeat the army of Charles I. Among these lower-class revolutionaries were radical, Protestant, dissenting groups: Quakers, Ranters, Diggers, and Levellers. They questioned the superiority of the upper classes and the power of the established church and aristocracy. After the war, the aristocrats and military leaders who had enlisted the poor against Charles I feared that, once emboldened, the poor would set up an alternative social order and "turn the world upside down," i.e., a world where the lower classes would direct the upper classes. The upper classes attacked the dissenting groups' radical ideas as a product of the lower classes, who were base, vulgar, stupid, but dangerous—the "mob."

The conflicts raised questions about the best form of government, the powers of the monarch, and the right of the people to resist unjust rulers. The questions challenged the medieval view that the people should obey God's rulers. The new theories were populist in tone.

One factor was the Reformation. It sanctioned an individualism that weakened medieval obedience and led to a populist view of knowledge: that individuals could obtain religious and other knowledge on their own. Yet on the question of obedience, one of the Reformation's leaders, Martin Luther, was thoroughly medieval. Luther agreed with the Augustinian view that humans are fallen creatures and should obey their secular masters. But what happens if rulers are tyrannical? In his "On Temporal Authority," Luther agrees that no one has a duty to do evil, as prescribed by a ruler. Yet he is pulled in the other direction by St. Paul's doctrine that citizens should not disobey a ruler since it is against the will of God, who ordains the rulers. Luther ends up with passive resistance: If a ruler commands you to do evil, you must refuse; if he punishes you for refusing, you must accept it, and thank God you can suffer for the sake of the divine Word. Tyranny, Luther says, is "not to be resisted but endured."[36] But doesn't this mean God is author of the evil committed by rulers against the people? Luther's reply, adopting Augustine's view, is that if the people suffer tyrannical rulers, it is their fault. It is "because of the people's sins."

The full implications of Luther's theory of passive resistance emerge when we consider how he treated the German peasant wars. Luther attempted, awkwardly, to both condemn tyranny and forbid resistance. In his "Sincere Admonition" of 1522, Luther warns all Christians "to guard against insurrection and rebellion" and counsels conciliation. One reason was his fear that the peasants and their Protestant leaders, such as Thomas Munster, would be seen as radicals, discrediting his own demands for religious change. By 1525 peasants had won victories in Thuringia and were pillaging across southern Germany. Luther responded brutally.[37] Luther argued that, because the peasants broke their oath of obedience, they merited death. The uprisings were the work of devil-inspired peasants who should be treated like mad dogs.

In the Reformation period, the theoretical basis of limited government was strengthened by the doctrine of constitutionalism, developed by philosophers and jurists. It "proclaims the desirability of the rule of law as opposed to rule by the arbitrary judgment or mere fiat of public officials."[38] Constitutional-ism opposed political absolutism—the claim that kings ruled alone by divine right. There is a populist core to constitutionalism: All political authority, and therefore all law, inheres in the body of the people. These laws, typically gathered into a constitution, give the people rights before the law and protect them from abuse of power. This ideology grounded the first wave of success-ful revolutions of modern times, in The Netherlands, England, and France.

The turmoil also prompted a sharp, conservative reaction from other politicians, theologians, and writers. They opposed social change. Montaigne (1533–1592) in his *Essays* expresses a thoroughgoing conservativism. Tired of the wars between the Catholics and the Huguenots (French Calvinists), Mon-taigne adopts skepticism toward knowledge and social change. He accepts the status quo. Other writers developed the notion of political absolutism. A ruler is "above the law" and not accountable to any other person or body. The absolute ruler is justified, especially when the matter is urgent, to violate existing law. In 1576, French jurist Jean Bodin (1530–1596), in *Six Books of the Commonwealth*, defines sovereignty as a supreme, perpetual power, with the capacity to make law without the consent of any other person or body. "The sovereign Prince is accountable only to God," he writes.[39] Bodin thought peace required a prince who wielded the absolute and indivisible power of state.

EARLY MODERN POPULISM

In the seventeenth and eighteenth centuries, populism entered the early modern era.

The seventeenth century in Europe was the age of experimental science, voyages of discovery, colonial wars, and economic and artistic progress in The Netherlands and other Western European nations. It would usher in the eighteenth-century Enlightenment, with its stress on reason and individual freedoms. By the end of the eighteenth century there had been populist revolutions in America and in France, leading to declarations of the rights of all citizens. Populist and democratic ideas could no longer be repressed; they were no longer expressed by short-lived revolts. From here on, popular sovereignty would be a foundational idea of Western politics. The rights of the people would be the rallying cry of statesmen, journalists, and the people themselves.

Populism within Nations

Populism would have to adapt, chameleon-like, to a new social and political climate in the West. Populism's impulses, originally so direct and raw, now existed within large centralized nations with rulers restrained by parliament. Politics was a search for popular power—support of the people—and power was exercised through impersonal institutions and parliaments, political parties, and the rest of the complex machinery of representative democracy. This was not face-to-face direct democracy in a small, relatively homogeneous city-state. It was politics in the bruising public sphere of evolving, competitive nations where journalism, through a new periodic press, grew in importance.

The definition of "the people" extended beyond the lower classes. Social classes, from the middle classes to the urban proletariat, grew in number and influence due to the rising fortunes of capitalism, international finance, free trade, and mass industrialism. These classes would want the right to be heard and to shape decisions. Also, new ideologies would come forward: liberalism for the middle classes; socialism for the proletariat; and nationalism, allegedly for all. The populist revolutionaries were a mix of intellectuals, middle-class journalists, agitators, merchants, soldiers, reformist clergy, and the poor. Meanwhile, nonpopulist, conservative thinking by an entrenched upper class remained a political force and a stern critic of populism and democracy.

Social Contract: Justifying Popular Consent

By the early 1600s the idea of popular sovereignty and parliamentary control of monarchs was ascending, but it was not universally accepted. It was an idea that had to be justified, often at the peril of one's life.[40]

The most important set of ideas was contract theory. It developed an ancient idea. In Book II of Plato's *Republic*, Glaucon explains justice as a social contract. Justice is a set of man-made laws to protect people from the unjust acts of others. However, social contract theory began in earnest in the seventeenth and eighteenth centuries. It was developed in different ways by Thomas Hobbes, Locke, Jean-Jacques Rousseau, and others. All versions explained the legitimacy of a ruler by imagining that, at some point, the people and the ruler entered into a contract to make society possible. In 1651, Hobbes used the idea of a contract to support a conservative view. Men, he said, had agreed to hand over power to a great ruler, a *leviathan*, who enforced contracts.[41]

The leviathan allowed men to leave an insecure state of nature for the peace, security, and benefits of society.[42]

Locke's famous *Two Treatises of Government*, on the limits of government, was composed in the 1680s. The topic was urgent as Charles II drifted toward absolutism, refusing to call parliaments and executing opponents, including Locke's Whig friends. Applying the natural law tradition, Locke developed a protoliberal view of social contract. He said men are by nature free, equal, and independent. In nature or in society, men have inalienable natural rights to liberty and justice.[43] The American Declaration of Independence would borrow such language. For Locke, the creation of society was voluntary and it left unaltered men's natural rights. Their sovereignty was delegated, not alienated. Men had the right to oppose, violently if necessary, a tyrant who violated men's natural rights.

Yet Locke was no liberal democrat. Locke did not argue that consent entailed the right for *all* to participate equally in politics. He did not call for the vote to be extended to all adult males, let alone to females, and he apparently had no scruples about slavery.

Romantic Populism

In the eighteenth century, Rousseau, in *The Social Contract*, would go further than Locke. He would lay down the ideas of popular will and the rights of all citizens. While Locke's *Treatises* justified parliamentary constraint on English kings, Rousseau's ideas inspired revolution.

Rousseau started from a contrarian view of society, not shared by his contemporaries, the Enlightenment philosophes. In a prize-winning essay, he argued that the arts and sciences had corrupted public morals.[44] Rousseau attacked central assumptions of the Enlightenment. Rousseau declared that science was *not* saving us; progress was an illusion; modern man was unhappy and corrupted by civilization. In society, men were in chains. In a prior state of nature, they were innocent and virtuous, unsullied by social ambition, manners, and luxury.

However, in *The Social Contract*, an older Rousseau, perhaps influenced by reading Hobbes on the fierceness of a state of nature, provided a more positive account of society. He advocates a democracy where the "general will" of citizens approves the laws. Hobbes said men had to choose between being ruled and being free. Rousseau disagreed. Men can achieve freedom and virtue *if* they live in a democratic society where they rule themselves. This is Rousseau's ideal, republican model of society, where citizens make decisions based on the common good.

Contract theory in Locke and Rousseau provides both a nonromantic and a romantic view, respectively, of the people as sovereign. Locke was the unromantic empiricist. Unlike Rousseau, Locke did not idealize ordinary people. Locke did not paint a romantic picture of "natural" man.

After Rousseau, the term *romanticism* would encompass a century-long movement of art, music, and thought. We associate it with creative minds from the late eighteenth century to the middle of the nineteenth century, such as Goethe, Blake, Wordsworth, Herder, Brahms, Fichte, and perhaps Nietzsche. We are familiar with its features: an emphasis on turbulent emotion, passion, and intuition; the value of authentic experience; descriptions of heroic, tormented individuals in nature; a celebration of will and creativity over reason, of individuality over conformity. As Isaiah Berlin said, the romantic mind-set rejected the Western philosophical tradition of natural law, universal truths, and objective values known by reason.[45] Romanticism emphasized peculiarity, individual distinctness, and cultural plurality.

Romanticism may seem far removed from populism. But not so. The romantic idea of uniqueness was used to develop a theory of culture. For German philosopher Johann Gottfried Herder, the natural unit for human society was *das Volk*, the people. The *Volk* of each nation are unique in their land, language, values, and customs. When Herder discusses the *Volk*, Berlin writes, "differences, peculiarities, nuances, individual character are all in all."[46] Nations should pursue their own culturally relative idea of happiness and development. There is no objective way to evaluate cultures. Moreover, there is no need of comparison since "every nation bears in itself the standard of its perfection, totally independent of all comparison."

Populist Revolution

The American and French Revolutions are iconic examples of how the idea of popular sovereignty could stand behind impassioned movements to eliminate monarchy, reduce aristocratic privileges, and form a society based on the rights of man.

The populistic nature of the French Revolution cannot be minimized. The idea of the rights of the people motivated the *sans-culottes* revolutionaries who took the lead in the early days of the revolution.[47] They attacked the Bastille, helped supporters to form and declare a National (Popular) Assembly, published the Declaration of the Rights of Man and of the Citizen, and held a women's march on Versailles that forced the royal court back to Paris.

As tensions built, law and order in cities broke down. Nobles who had fled to neighboring countries called for military intervention by a foreign power. Amid this chaos, the spirit of popular sovereignty spread across France, incited by a passionate revolutionary journalism. Within a relatively short time, the revolutionaries had passed laws that gutted aristocratic society from top to bottom. They ended monarchy; curtailed aristocratic privileges; outlawed feudalism and serfdom; abolished slavery in French colonies; and popularized the idea of the freedom, equality, and fraternity of all citizens. Populism had been transposed from a lower-class preoccupation into the new political key of mass democracy, expressed in a manner and strength never seen before.

But the revolutions, or attempts at revolution, did not stop with the American and French Revolutions. They inspired movements and revolutions across the nineteenth and twentieth centuries, including the revolutions that rippled across Europe in 1848, from France to Germany and beyond. The revolutions were liberal and populist in seeking to replace a monarch or to place government under greater democratic control. Most of the revolutions failed, but they pointed to a future when liberal democracies would become the norm for Western countries.

At this point, it seemed that democracy would steamroll over conservative Western regimes, one by one. But this did not happen. The story is more complex. First, after the French Revolution, revolutions did not occur in all major nations, such as England. Second, the revolutions did not result in stable governments, as witnessed in France after the revolution. Robust democratic regimes would not exist in most of Europe until the late 1800s. Third, conservative forces did not simply melt away. In countries such as England, slow, difficult reform—not revolution—occurred. Parliaments were controlled by the bourgeoisie, wealthy capitalists, and aristocracy.

No one better expressed the conservativism of the ruling upper classes than the Whig politician and intellectual Edmund Burke, especially in his criticism of the French Revolution. Burke said the French, inspired by Rousseau, had mistakenly tried to create a new state from scratch, cutting the people off from their established institutions.[48] To let the "lower orders" assume power was to let loose the mob, to give free rein to anarchic impulses that could not be restrained by reason. Similar conditions for revolution, Burke warned, existed in England.

After Revolution: Populism Untrammeled?

The story of democratic revolutions in the eighteenth century is not only a narrative about the rise of populism and democracy. It is also a story of how enthusiasm for popular sovereignty became a *problem* for those who would rebuild government after revolts and revolutions. Having set loose the anger of the people upon monarchs, barons, and elites, the revolutionary leaders began to worry where the movement might lead. How much populism is too much populism? How can modern democracies avoid Polybius' cycle of regimes?

Among the American Constitution's Framers, there were those who had a critical view of "the people." Take one incident from the United States. The stirring beginning of the Constitution of the United States, "We the People"— that most populist of phrases—was not the first choice. The original version began prosaically as "The people of . . ." followed by a list of thirteen states. But then New York and Rhode Island refused to sign the document for various reasons. So Gouverneur Morris of New York, called a "penman" of the new constitution, rephrased it to "We the People." Morris did so not because "We the People" was a better opening for a democratic document. He settled on this phrase to avoid naming states. He felt that with a less specific introduction the document would be more acceptable to states reluctant to sign. Morris was no populist. He once referred to the people as "reptiles."[49]

Fear of "the people" among middle- and upper-class Americans was clear during Shays' Rebellion in the late 1780s.[50] A group of merchants, financiers, and political officers passed a new constitution for Massachusetts that increased the property qualification for holding political office, effectively disqualifying ordinary Americans. To make matters worse, an economic recession had forced many farmers into debt as they struggled to pay the bankers' usurious loan rates. The answer, according to the government? Build debtor prisons and have judges fill them with farmers. On Aug. 29, 1786, Daniel Shays, a farmer and Revolutionary War veteran, led 1,500 men to a Northampton courthouse with a petition demanding the adjournment of a meeting of judges to imprison debtors.

The judges broke up their meeting. But the response from other elites was harsh. Governor James Bowdoin, using an idea from Polybius, condemned the farmers' efforts to "subvert all law" and "introduce riot, anarchy, and confusion, which would probably terminate in absolute despotism."[51] The farmers might "throw the whole union into a flame." Indeed. By the end of 1786 almost 9,000 militants had joined Shays' Rebellion. But a federal force ended the insurrection after several skirmishes. All militants were apprehended by the summer of 1787 when the Founding Fathers convened in Philadelphia to draft a constitution. The significance of Shays' uprising was not the threat of his militant group, but how it panicked some of the Constitution's Framers. General Henry Knox, in a letter to George Washington, said: "This dreadful situation has alarmed every man of principle and property in New England . . . What is to afford us security against the violence of lawless men?"[52] At the bottom of it all was class conflict: "one class defending itself against another."[53]

Among the Framers of the Constitution, there were deep differences in how populist they believed the new country should be. Jefferson wanted a citizen-led democracy and a "populist constitution."[54] The democratic-loving character of the people was the ultimate safeguard of the constitution, not soldiers or governors.[55] Thomas Paine, liberal journalist of the Revolutionary War, agreed. The country's constitution was an act "of the people constituting a government."[56]

Against Jefferson's populism were skeptics like Charles Pinckney of South Carolina, who said the House of Representatives should be selected by state legislatures because "the people were less fit judges."[57] Edmund Randolph, in presenting the "Virginia Plan" to the Framers, warned that "our chief danger arises from the democratic parts of our constitutions."[58] Others talked of the "democratic licentiousness" of state legislatures.[59] Madison had grave fears of the people dividing into factions. Alexander Hamilton at one point proposed that the United States should be a sort of aristocratic monarchy with the president and senators holding office for life. In *The Federalist Papers*,[60] Hamilton worried about "the military despotism of a victorious demagogue." The fear of an American Cleon was real.

When one steps back from the constitution that was approved, its democratic faith is clear. Yet from another perspective, it is a document grounded in upper-class concern about too much populism. Democratic yes, but democracy tamed by vetoes and other mechanisms. The Framers prevented the people from directly electing the president. The public's will must be vetted by an electoral college, an "elite barrier."[61] They created an unelected high court. The Framers decided senators would be selected by state legislatures, not directly by the people. Madison asserted that checks and balances would control "the followers of different Demagogues."[62] Yet the Constitution, and the nation, would evolve. Jefferson's Bill of Rights, with subsequent amendments, would further democratize the Constitution.

Not long after the Constitution was approved, it seemed that the fear of an American Cleon would be realized by Andrew Jackson. A true American demagogue, Jackson arrived in Washington as a Tennessee congressman in 1796 and went on to become president in 1828. Jackson, a self-described "common man," cut quite a figure on the public stage with his long hair, gruff manner, and the clothes of a frontiersman. He had the demagogue's streak of violence in him—a huge temper that prompted him to hold duels. He became a military celebrity. He prosecuted a bloody war against Native Americans, helped America defeat the British in the War of 1812, and was the heroic commander of the Battle of New Orleans. Fears of a populist revolution that would swamp the Constitution were exacerbated by Jackson's inauguration, when excited people stormed the White House, climbing in and out of windows. Jackson had to retreat down a back stairway to a boardinghouse. Supreme Court Justice Joseph Story declared that the "reign of KING MOB" had begun.[63] Senator Henry Clay saw in Jackson the ancient Greek demagogue whose election as president guaranteed that "the republic will march in the fatal road which has conducted every other republic to ruin."[64] Jefferson told Daniel Webster: "He is one of the most unfit men I know of for such a place . . . he is a dangerous man."[65]

As president, Jackson launched "Jacksonian democracy," which included attacks on the Bank of the United States as an unelected board. He widened the voting franchise, required civil servants to rotate their positions, and cut federal programs that made the rich richer, e.g., federal road building. No cycle of regimes occurred. To the contrary, stability seemed possible. Yet tests of the democratic constitution lay ahead.

Liberty and . . . Fear

In France, after the first success of the revolution, the problem of populism was posed in a dramatic and visceral manner: How could the revolution, being pushed forward by demagogues and radical agitation, avoid a bloodbath of fanatical ideologies? It couldn't. The French Revolution descended into a reign of terror that beheaded up to 40,000 people, including a king and his wife, and Enlightenment thinkers such as Nicolas de Condorcet. Confused and divided, the revolution would be led by the icy Maximilien Robespierre and the feared Committee of Public Safety. Demagogues, those Platonic tyrants-in-waiting, would abound. Georges Danton and Jean-Paul Marat used the press, the latter calling his journal *L'Ami du peuple*. Robespierre made bold to say that he *was* the people, a claim made by absolute monarchs.

The revolution eventually fell into the hands of another strong man—a military despot called Napoleon who began as the savior of revolutionary ideals. Napoleon would skillfully appeal to the people, for whom he claimed he did everything—even while his wars killed countless lower- and middle-class Frenchmen. The French Revolution, initially full of Enlightenment love of the people and the humanistic ideal of the rights of man, would become a case study for Polybius' cycle of regimes.

MODERN POPULISM

Critic of Democracy

After stirring revolution, populism entered the modern era of the nineteenth and twentieth centuries. Once again, populism had to adapt to a new political environment. Politics in many Western countries was a contest between liberals and conservatives within dueling political parties. At about the same time, "right" and "left" came to apply to politics, the terms originally referring to how groups were seated in the postrevolutionary French assembly. The Rightists—typically, Catholics, aristocrats, bishops, kings, and anyone dependent on these groups—were conservatives who rejected the principle of popular sovereignty. The Leftists—Whigs, liberals, socialists, anarchists, and democrats—demanded greater popular sovereignty, democracy (e.g., universal male suffrage), or the rights of the proletariat.

In this competition between right and left, between liberal and conservative, the voices of the bourgeoisie and the upper classes were frequently heard. Yet populism did not fade away. It found a new voice as a critic of democracy. Populists criticized democratic countries as not sufficiently populist, as controlled by elites. Populism finds expression in two forms: as an *internal* or *external* critic of modern democracy. As an internal critic, populists sought to reform democracy from within. As an external critic, populists sought to replace democracy with some other system, either socialism or right-wing nationalism.

An example of internal populism was the worker revolts in nineteenth-century England. A mixed parliament where aristocratic traditions held sway was challenged by the Chartist movement, from 1838 to 1857. The movement took its name from the People's Charter of 1838. It became a national protest movement, with strong support in Northern England, the East Midlands, the Staffordshire Potteries, the Black Country, and the South Wales Valleys. Support for the movement was at its highest between 1839 and 1848, when petitions signed by millions of working people were presented to the House of Commons. The Chartists pressured politicians to agree to universal manhood suffrage, secret election ballots, and annual parliamentary elections to limit corruption.

In the economically distressed 1870s and 1880s, popular dissatisfaction with the political leadership, courts, and other institutions became so widespread that many people predicted an English revolution, a century after France's.

Populist Socialism

On the left, a major critic of democracy was socialism, in Germany, England, France, Russia, and elsewhere. Socialists drew out the logical implications of populism: If the people *as a whole* should govern and each citizen is equal, then social hierarchies should be leveled. Populism seems to entail a classless society.

In nineteenth-century Russia, populist socialism anticipated the Communist revolution of 1917. Lenin's Bolsheviks were the inheritors of decades of dissent against the tsar, who had hanged Lenin's older brother for his political activism.

One group is of particular interest: the Russian *narodniki* in the late nineteenth century. Their ideology of *Narodnichestvo* is translated as populism. *Narod* meant people or folk, and so connects with Herder's *Volk*. The Narodniks were a revolutionary movement of the Russian middle class and intelligentsia in the 1860s and 1870s. Many Narodniks thought, contra Marx, that it was possible to skip the capitalist phase of Russia's development and proceed directly to socialism. Narodism arose after Tsar Alexander II emancipated the serfs in 1861. The Narodniks saw the peasantry as the revolutionary class that would overthrow—with the help of the Narodniks—absolute monarchy. The village commune would be the embryo of socialism. In the spring of 1874, the Narodnik intelligentsia left the cities for the villages, to "go to the people" in an attempt to teach the peasantry their duty to revolt. The "to the people" movement worked with an unreal, romantic image of the peasant. They found almost no support. The peasants were suspicious of these city folk and thought the tsar was on their side.

Authorities cracked down on the Narodniks, prompting them to form Russia's first revolutionary (and terrorist) party, Narodnaya Volya ("People's Will"), in 1879. Adopting terrorism, they assassinated Tsar Alexander II in 1881. The peasantry were horrified by the murder, and the government had Narodnaya Volya leaders hanged, decimating the movement.

Yet populist dissent would recover and grow even more intense, resulting, in 1905, in "Bloody Sunday." Tsar Nicolas II ordered troops to fire on a large gathering of citizens in St. Petersburg who demanded reforms and protested living conditions, including lack of food. The shooting forever damaged Nicolas II's reputation. Nicolas II did set up a popular assembly, the Duma, but he granted himself the power to veto any Duma law.

When the Russian Revolution came in 1917, the problem of "what next?" reoccurred. Inside the revolutionary leaders' camp, Lenin and the Bolsheviks worried about the power of the peasants. Maxim Gorky, artistic voice of the revolution, wanted a "politically literate" proletarian dictatorship in "close alliance with scientific and technical intelligentsia." Unlike Tolstoy, who idealized the Russian peasant, Gorky considered peasants lazy and anti-intellectual, a dark, uncontrollable force.[66] At the same time, Russian writers, artists, and intellectuals struggled with how to support or critique a socialist revolution that declared itself to be the vanguard of worker's populism around the world.[67] Could they change the system from within, or should they depart for the West? At least from Stalin onward, Russian communism was a faux populism; in reality, it was a brutal party dictatorship using the rhetoric of popular socialism.

Historically, the relationship between Marxian socialists and democracy was never strong and unambiguous. Many Marxists distinguished between politics and society, or, in this case, between political democracy and society. They thought that to bring about radical social change—a socialist revolution—democracy may have to be jettisoned for some period of time. Perhaps, as Lenin thought, Russia in 1917 needed a dictatorship of socialist leaders to create a democracy of, and for, the workers and the poor. How that was possible was never clear. History has shown, in Russia, China, and elsewhere, that this is a vain hope. Creating democracies from authoritarian leadership, or making democracies more democratic by undemocratic means, leads to regime crisis and paves the way to autocratic rule.[68]

U.S. Agrarian Populism

Far from the Russian turmoil, in the United States, an important development in left-wing populism was occurring at about the same time.

The American Populist Party was formed in 1891 with support in mid-western and some southern states. The party is given credit for being the first to invent and popularize the terms *populism* and *populist*.[69] The party brought together wheat and cotton farmers, laborers, populist politicians, and eventually unions. They believed that elites, e.g., eastern bankers, trusts, and transportation conglomerates, were driving the agrarian class into debt. The two major parties, Democratic and Republican, were beholden to the interests of the upper classes. Under the democratic system, "the fruits of the toil of millions are boldly stolen to build up colossal fortunes for a few."[70]

The party's ideas, known as the Omaha Platform, called for the abolition of national banks; a graduated income tax; direct election of senators; civil service reform; a working day of eight hours; and government control of all railroads, telegraphs, and telephones. From 1892 to 1896, the party was a force in American politics. The party reached its peak in the 1892 presidential election, when its ticket of James B. Weaver and James G. Field won 8.5 percent of the popular vote and carried five states. In the election, the party's slogan was "Equal rights to all; special privileges to none." The party merged with the Democratic Party in 1896.

In *The Tolerant Populists*, Walter Nugent argues that, from the 1950s onward, writers such as Richard Hofstadter, especially his 1955 book *The Age of Reform*, falsely characterized these populists as narrow-minded nationalists and anti-Semites, the forerunners of Joseph McCarthy's anti-Communist crusade in the 1950s. Who were these populists, for Nugent? They were people "who believed in the ideals of democratic republicanism, of economic democracy, and of freedom from the European conditions of life."[71] The populists were a source for twentieth-century liberalism, manifested in the progressive movement in the early 1900s, in the popular style of Teddy Roosevelt (despite his patrician upbringing in New York), and in Franklin Roosevelt's New Deal.[72]

It is important not to confuse the American populists with the American progressives, although both were active in same period and shared liberal beliefs. Both sought to widen democracy and were worried about the power of big business. However, progressives were upper-class Republicans, mainly from northeastern states such as Massachusetts, who by 1880 were unhappy with the direction of their party. These Mugwumps, as they were called by conservative Republicans, believed, as John Stuart Mill did in England, that social reform and social planning should be directed by educated, liberally minded elites. By the early 1900s the progressives were ascending. The leader of the Progressive Party, Theodore Roosevelt, was president. Presidents Wilson and Hoover were progressives also.

By the 1920s there was a deep split between the progressives and populists. They disagreed on entering the First World War. They divided over the Scopes "monkey trial," about the teaching of evolution, where the populist and anti-evolutionist lawyer William Jennings Bryan faced the progressive lawyer Clarence Darrow. Later, progressives were shocked by the populists' strong nationalism and their support for laws that would censor books.

Twentieth-Century American Demagogues

In the early twentieth century, populism in the United States was led by demagogues on the left and right of politics.[73] For example, in the 1930s, there were more than 800 far-right groups in the country.

Theodore Roosevelt was an energetic, canny demagogue who was popular because of his brash style and his restrictions on the business trusts that controlled the economy. In the 1930s, left-wing populism was advanced by two powerful orators, Louisiana governor Huey Long and Father Charles Coughlin of Michigan. Using the new medium of radio, they wanted the people to control the "faceless" elites who ran Wall Street, the international bankers who distorted financial policy, and the other wealthy groups who had led the country into the Great Depression.[74] Long and Coughlin, both isolationists in foreign policy, were a serious political obstacle to President Franklin Roosevelt as he sought to bring the United States into the Second World War.

Elected governor in 1928, Long created his own political fiefdom in Louisiana and flouted political rules to push forward his agenda.[75] He was both admired for his bold populist platform and feared as a Cleon of American politics. Long advanced a progressive program: free textbooks, more hospitals, large funding for the state's university, and a tenfold extension of the state's paved highways. After installing a puppet governor in Louisiana to maintain his influence, Long moved to the United States Senate in 1932. Now the "Kingfish" (Long's favorite nickname) reached national audiences on radio. He asserted that the FDR administration was "mired in the mud of Wall Street and the House of Morgan." After a typical broadcast in 1935, he received up to 60,000 letters.

In the view of Long and Coughlin, Roosevelt failed to exploit the financial crisis of the Depression to introduce radical economic changes. In 1934, Long unveiled his "Share Our Wealth" program that would redistribute money from the rich to the poor. He would impose high taxes on the rich and provide an annual guaranteed income for all. The slogan for the program was "Every man a king." He was assassinated in 1935 before he could run for president.

Father Coughlin was one of the first political leaders to use radio to reach a mass audience. Up to 30 million listeners tuned to his weekly broadcasts during the 1930s. Early in his career he was a supporter of Roosevelt and his New Deal. But by 1934 he accused the president of being too close to the banks. He created an organization called the National Union for Social Justice that called for monetary reforms, nationalization of major industries, and protection of the rights of labor. Membership ran into the millions, but it was not well organized at the local level.

In the late 1930s, Coughlin's demagoguery turned ugly and would end his career. He broadcast anti-Semitic messages on his radio program and in his newspaper, recycling old charges of a Jewish plot to impose financial slavery on the world. He set up an ominous-sounding "Christian Front" that attracted violent members. The latter collected guns and at times smashed the windows of Jewish stores or engaged in Nazi-like street brawls with Jews. Coughlin spoke approvingly of Hitler and Mussolini, praising Hitler's regime for imposing a new moral purity on Germany and arguing for the superior strength of the Axis powers in comparison to the "sleazy Britishers."[76] Coughlin was not alone in his views. During the Depression, many Americans admired the way that Hitler and Mussolini reorganized their countries. In 1937, Henry Luce, creator of *Time* magazine, called Mussolini "the ablest manager a poor nation ever had."

Many American bishops, as well as the Vatican, wanted Coughlin silenced. After the outbreak of World War II in 1939, the National Association of Broadcasters adopted new codes that limited the sale of radio time to "spokesmen of controversial public issues." Then, in 1942, Postmaster General Frank Walker barred the publication of Coughlin's paper, *Social Justice*, and Attorney General Francis Biddle warned that Coughlin would be charged with sedition if he did not cease publication. Coughlin lost access to the radio and to the press. Coughlin announced he was ceasing political activity.

Alan Brinkley has argued that Long and Coughlin (before he descended into anti-Semitism) were "constructive demagogues." They were the last voices to engage Americans in reform of an economic system that was moving out of their control. They raised issues of privilege, wealth, and centralized power, keeping alive the spirit of the 1890s.[77] Not all of the American demagogues were constructive. In the nineteenth and twentieth centuries, racist politicians pushed the country down a dark path of cruel, institutional discrimination. For example, in the first half of the 1900s, "Pitchfork Ben" Tillman, senator for South Carolina, said "we" Americans had never believed the Negro was equal to the white man and that "we will not submit to his gratifying his lust on our wives and daughters without lynching him." In the 1950s, Senator Joseph McCarthy was a feared demagogue, accusing many Americans of being Communists.[78] In 1963, Governor George Wallace of Alabama declared in his inaugural gubernatorial address: "Segregation now, segregation tomorrow, segregation forever."

In the United States, right-wing political movements and leaders have been growing since the 1980s. The Tea Party, beginning in 2009, has used populist language, strategies, and symbols. The party's name recalls the populist protest of colonial America called the Boston Tea Party. The party's other populist elements include its large outdoor rallies and its use of patriotic symbols, such as the "Don't Tread on Me" Gadsden flag.

POPULISM AND NATIONALISM

Populism from the right wing of politics also grew in the nineteenth and early twentieth centuries. It began with the idea that the Germans were a unique

Volk. This *völkisch* philosophy was later transformed from a cultural movement into the ideological basis of extreme nationalism in the hands of Hitler. The *Volk* movement was anticipated by Herder's idea of the *Volk,* while its nationalist side could look back to the German philosopher Johann Gottlieb Fichte. With Fichte, patriotism was refashioned as nationalism, or love of nation.[79]

In his famous lectures on the German nation, Fichte claimed that Germans were a distinct people and their first duty was to love their nation. Fichte's ideas, a mixture of romanticism and Kantian idealism, stressed the spiritual value of a people and a nation. His fourteen lectures were delivered to the Academy of Sciences in Berlin in 1807–1808. Fichte courageously spoke of justice and freedom as Napoleon's troops occupied the city. Throughout the first seven lectures, Fichte probed what it was to be German, contrasted with other peoples of Teutonic descent. Then, in his eighth lecture, he asked the large question: What is a people? He said this question was answered by answering another question: What is the love of the individual for his nation or his love of the fatherland?[80]

The *Völkisch* Movement

The *völkisch* movement was characterized by frustration at the status of Germany amid modernization. Advocates shared a longing for German unity and spiritual renewal against the "material" and alienating forces of modernity—industrialization, liberalism, and capitalism—about which Marx had written. Politically, the movement protested Germany's fragmented state and its second-rate status among European powers, which, in their view, was not corrected by the Treaties of Paris in 1814–1815 or the leadership of Otto von Bismarck. After the First World War, the imposition of the Treaty of Versailles, the weakness of the Weimar Republic, and an economic crisis would rub more salt on the pride of German volkists.

Volk *as Rootedness*

Since German romanticism in the late 1700s, *Volk* meant more than "the people." It meant the unity of the German people as part of some transcendental reality, such as nature or the cosmos. Nature was not regarded as an external, material system. It was regarded, in pantheistic terms, as something alive, a source of German creativity and feeling. The essence of the German *Volk* is to be "rooted" in a particular landscape.

The movement, which evolved in stages across the 1800s, consisted of an unlikely and odd collection of individuals and groups. Among the shapers of the ideology were frustrated academics, social misfits, philosophers who embraced "irrationalism," theorists of culture and race, and people who claimed to intuit the spiritual essence of the *Volk*. Some groups delved into the occult and practiced nature mysticism, sun worship, and theosophy. Some called for a Germanic religion, while attacking the entire Western tradition of rationalism and science. Some German utopians set up "back to the land" communities to escape modernity.

The belief in a mystical *Volk* relied on the questionable view that there was a homogeneous Germanic race going back to a golden age in medieval times. Writers like Berthold Auerbach (1812–1882) and Dietrich Eckart (1868–1923)—the latter later to become Hitler's crazed mentor—wrote popular novels and plays that idealized the simple, honest German peasant close to nature, in the tradition of Rousseau and Tolstoy.[81] Other adherents looked to Wagner's music to speak for the greatness of the *Volk*. Importantly, educators created a youth movement that carried the *Volk* ideas forward. Toward the end of the 1800s, Aryan theories of race, using anthropology and phrenology, became popular and were deemed "scientific." One could determine the inner quality of a race's (or a person's) character from their external features and appearance. Not surprisingly, writers claimed that the Aryan race was the most beautiful and "pure" and that there should be no mixing of races. The Jew, the lowest race according to this scale, threatened the purity of the German people.

By the time of National Socialism, the idea of a unique, superior, German *Volk*, exclusive of Jews and wealthy capitalists (and liberals), was accepted across much of the nation, ready to be exploited by Adolf Hitler.

Extreme Nationalism

We are all too familiar with the Nazis' rise to power in the 1930s and 1940s. A terrifying right-wing populism, with a totalitarian mind-set supported by massive military power, strutted across Germany and the world's stage.

Toward the end of the 1800s, nationalism and socialism merged in Germany and Austria, with nationalism taking the lead. By 1890 various Christian Socialist parties were formed in Germany and elsewhere. "Christian" meant white Christians with a suspicion of Jews. Then, 10 years later, there were the first, small National Socialist parties.[82] Secret societies grew in number, such as the Teutonic Order, founded in Berlin in 1912. It required candidates for membership to prove that they had no "non-Aryan" bloodlines and to promise they would maintain the purity of their race in marriage. Members of the anti-Semitic Thule Society, founded in 1918 by Rudolf von Sebottendorff, were occultists who believed in the coming of a "German Messiah" who would redeem Germany after its defeat in World War I.

Hitler said that by the time he was fifteen he understood the difference between patriotism and *völkisch* "nationalism" and that, even then, "I was interested only in the latter."[83] Patriotism, for Hitler, belonged to an earlier age when Germany was divided into many principalities. Patriotism did not fit a nationalist age or Germany's need for unity.[84] Hitler wrote that the "basic ideas of the National-Socialist movement are populist (*völkisch*) and the populist (*völkisch*) ideas are National-Socialist." Hitler later said he was a populist socialist, not an international one. But it was his nationalism that galvanized Germans.

Hitler: "Move the Masses"

The key to Hitler's rise to power was his ability to turn the populist *völkisch* ideas into a disciplined, practical, political movement. In 1924, after his release from prison for his Munich putsch, he decided to come to power constitutionally. Once in control of the Reichstag, he would take control of Germany.[85] He did so by exploiting one "hot button" issue that united all *völkisch* groups: hatred of the Jew as inferior, as "unrooted" to any *Volk*, and as a threat to the purity of the German race. At the same time, Hitler knew he needed a broad base of support to undermine the Weimar Republic. He had to appeal to the masses. He recognized the importance of a strong populist message, using stirring slogans, rallies, and mass media. In 1920, he created a twenty-five-point plan for the National Socialist party that pandered to the masses. The platform would abolish any income derived not from labor and would nationalize trusts. Hitler wrote: "An agitator who demonstrates the ability to transmit an idea to the broad masses must always be a psychologist, even if he were only a demagogue. Then he will still be more suited for leadership than the unworldly theoretician, who is ignorant of people. *For leading means: being able to move the masses.*"[86]

Standing back from the details, how might we view, overall, this madness that had overcome Germany? George Mosse, in his seminal work on the origins of Nazi ideology, regarded this "German Revolution" as a revolution of the middle-class bourgeoisie.[87] They did not want a radical socialist revolution because it would threaten their status and property. But they were dissatisfied with the cultural and political state of Germany. A *Volk*-led revolution was an ideal revolution for them since it meant cultural revival, not material or structural reform.

If the Nazis had not taken the lead, other right-wing parties were ready to do so, since by the 1930s *völkisch* thought, as Mosse says, had captured "the entire powerful German right." The *völkisch* scorn for parliamentary democracy helped to undermine the Weimar Republic. Parliaments with their partisan parties divided the *Volk*, and they dealt with mundane, "material" matters that had nothing to do with a spiritual revival—something greater for Germany than successful industrialization.

Many Germans were ready to hand the struggling German government to a strong man. Even the German philosopher Martin Heidegger would join the Nazi party. It was a cultural movement, a revolt against democracy, and a response to wartime humiliation. Generations had come to believe that some implementation of *Volk* ideals was the *only* solution to Germany's problems.[88] Respectable, educated people became so wedded to an ideology that they "lost sight of civilized law and civilized attitudes toward their fellow men."[89] From a politics of "cultural despair" in the nineteenth century would arise a politics of steel, power, and racial hatred.[90] The pogroms and massacres by the Nazis were the massacres that Polybius had predicted would occur when democracy failed and turned to dictatorship.

POPULISM AND JOURNALISM

Journalism has played an important role in the history of populism. Populists have used journalism to propagate their ideas. Journalists have supported or opposed populist leaders; they have created populist news media. Journalists have been a mouthpiece for demagogues and have helped to spark revolutions of the people.

The seeds of populist journalism were planted in the sixteenth century.

The propagandist potential of Gutenberg's printing press was not lost on groups caught up in the religious and political turmoil of the era. Protestants in city-states during the Reformation, such as Nuremberg and Strasbourg, gave printed matter its first ideological role. In 1517, pamphlets ignored official censors and spread news of Martin Luther's *Ninety-five Theses*. Reformers took part in a vicious pamphlet campaign against the pope. Printed texts used images of Luther with a halo around his head. A pamphlet war erupted in France during the sixteenth-century conflict between Catholics and Huguenots, and again in The Netherlands during its revolt against Spain. Between 1614 and 1617, when French nobles rebelled against their king, 1,200 anti-monarchy pamphlets appeared.

Kinds of Populist Journalism

Yet this publishing did not constitute a popular or a populist press.[91] Populist journalism did not really exist until the newspapers of the eighteenth-century Enlightenment.

Before a modern populist press could emerge, three big things had to occur: First, the technological conditions for a periodic news press had to exist, e.g., transportation systems to gather information at a distance and to distribute papers. Second, social conditions had to be satisfied—sufficient numbers of readers had to be literate, able to pay for newspapers, and with a need for news they could not easily obtain on their own. Also, demand for newspapers increased as citizens came to see themselves as members of a public with a right to be informed. Third, politically, there had to be a significant, if gradual, drift away from authoritarian government and hierarchical society sufficient for liberty of the press.

All three conditions were falling into place by the eighteenth century in Europe and America. Journalists declared themselves to be "tribunes" of the people—a reference to the Roman tribunes. Philosopher Jeremy Bentham argued that representative government depended on "publicity" from the press.[92] In the 1720s, London editor Nathaniel Mist portrayed his *Weekly Journal* as a moral educator of the public. Pierre-Louis Roederer, French revolutionary politician and journalist, said in 1796 that newspapers reached more readers than books and taught the same truth "every day, at the same time . . . in all public places." After fomenting discontent and revolutions, journalists would be called a fourth estate of the realm.

From the eighteenth to the twentieth century, there were at least three types of populist journalism with different ideas on how to serve the public. There were (1) reformist-activist journalists, for whom service to the public meant service to the correct political cause or party; (2) revolutionary journalists, for whom serving the public meant creating a new political order; and, later, (3) reporters for a mass, populist press, for whom serving the public meant factually informing people about news of the world.

Reform for the People

In the category of reform journalists, we can place the sharp, attention-grabbing editorials (or essays) in the London papers of the early 1700s. Essayists from Daniel Defoe to Jonathan Swift critiqued government in the name of the people. From 1720 to 1723, John Trenchard and Thomas Gordon published anonymously the famous Cato letters, 144 in total, in the *London Journal*. In the name of Cato, the Roman republican, Trenchard and Gordon warned government to pay attention to the reasonable demands of the people. The letters, republished in the American colonies by Benjamin Franklin, played a role in the acquittal of John Peter Zenger in 1735 for criticizing the governor of New York. Zenger's lawyer, Alexander Hamilton, argued that the people had a right to expose arbitrary power by speaking and writing the truth.

Reform journalism took demagogic form in England during the turbulent late 1700s. Journalists tapped into deep reservoirs of popular resentment against George III and his government. Two examples of this strident journalism are the anonymous letters of Junius and the protests of editor John Wilkes, London M.P., self-proclaimed defender of the people's liberty.

The seventy Junius letters—who wrote them is still debated—were published between January 1769 and January 1772 in London's popular *Public Advertiser*.[93] Junius' first letter attacked the Grafton government on behalf of "a nation overwhelmed with debt; her revenues wasted . . . the whole administration of justice become odious . . . to the whole body of the people." Junius told the king it was "the misfortune of your life . . . that you should never have been acquainted with the language of truth, until you heard it in the complaints of your people."

Meanwhile, the editor-demagogue Wilkes used his appeals to the liberty of the people to ride a wave of dissent to notoriety, public office, and journalistic immortality. On April 25, 1763, the famous No. 45 issue of Wilkes's *North Briton* newspaper criticized the king's speech to parliament for repeating the falsehoods of Lord Bute and other corrupt ministers. The government charged Wilkes for seditious libel, raided his premises, seized documents, and threw him into the London Tower. Such treatment made Wilkes and the "liberty of the press" a cause célèbre. "My Lords," Wilkes cried at his trial, "the liberty of all peers and gentlemen, and what touches me more sensibly, that of all the middling and inferior set of people, who stand most in need of protection, is in my case this day to be finally decided upon a question of such importance as to determine at once whether English liberty shall be a reality or shadow." The charge was dismissed because Wilkes, as an M.P., was judged to be immune from libel. A crowd of Wilkes supporters left the court shouting "Wilkes and Liberty!"

Reform journalism would appear in many guises in the future. Across Europe in the nineteenth century, there would be a press devoted to working-class and lower-class readers, from socialist papers to Chartist pamphlets. In England, the government, until about 1850, would try to limit the distribution of populist papers by taxing newsprint and circulation, among other measures. Also, as seen, left-wing American demagogues in the 1930s, such as Long and Coughlin, would use newspapers and radio to reach the populace. In the United States, the populist, magazine muckrakers of the early 1900s would expose public wrongdoing.[94] Then the investigative journalists of the 1970s and 1980s—their status enhanced by their role in the Watergate crisis—would investigate corruption in public places. At the same time, advocacy journalists took up the cause of the American civil rights movement, finally providing what much of the white-dominated mainstream press would not offer—an activist journalism against racial discrimination among the populace.

Fomenting Revolution

Revolutionary journalists took the polemical energies of reform journalism to a higher level of intensity and engagement. The point of revolutionary journalism was not to simply inform readers or to seek reform. It was to replace the political system, not to modify it.

In America, the newspapers were a driving force behind anti-British feeling long before the first shots of the War of Independence were fired in 1775. By the 1760s there were more than forty-five American newspapers. Samuel Adams, writing in the *Boston Gazette and Country Journal*, covered the meetings of independence groups and attacked colonial authorities. The Boston Tea Party was planned in the house of Benjamin Edes, editor of the *Boston Gazette*. When the war was won, the American papers took credit for helping to create a free nation. Jefferson called the newspaper "the only tocsin of a nation."

In France, press censorship in the eighteenth century restricted reformists and produced an official press that was scientifically and informationally sophisticated but politically cautious. However, a revolutionary press began in the late 1780s, as activists across France prepared for a dramatic meeting of the Estates-General to deal with France's deteriorating financial situation. The government lifted censorship.[95] Leading deputies, such as Jacques Pierre Brissot and Honoré Gabriel Riqueti, comte de Mirabeau, published their own papers and called for a free press. A staggering number of pamphlets appeared. The total number of copies of pamphlets circulated in France in the year before the Estates-General met in May 1789 was more than 10 million.

But it was the unexpected fall of the Bastille and establishment of a provisional government that created, almost overnight, a revolutionary press. The *Revolutions de Paris* gave hurried summaries of the Bastille crisis. Marat put out his *Ami du peuple* in September 1789. In the provinces, the "affiches" added political news and published more frequently. In the years of press freedom, from 1789 to 1792, up to 1,000 papers are known to have existed, spanning the political spectrum.[96] The revolutionary press's rhetoric could be red-hot: "In fighting against the enemies of the state, I attack the cheats without fear, I unmask the hypocrites, I denounce the traitors," railed Marat.[97] Revolutionary journalists argued that the authority of church and king had been transferred to a public or "re-public" of citizens.

The revolutionary's interest in journalism carried forward. Karl Marx edited left-wing journals and wrote essays for the *New York Daily Tribune*. The first thing that Lenin did when he set out in 1901 to promote revolution in Russia was to start a newspaper as a "collective propagandist and a collective agitator." In a series of articles after the Russian Revolution, Lenin stressed that the workers' press should write concise, factual articles in "telegraphic" form on the revolution—a style found in Western bourgeoisie newspapers.[98]

A Popular Press

The populist press was not confined to activists and revolutionaries. For much of the nineteenth century, elite liberal papers, such as *The Times* of London, were dominant, advocating free trade and freedom of the press. In the late 1800s, a different liberal press arose that was both popular and populist: mass commercial newspapers that, instead of being financed by elites, were financed by sale to the people as a whole, and by ads that sought to reach the populace. This genre of publishing included the popular newspapers of Joseph Pulitzer, such as the *New York World*, and the new "tabloids" directed at the lower and middle classes. These papers were in the business of news, not opinion. Ideologically, they claimed their service to the public was to factually inform the populace on events and on the actions of government.

We should not forget that populists and their publications faced resistance. Conservative forces in society did not melt away. A good deal of journalism in the elite press was *against* populist ideas. Even in "liberal" times, one never knew when criticism of an existing institution could roil the public sphere. For example, in the United States, Paine was a powerful and popular agitator for independence from Britain. But then he turned his liberalism to religion in *The Age of Reason*, arguing that Christianity would give way to science. Paine was attacked by newspapers for undermining religion. One U.S. newspaper called him a "loathsome reptile."[99]

The Mob Returns

The growth of mass democracy sparked criticism from intellectuals and journalists in the late 1800s and early 1900s.

Their first target was the intelligence and character of the "ordinary" person. As more citizens got the right to vote, including women, conservative writers revived the ancient idea of the people as an irrational mass, a mob. Journalist H. L. Mencken lampooned democracy and "homo boobus"—the average person. Among the intelligentsia, conservative Gustave Le Bon of France, in his groundbreaking book on crowd psychology, wrote that the modern public was a crowd "little adapted to reasoning." Everett Dean Martin's popular *Behavior of Crowds* of 1921 shared LeBon's anti-egalitarian social psychology, which influenced Hitler and Freud. The masses were intellectually lazy or cognitively overwhelmed by issues. *The Revolt of the Masses*, by philosopher José Ortega y Gasset, and *End of Economic Man*, by Peter Drucker, worried that the masses would follow fascist leaders.

If the people were a mob, then public opinion, the key mechanism of democracy, was irrational or unreliable. The success of war propaganda in maintaining support for the slaughter of the First World War showed how government could manipulate public opinion. Historian Jack Roth called the war the "first modern effort at systematic, nation-wide manipulation of collective passions."[100] Meanwhile, in the 1920s and 1930s, a cadre of American press agents, led by Ivy Lee and Edward Bernays, put wartime propaganda techniques to work for government, leaders, and corporations. The conservative Leo Strauss, who escaped Nazi Germany and taught at the University of Chicago, revived Plato's skepticism of democracy. In an essay on Plato's *Republic*, Strauss wrote: "The end of democracy is not virtue but freedom, i.e., the freedom to live either nobly or basely according to one's liking."[101] Ideally, the unwise masses would consent to be governed by the wise. But, Strauss adds, it is unlikely that this will "ever be met."[102]

Walter Lippmann, a progressive philosopher-journalist, supported citizen-led democracy but became a worried analyst of mass opinion and democracy. In his *Public Opinion* of 1922, Lippmann argued that people understand events through the prism of general ideas, or "stereotypes." They struggle to see the world from behind a veil of ideas, emotions, and interests. Democracy is unrealistic because it expects citizens to arrive at informed opinions on matters beyond their personal experience, expertise, or interests—military operations, international affairs, and economic policy. To rectify this situation, society should assign the analysis of important issues to objective experts employed by "intelligence bureaus."[103] The press would relay their knowledge to the masses. For Lippmann, too much populism was a bad thing.

Pragmatist John Dewey tried to answer Lippmann's skepticism about mass democracy. But even Dewey lamented that "we live exposed to the greatest flood of mass suggestion that any people has ever experienced . . . sentiment can be manufactured for almost any person or any cause."[104]

In the decades after the Second World War, journalism moved away from its brash origins in popular movements. In wealthy Western nations, journalism became increasingly professional, embedded in a complex industrial process dominated by large corporations. Journalists became better educated and better paid, and many of them joined the elites. Journalists never gave up their claim to publish for the people, but the distance between newsroom and audience grew.

NOTES

1. Aristotle, *Politics*, trans. Carnes Lord (Chicago: University of Chicago Press, 2013), Book V, chapter 4, 1240.

2. John Lukacs, *Democracy and Populism: Fear and Hatred* (New Haven, CT: Yale University Press, 2006), 11.

3. By the third quarter of the fourth century BC, as Aristotle was writing *Politics*, there were about 1,100 city-states in the Greek world. The most important were Athens, Sparta, Corinth, Thebes Syracuse, Aegina, Rhodes, Argos, Eretria, and Elis. The extended Greek world under Alexander the Great contained more than 8 million people. Among the largest city-states was Athens, of some 2,500 square kilometers, about the size of Orange County in southern California. Most city-states were small. Plataea, northwest of Athens, was only 170 square kilometers, with fewer than 10,000 people. See Josiah Ober, *The Rise and Fall of Classical Greece* (Princeton, NJ: Princeton University Press, 2015), 6–7.

4. See Humfrey Michell, *Sparta* (Cambridge, UK: Cambridge University Press, 1964). During the classical era, other Greek city-states had forms of government similar to Athens, such as Corinth, Megara, and Syracuse. Athens, however, is the best-understood example of Greek democracy.

5. John Boardman, Jasper Griffin, and Oswyn Murray, *The Oxford History of Greece and the Hellenistic World* (Oxford: Oxford University Press, 1991), 27.

6. Boardman et al., *The Oxford History of Greece and the Hellenistic World*, 96.

7. The archaic period extends from the eighth century BC to the second Persian invasion of Greece in 480 BC. It was followed by the classical period.

8. The first occurrence of the word in surviving Greek literature is in Herodotus, *The Histories*, trans. Robin Waterfield (Oxford: Oxford University Press, 1998), especially Book III, 204–206.

9. David Stockton, *The Classical Athenian Democracy* (Oxford: Clarendon Press, 1990), 1.

10. Stockton places Solon's reforms in the 570s BC. See *The Classical Athenian Democracy*, 20.

11. Herodotus, *The Histories*, Book V, 327–329.

12. For details on the reforms, see Stockton, *The Classical Athenian Democracy*.

13. The Pnyx, which looked down on the agora, was used for popular assemblies as early as 507 BC, when Cleisthenes transferred power to the citizenry.

14. Thucydides, *The History of the Peloponnesian War*, trans. Martin Hammond (Oxford: Oxford University Press, 2009), 145.

15. Stockton, *The Classical Athenian Democracy*, 15–16. See also Arnold Jones, *Athenian Democracy* (Oxford: Oxford University Press, 1957).

16. See Plato, "The Apology," in *The Complete Works*, 17–36, ed. John M. Cooper (Indianapolis, IN: Hackett Publishing, 1997).

17. Ober, *The Rise and Fall of Classical Greece*, xiii.

18. Plato, *The Republic*, trans. Francis Cornford (New York: Oxford University Press, 1968), part IV, chapter XXXI, 283.

19. Aristotle, *Politics*, 106.

20. Plato, *The Republic*, Books VIII and IX, 265–301; Aristotle, *Politics*, Books IV–VI, 97–186.

21. Polybius, *Histories* (Oxford: Oxford University Press, 2010), 372, 373.

22. Polybius, *Histories*, 372, 373.

23. Polybius, *Histories*, 373.

24. Josiah Ober, *Mass and Elite in Democratic Athens: Rhetoric, Ideology, and the Power of the People* (Princeton, NJ: Princeton University Press, 1989), 85–90.

25. Cicero, *The Republic and the Laws*, trans. Niall Rudd (Oxford: Oxford University Press, 2008), 19.

26. For an overview of the structure and the social classes, see Paul A. Zoch, *Ancient Rome: An Introductory History* (Norman: University of Oklahoma Press, 1998).

27. See Peter Baehr, *Caesar and the Fading of the Roman World: A Study in Republicanism and Caesarism* (Piscataway, NJ: Transaction Publishers, 1998).

28. See Richard Alston, *Rome's Revolution: Death of the Republic and Birth of the Empire* (Oxford: Oxford University Press, 2015).

29. Stockton, *The Classical Athenian Democracy*, 56.

30. See Arthur O. Lovejoy, *The Great Chain of Being* (Cambridge, MA: Harvard University Press, 1978).

31. On the historical inaccuracy of this image, see Francesco Maiolo, *Medieval Sovereignty: Marsilius of Padua and Bartolus of Saxoferrato* (Delft, The Netherlands: Eburon Academic Publishers, 2007).

32. See Alan Gewirth, *Marsilius of Padua: The Defender of Peace* (New York: Columbia University Press, 1964), and Quentin Skinner, *The Foundations of Modern Political Thought* (Cambridge: Cambridge University Press, 1978).

33. Cited in Maurizio Viroli, *For Love of Country: An Essay on Patriotism and Nationalism* (Oxford: Clarendon Press, 1996), 26.

34. Francesco Petrarch, "On His Own Ignorance and That of Many Others," trans. Hans Nachod, in *The Renaissance Philosophy of Man*, ed. Ernst Cassirer, Paul Oskar Kristeller, and John Hermann Randall Jr. (Chicago: University of Chicago Press, 1948), 104.

35. Ernst Cassirer, Paul Oskar Kristeller, and John Hermann Randall Jr., eds., *The Renaissance Philosophy of Man* (Chicago: University of Chicago Press, 1948), 4.

36. Martin Luther, "On Temporal Authority: To What Extent It Should Be Obeyed," in *Luther's Works*, ed. Walther Brandt, trans. J. J. Schindel (Philadelphia: Open Court, 1962), Vol. 45, 112.

37. See Martin Luther, "Against the Murderous, Thieving Hordes of Peasants," in *Luther's Works*, ed. Jaroslav Pelikan and Hilton C. Oswald (St. Louis and Philadelphia: Concordia Publishing House and Fortress Press, 1955–1986), 50–51.

38. See David Fellman, "Constitutionalism," in *Dictionary of the History of Ideas: Studies of Selected Pivotal Ideas*, ed. Philip P. Wiener (New York: Charles Scribner, 1974), Vol. 1, 485, 491–492.

39. Jean Bodin, *Six Books of the Commonwealth* (Cambridge, MA: Harvard University Press, 2014). See, especially, Book I, chapters VII and X.

40. Locke had to flee to Europe for fear of his life after writing his *Two Treatises of Government*.

41. See Thomas Hobbes, *Leviathan* (London: Penguin Books, 1968).

42. I explain Hobbes's social contract in "Thomas Hobbes: The Ethics of Social Order," in *Ethical Communication: Moral Stances in Human Dialogue*, ed. Clifford Christians and John Merrill (Columbia: University of Missouri Press, 2009), 158–164. On contractualism, see Stephen Darwall, ed., *Contractarianism/Contractualism* (Malden, MA: Blackwell Publishing, 2003), and Nicholas Southwood, *Contractualism and the Foundations of Morality* (Oxford: Oxford University Press, 2013).

43. John Locke, *Two Treatises of Government*, ed. Mark Goldie (London: J. M. Dent, 1996), 163.

44. Jean-Jacques Rousseau, "Discourse on the Sciences and Arts," in *The First and Second Discourses*, ed. Victor Gourevitch (New York: Harper Torchbooks, 1990).

45. For detailed historical studies of romanticism, see Isaiah Berlin's *Political Ideas in the Romantic Age: Their Rise and Influence on Modern Thought* (Princeton, NJ: Princeton University Press, 2008) and *The Crooked Timber of Humanity* (London: Fantana Press, 1991).

46. Berlin, *The Crooked Timber of Humanity*, 39.

47. They were so called because they did not wear the upper-class culottes, or breeches.

48. On Rousseau's ideas as leading to the "shameful evil" of the revolution, see Edmund Burke, *Reflections on the Revolution in France* (Oxford: Oxford University Press, 2009), 274.

49. Lukacs, *Democracy and Populism*, 9.

50. See David P. Szatmary, *Shays' Rebellion: The Making of an Agrarian Insurrection* (Amherst: University of Massachusetts Press, 1980).

51. Marion L. Starkey, *A Little Rebellion* (New York: Knopf, 1955), 33.

52. Michael Signer, *Demagogue: The Fight to Save Democracy from Its Worst Enemies* (New York; Palgrave Macmillan, 2009), 80.

53. Signer, *Demagogue*, 81.

54. Signer, *Demagogue*, 87.

55. David N. Mayer, *The Constitutional Thought of Thomas Jefferson* (Charlottesville: University Press of Virginia, 1994), 318.

56. Thomas Philip, ed., *Thomas Paine: Rights of Man, Common Sense, and Other Political Writings* (New York: Oxford University Press, 1995), 122.

57. James Madison, *Notes of Debates in the Federal Convention of 1787* (New York: Norton, 1987), 73.

58. Wilbourn Benton, ed., *1787: Drafting the U.S. Constitution* (College Station: Texas A&M University Press, 1986), Vol. 1, 89.

59. Benton, *1787*, 456.

60. Signer, *Demagogue*, 94. *The Federalist Papers* were essays organized by Hamilton to defend the proposed constitution. Written by Alexander Hamilton, John Jay, and James Madison, the essays began appearing in *The Independent Journal* in 1787.

61. Signer, *Demagogue*, 87–88.

62. Benton, *1787*, 802.

63. Sean Wilentz, *Andrew Jackson* (New York: Times Books, 2005), 55.

64. Wilentz, *Andrew Jackson*, 47.

65. Arthur M. Schlesinger Jr., "An Impressive Mandate and the Meaning of Jacksonianism," in *Andrew Jackson: A Profile*, ed. Charles Sellers (New York: Hill & Wang, 1971), 50.

66. Solomon Volkov, *The Magical Chorus: A History of Russian Culture from Tolstoy to Solzhenitsyn*, trans. Antonina W. Bouis (New York: Vintage Books, 2009), 74–76.

67. For a revealing account of Russian cultural history at this time, see Volkov, *The Magical Chorus*.

68. Juan Linz, *The Breakdown of Democratic Regimes* (Baltimore: Johns Hopkins University Press, 1978), 97.

69. On American populism, see Lawrence Goodwyn, *Democratic Promise: The Populist Moment in America* (New York: Oxford University Press, 1976).

70. See Michael Kazin, *The Populist Persuasion: An American History* (Ithaca, NY: Cornell Paperbacks, 1998).

71. Walter Nugent, *The Tolerant Populists: Kansas Populism and Nativism* (Chicago: University of Chicago Press, 2013), 178.

72. Populism in the American Midwest was not alone in the Americas. Across the border in Canada, farmers in Alberta created the conservative, populist "social credit" movement in the 1930s as they struggled to survive the Great Depression. It led to provincial and federal social credit parties and governments that were a political force until the 1960s.

73. See Steven J. Rosenstone, Roy L. Behr, and Edward H. Lazarus, *Third Parties in America* (Princeton, NJ: Princeton University Press, 1984), and Ronald P. Formisano,

For the People: American Populist Movements from the Revolution to the 1850s (Chapel Hill: University of North Carolina Press, 2012).

74. Alan Brinkley, *Voices of Protest: Huey Long, Father Coughlin & the Great Depression* (New York: Vantage Books, 1983).

75. For a novel based on Long's life, see Robert Penn Warren, *All the King's Men.*

76. Brinkley, *Voices of Protest*, 266–268.

77. Brinkley, *Voices of Protest*, 261.

78. See Tom Wicker, *Shooting Star: The Brief Arc of Joe McCarthy* (New York: Harcourt, 2006).

79. Patriotism is ancient; nationalism is a late development. The terms *nationalism* and *nationalist* only appear in French and English in the late 1800s.

80. Johann Fichte, *Addresses to the German Nation* (Whithorn, UK: Anodos Books, 2017), 99.

81. In 1912, Eckart adapted, with popular success, Ibsen's Norwegian tale of peasant Peer Gynt. Gynt was now portrayed as an honest German peasant struggling for salvation.

82. Lukacs, *Democracy and Populism*, 39.

83. Adolf Hitler, *Mein Kampf*, trans. Ralph Manheim (Boston: Houghton Mifflin, 1943), 13.

84. Hitler, *Mein Kampf*, 424.

85. William L. Shirer, *The Rise and Fall of the Third Reich: A History of Nazi Germany* (New York: Exeter Books, 1987), 45.

86. Hitler, *Mein Kampf*, 580. Italics in the original text.

87. George L. Mosse, *The Crisis of German Ideology: Intellectual Origins of the Third Reich* (New York: Grosset and Dunlap, 1964), 7–8.

88. Mosse, *The Crisis of German Ideology*, 202–203.

89. Mosse, *The Crisis of German Ideology*, 8–9.

90. Fritz Stern, *The Politics of Cultural Despair: A Study in the Rise of Germanic Ideology* (Berkeley: University of California Press, 1961), xi.

91. By popular, I mean a press that is popular with the people, i.e., enjoys wide distribution and readership. By populist, I mean a press that claims to serve the

public politically, i.e., informing the public of events, promoting populist ideas, and representing the public to goverrment.

92. Jeremy Bentham, "Constitutional Code," in *The Collected Works of Jeremy Bentham*, ed. Frederick Rosen and James H. Burns (Oxford: Clarendon Press, 1983), vol. I, 10.

93. Junius appears to have been chosen because it was part of the name of Lucius Junius Brutus, a founder of the Roman republic and one of the first Roman consuls in 509 BC.

94. The American muckrakers wrote more than 2,000 magazine articles between 1900 and 1915. Ida Tarbell wrote a long, critical series on John D. Rockefeller's Standard Oil Company. Lincoln Steffens's *The Jungle* exposed problems in the meat-packing industry. See Louis Filler, *The Muckrakers* (Stanford, CA: Stanford University Press, 1993).

95. Jeremy D. Popkin, *Revolutionary News: The Press in France, 1789-1799* (Durham, NC: Duke University Press, 1990), 25.

96. Popkin, *Revolutionary News*, 33. At least 250 French newspapers were established in the last six months of 1789, aimed at different audiences. Some 335 newspapers appeared in Paris in 1790 alone.

97. Anthony Smith, *The Newspaper: An International History* (London: Thames & Hudson, 1979), 197.

98. Lenin, "Where to Begin," 16.

99. Thomas Paine, *The Thomas Paine Reader* (London: Penguin Books, 1987), 16, 17.

100. Cited in William A. Gamson, "The 1987 Distinguished Lecture: A Constructionist Approach to Mass Media and Public Opinion," *Symbolic Interaction*, vol. 11, no. 2 (1988): 161–174.

101. Leo Strauss, "Plato," in *An Introduction to Political Philosophy: Ten Essays by Leo Strauss* (Detroit: Wayne State University Press, 1975), 210.

102. Leo Strauss, *Natural Right and History* (Chicago: University of Chicago Press, 1999), 141.

103. Walter Lippmann, *Public Opinion* (New York: Macmillan, 1922), 182, 399.

104. John Dewey, *Individualism Old and New*, 42–43.

Extreme Populism and Journalism

All power comes from the people. But where does it go?

—*Bertolt Brecht*

DEFINING POPULISM

Populism as a Concept

One reason to define populism is that many people think *populism* and *populist* are well-understood terms. In fact, our ordinary usage of *populism* and its associated terms, *populist* and *demagogue*, is vague and too accommodating—almost everyone is a populist. Things are not much better in theory. Political scientists disagree on the definitions of these terms. Moreover, in defining populism it is important to avoid mistakes, such as the pervasive tendency to regard populism as always bad, or identical to dangerous demagoguery.[1]

Etymology helps, to a degree. Populism comes from the Latin word *populous*, meaning "people," and suggests a concern for people. Which people? A frequent reply is *ordinary* or *common* people. The American Heritage Dictionary entry for populism states: "A political philosophy directed to the needs of the common people and advancing a more equitable distribution of wealth and power." Populism promotes the things that common people would seek if they were to rule. Yet who is "common" varies across populism's history.

Some people restrict the reference of populism to the actions of one group. Populist scholar Walter Nugent, discussed in chapter 2, thinks populism should be applied only to the Midwest farmers who started the left-wing American Populist Party in the 1890s, since they popularized the term *populist*.[2]

But we should not confuse concept and term. Even if the term *populism* did not enter general usage until the late 1800s, this does not mean that the concepts that give meaning to the term came into being at the same time. Many concepts have preceded their explicit linguistic formulation and general usage, e.g., "objectivity" and "nationalism." The ideas of populism are as old as antiquity, and populism took many forms before and after the Populist Party.

Yet if we admit a plurality of forms of populism, the definitional problem returns. What are the essential, shared features? Defining populism is made difficult because of its association with democracy and its many forms.[3] Across history, the trajectories of populism and democracy crisscross each other. We may think, incorrectly, that populism and democracy are identical since both subscribe to governance by the people.

Can we solve the problem by defining populism by reference to *populist*, e.g., define populism as the philosophy of populists? Regrettably, *populist* has the same imprecision as *populism*. One Oxford dictionary says a populist is "a person, especially a politician, who strives to appeal to ordinary people who feel that their concerns are disregarded by established elite groups." But as chapter 2 showed, who are "the people" is a moving target, and it seems that populism must be more than simply "appealing" to the people. Further, to add to the confusion, *populist* is applied to things other than political leaders and their platforms. We speak of populist newspapers and populist art, novelists, and music. *Populist* is ascribed to attempts to make one's activities or products popular with the people, such as a chamber orchestra's decision to perform in shopping malls. Like populism, *populist* is applied to the left, center, and right of politics. In the 2016 U.S. presidential election, both Donald Trump and Bernie Sanders were called populists because of their antiestablishment rhetoric. In recent years, both the left-wing Occupy movement and the right-wing Tea Party have been called populist. Left-wing alliances, like Syriza in Greece, are considered populist because they oppose the elites of the European Community and their calls for budget cuts. To complicate matters, populists do not always call themselves populists, and people who are not populists adopt the label to gain support.[4]

Here is a paragraph from a story in *The New York Times* on the drift of populism from Western to Eastern Europe. The story quotes Jiri Pehe, a Czech scholar, on populist leaders in the four Visegrad countries of Eastern Europe.

> Prime Minister Viktor Orban of Hungary "is a right-wing nationalist"; the Polish leader Jaroslaw Kacynski "is an ideologue" obsessed with Russia and the death of his twin brother; Prime Minister Robert Fico of Slovakia "is a left-wing populist"; and Mr. (Andrej) Babis (of the Czech Republic) is closer in spirit, Mr. Pehe said, to figures like President Trump and the former Italian Prime Minister Silvio Berlusconi, promising to rid the country of corruption and run it like a business.[5]

Similarly, in the *New York Times* coverage of the Italian election in March 2018, as mentioned in chapter 1, the main reports labeled all of the right-wing and far-right parties as *populist* apparently because they opposed established parties.[6]

What prompts Pehe or *The New York Times* to call these different politicians populist? With populism brandished so liberally, I am led to ask, with Jan-Werner Müller: Is everyone a populist?[7] We are close to conceptual chaos. We barely know what we are saying.

How to develop a better definition?

Criteria for Definition

By a definition, I do not mean a formal sentence that provides necessary and sufficient conditions for applying a term, a definition that cleanly—without gray areas—separates those things we call populism from those we do not. Precise definitions may be available in mathematics and science, but in political philosophy, basic terms are more imprecise and disputable. There are gray areas no matter what definition of populism is offered. It would be convenient if we could simply note, linguistically, the way *populism* is used. But this provides only a list of different meanings, like a dictionary. One still has to decide which meaning is best. But how? Definitions should be judged pragmatically. As I have said elsewhere,[8] definition amounts to constructing a meaning to clarify our understanding of a term for some phenomenon. We are not *discovering* the meaning; we are not discovering a preexisting fact; we are attempting to clarify and regulate our use of a term. Definition is a conceptual proposal on how we *ought* to understand a term. It stands or fall on its usefulness for theory in general. Defining is not an idle pastime of philosophers, a word game, or "just semantics." Words matter.

A political definition is useful if it meets four criteria:

1. *Cites general, important features:* It captures features of paradigmatic cases of the phenomenon, even if the features are not universal for all instances. This gives the definition empirical and historical validity.
2. *Explains the phenomenon:* It helps us understand the phenomenon and to see similarities and differences between it and other phenomena. It may also explain puzzling features, e.g., the attraction of some populists to conspiracy theories.
3. *Fallible result of inquiry:* It comes after rigorous examination of the phenomenon, not imposed on phenomena from the start. As Aristotle reminded us, good definitions come after inquiry. Definitions are fallible and revisable results of ongoing inquiry.
4. *Logically valid:* It avoids the many pitfalls of defining outlined in logic.

There is a pervasive type of definition that violates these criteria. It is reductionist definition—the reduction of populism to one feature. As an example of violating criterion 1, a reductionist definition may reduce populism to an anti-elite attitude. Anti-elitism does characterize populism, but anti-elitism is not sufficient as a defining feature. Many people are critical of elites. Elites are critical of other elites. Almost *every* politician in the United States today runs "against" the elites of Washington. As an example of violating criterion 2, reductive definitions may identify populism with left-wing or right-wing movements. However, as noted, populist movements exist on the left, right, and center of the political spectrum. Or populism may be reduced to a psychological or sociological feature, such as "angry" voters; or populists are said to be people who have an "authoritarian personality," i.e., a desire to be governed by a strong man. But being angry is not a defining feature of populists. Many people are angry at their political system. Also, not all populists suffer from some authoritarian personality complex.

As an example of violating criterion 3, a reductive definition may be too simple. It may say that populism is a love of the people but fail to note who the people are and in what that love consists. Or the definition fails to note that populism can have antidemocratic impulses, such as a dislike of ethnic or cultural pluralism. As an example of violating criterion 4, the definition may use a pejorative (and empirically false) description of populism, such as the politics of uneducated, unreasoning masses. In 1963, Seymour Martin Lipset, in attacking Senator Joseph McCarthy and the right-wing John Birch Society, called populists "the disgruntled and psychologically homeless . . . the personal failures, the socially isolated . . . the undereducated, unsophisticated, and authoritarian personalities."[9] Populists are the mob.

Core Ideas

If these avenues lead to definitional dead ends, how *should* we define populism?

Müller advises that we avoid thinking about populism as one feature. Rather, we should think about populism as a core of several ideas. This core has what he calls an "inner logic," i.e., it leads to other notions and attitudes.[10] This is a step forward. A core avoids reductionism. But we need to add an important point: This core is a highly general set of ideas. The ideas are so general that populism can be ascribed to many forms of political action. Populism can be realized in varying ways.[11] Also, populism is not a rigorously codified or fixed doctrine. Often, populism is a viewpoint that is more emotive than intellectual—a basic impulse to see all people treated equally. Philosophers develop such convictions into complex political views, such as theories of egalitarian democracy.

So how does this help us define populism? First, we recognize populism as a type of political ideology, and second, we define that ideology in terms of a core of general ideas.

For some people, ideology is a dirty word. It refers to the beliefs of ideologues—people who have narrow and unchangeable views of society and politics—or to ideology as a system of belief that elites impose on the masses to justify their power, such as leaders of fascist states. For Marx, ideology was the means by which capitalists justify their control of society's means of production and their unethical treatment of the proletariat.

This is not my sense of ideology. My sense goes back to the originator of the term, Antoine Destutt de Tracy, writing after the chaos of the French Revolution, where ideology referred to a set of ideas. With fellow French "ideologues," Destutt de Tracy hoped to create a rigorous science of human ideas. I do not dream of such a science, but I do think of ideology as a set of ideas. By ideology I mean ideas—religious, philosophical, economic—by which we understand some area of life. A political ideology is a view that helps us comprehend, rightly or wrongly, adequately or inadequately, what happens in the domain of politics. To be more precise, a political ideology is a set of "action orientated ideas concerning human communities seeking to achieve public influence and control."[12] Ideologies guide political action.

For example, if we walk around a corner and come across an angry group of protesters outside the governor's mansion, waving pickets and surrounded by police, we need some set of ideas to interpret what we see. An anarchist might think of the demonstration as an act of the popular will against the oppressive control of elites. But a conservative might regard the event as a dangerous attempt to achieve goals outside the normal structures of politics. Anarchism and conservatism are political ideologies that interpret events.[13] *Some* interpretation is necessary since the bare facts of observation, e.g., perceiving people in front of a mansion, do not by themselves tell us what is occurring. Interpreting actions according to ideology is the universal human phenomenon of giving events meaning by placing them under a pattern.

Populism, as political ideology, consists of five core ideas.

1. Populism is love of the people. I use "love" intentionally, not in a sentimental manner but in a psychological sense to indicate that it is an emotion-charged conviction. Populism is not just a logical principle that earns someone's intellectual assent. Also, all forms of populism have to decide who the people are—the objects of this love. Candidates for "the people" include (a) all of the people living in a country, or the "body politic," regardless of social status or ethnicity; (b) the common people who belong mainly to the lower classes; (c) the people as a *Volk*, a folk of a nation, which excludes people of different origins; or (d) all citizens.

2. Populism affirms popular sovereignty. Populism thinks the people, however defined, are the ultimate source of political validity. A political system and its basic laws and institutions are valid if they are based on the consent and interests of the people. This is the principle of popular sovereignty, interpreted as the people's right not only to be part of a self-governing citizenry, e.g., having the right to vote, but also to enjoy freedom and equality before the law.

3. Populism is anti-elitism. Popular sovereignty is asserted by populists against individuals or groups who would place their own interests ahead of the people. Among these groups are elites such as the intelligentsia, military leaders, the rich, business monopolies, leaders of state religions, and government bureaucrats and politicians. Populism typically depicts these elites as self-interested and/or corrupt. In this way, populism takes on a moral sense. Honest, hard-working people are morally superior to fat-cat elites. Populism "pits a virtuous and homogeneous people against a set of elites and dangerous 'others' who together are depicted as depriving (or attempting to deprive) the sovereign people of their rights, values, prosperity, identity, and voice."[14]

4. Populism implies class competition. The need to protect popular sovereignty against elites typically presumes a rivalry among social classes. Populism's long struggle with monarchs, nobles, bishops, and the rich bourgeoisie makes social history appear to be a perpetual clash between social classes for power, rights, and benefits. Populist rebellions have arisen in a context of class tensions: the rich versus the poor, the intelligentsia versus the practical people, the upper classes versus the lower classes, the cultured versus the masses. Populism began in ancient Athens with the lower class's efforts to check the power of the aristocrats. Some Western populists today might not describe populism as class warfare, perhaps because it sounds too close to Marx.[15] Yet it *sounds* like class struggle when political leaders say a country must free its political system from control by "privileged elites."[16]

5. Populism is not identical to democracy. Advocacy of the people is not identical to advocacy of democracy. In fact, some populists have criticized or rejected democracy. Both political views start from the same place: concern for the people as self-governing. But then we have to decide *how* the people "get" to govern. Populism does not say, precisely, what sort of rule by the people is in question.

This is where political theories of democracy enter. Democracy is a political philosophy of *how* the people should govern their nation. The varieties of democracy are various ways of imaging how the people should govern and be governed. The different kinds of democracy, from direct to representative to participatory, propose different ways in which the populist impulse—the love of the people—is to be practically expressed in daily politics.

That democracy is not identical to populism can be appreciated by considering some facts. First, the people (or populist movements) have supported nondemocratic leaders and parties. The German people, disgruntled with the Weimar Republic after World War I, exchanged democracy for the dictatorship of Hitler. Second, it is possible for other political structures to express a love of the people, e.g., a benevolent monarch. Third, democracy can be elitist. In the past, liberals agreed on popular sovereignty, but they thought that educated liberal elites should direct democracy. They thought the vote should not be extended to women or to people who do not own substantial amounts of property.

Populism is simple; democracy is complicated. It is easy to shout out "Power to the people" or wax poetic about the virtues of the common person. The impulse to favor everyday people over elites is, at least in our times, an impulse bolstered by a robust popular culture. But democracy is complex because it must decide how to structure daily politics to make popular sovereignty real, fair, and effective; and then citizens must participate regularly in the grinding processes of democracy. Democracy is a hardheaded view of how the people should participate in democracy, what form of democracy is preferred, what rights and duties belong to the public, what institutional mechanisms will guide popular participation, and so on. The preference for democracy is a populist impulse, realized by some democratic system.

In summary, populism is a political ideology with five general features: love of the people, popular sovereignty, anti-elitism, typically a context of class tensions, and an impulse to support the people that may or may not issue into democracy. Given this definition, we can define a populist as someone who supports the core ideas of populism.

Problems of Populism

In chapter 2, I showed how, in history, populist and democratic leaders struggled with their own political creed. One problem was how to incorporate populism into a democratic structure. The issues can be summarized as a set of questions:

How much populism? Should the people vote directly, e.g., through plebiscites, on all significant issues? Should the people directly elect (or remove) the president and the most significant officials, from court prosecutors to senators? What should be done if the populace is racist, anti-Semitic, or willing to deny rights to minorities? Some democrats think populism should be restrained by such means as unelected senators, electoral colleges that help to choose the president, an independent judiciary that strikes down laws of Congress, and a Bill of Rights that restrains popular majorities.[17]

Are the people sufficiently willing and wise? We do not need to regard the people as an irrational mob to recognize that asking people to be self-governing places duties on citizens. Are the majority of citizens sufficiently informed and wise to make the right democratic decisions? Are they motivated to follow politics and developments in civil society? Or do they tune out politics except for every four years when they vote? Are the people sufficiently virtuous to put the common good ahead of their self-interest? In a polluted public sphere, how reliable is the people's judgment? Does journalism provide citizens with the information they require? Are the people prepared to defend their constitution against undemocratic demagogues?

How to use the emotive power of populism? Populism is a two-sided sword. It can be used to advance good or bad causes. On the positive side, populism can be a grassroots movement against a tyrannical government. On the negative side, the term can be taken captive by demagogues who silence dissent, wrap themselves in a patriotic flag, and claim that the "people" are threatened by foreigners. Populism can be a thin veil for xenophobia, extreme nationalism, and moral tribalism.[18]

Demagogues: Heroes or Monsters?

Another problem is how to respond to populist demagogues. Demagogues are portrayed as either saviors of the people or "monsters" who threaten democracy—dangerous rabble-rousers.[19]

In 1838, James Fenimore Cooper listed four fundamental features of demagogues, portraying them as dangerous people.[20] The four features are as follows:

(1) They fashion themselves as a man or woman of the common people, opposed to the elites. (2) They connect with the people. In some cases, the people feel a close relationship with the leader, sensing that he or she is "like us." (3) They manipulate this connection for their own benefit. And (4) they threaten or break established rules of conduct, institutions, and even the law.

Here is a more recent derogatory definition of the demagogue:[21]

> He is a politician skilled in oratory, flattery and invective; evasive in discussing vital issues; promising everything to everybody; appealing to passions rather than the use of reason; and arousing racial, religious, and class prejudices—a man whose lust for power without recourse to principle leads him to seek to become a master of the masses. He has for centuries practiced his profession of "man of the people." He is a product of a political tradition nearly as old as western civilization itself.

These descriptions are true of numerous demagogues across history—those demagogues who, like Cleon or Hitler, undermined democracy and metaphorically led the people down the rocky road to hell. But logically speaking, such descriptions are not good general definitions—definitions that apply to all demagogues. They violate my definitional criterion 4, stated above. They fail to leave room for a positive form of demagoguery. For every fearful Joseph McCarthy, there is a freedom-loving Thomas Paine. Against Hitler's dangerous demagoguery, we can place Churchill's populist oratory skills during England's darkest days of the Second World War. For every anti-Semitic Father Coughlin, there is an inspiring Rev. Martin Luther King Jr. Rhetoric and oratory can advance what is true and just as easily as it can advance falsehood and injustice.

Aristotle, who wrote the first systematic treatise on rhetoric, defined rhetoric as the "faculty of observing in any given situation the available means of persuasion." The available means include the mood and emotions of the crowd, the nature of the incident under discussion, the audience's beliefs, and the ways in which an orator can exhibit his honesty and moral character to the crowd. Aristotle asks why a man should be able to defend himself physically with his body but not be able to defend his ideas by rhetoric. Why should falsehood alone enjoy the power of persuasion?[22] As noted in chapter 2, Renaissance humanism believed that truth and eloquence must join forces if people are to be "incited" to acts of civil virtue. Similarly, today, populists may be a positive influence, giving voice to legitimate issues not stressed by the news media; they may mobilize once-apathetic citizens; and they may force politicians to pay more attention to popular opinion.

Therefore, we need to define the demagogue in more general terms as someone skilled in public oratory who appeals to the people while advocating populist causes. He appears to embrace, or actually does embrace, the core ideas of populism.[23] A demagogue can use his oratory skills for good or ill.

EXTREME POPULISM

Given this understanding of populism, we can define extreme populism. As discussed in chapter 1, "extreme" in "extreme populism" is relative to the principles of moderate, egalitarian democracy. Extreme populists use extreme speech, defined by its disrespectful view of people who hold contrary views and its deep bias against people who belong to other social groups.

Core Ideas

What, then, are the core ideas of extreme populism?

The Exclusive People Thesis

Extreme populism defines the "the people" as an exclusive *subset* of the total inhabitants. They are considered the authentic, true patriotists. These "real" nationals are not necessarily identical to the common people or the poor.

Historically, the subgroup has been defined by race, ethnicity, religion, common place of birth, or some other criteria. Membership in the category of authentic nationals may exclude Muslims and transgendered people. The "authentic" people may be limited to descendants of the early white settlers of the land, or colonials. In Quebec, for example, during the heat of several referenda on whether to stay in Canada, some separatist politicians talked about the "pure" Quebecois who settled the province from France in the sixteenth and seventeenth centuries. Federalists attacked the politicians as extremists. They said that talk of French "purity" was racist and implies that the aboriginals, who preceded the settlers, and recent immigrants from non-European countries are not first-class citizens. Putting Quebec aside, we can say that, for extreme populists, it is *their* group that enjoys popular sovereignty. Laws are valid if they reflect their interests.

Whether someone is "one of us" is a question of tribalism. Margaret Thatcher, when British prime minister, was fond of asking if some candidate for cabinet or some civil servant was "one of us"—i.e., shared her conservative views. When heated topics arise, some people feel a need to identify the "real" patriots. Demagogue Nigel Farage of the U.K. Independence Party celebrated the Brexit vote by saying it was a "victory for real people," apparently making the 48 percent of British citizens who voted against leaving Europe less than real. In May 2016, at a presidential election rally, candidate Donald Trump said that "the only important thing is the unification of the people—because the other people don't mean anything."[24] Who the "other people" are was not clear.

The Anti-Pluralism Thesis

Extreme populism tends to portray the public as a relatively homogeneous, unchanging group of the "right" people, having features not shared by the excluded groups. Extreme populists take a dim view of pluralism, or more precisely, a dim view of normative pluralism. Pluralism is not considered a positive feature of a country. It is regarded as a problem. It is undeniable that today's societies are plural. They contain many types of people with many different interests and values. What matters is what we make of this fact. Normative pluralism thinks pluralism is a good thing, a strength for a country, giving the nation a variety of views, talents, and resources. As much as possible, democracies *ought* to include these many groups as equal participants in society and politics. Morally, it would be wrong to deny groups the right to be part of their country's political deliberations. This is fundamental justice, and it follows from the populist adage that whatever touches all should be approved by all. Practically speaking, normative pluralists believe that democracies that are open to all groups are more stable than nations that exclude groups from meaningful participation. Extreme populists can hardly be pluralists because they intensely dislike some of the social groups. Moreover, these "other people" get in the way of the extreme populists reaching their goals.

The People's Will Thesis

Extreme populists frequently claim to know and represent the will of the people. All populists take the people's will as fundamental. But some extreme populists go further to adopt an implausibly strict or extreme view of the people's will. They talk as if there is one unified public will. On major issues, the people have one will, or one view, rather than different views that need to be compared, altered, or reconciled. Moreover, the extreme populist claims to know what that will is. The view of the extreme populist or demagogue becomes, magically, *the* view of the people.

The Truth Thesis: Absolutism

The epistemology of extreme populists tends toward absolutism. They regard their beliefs as true, absolute, and self-evident. What is in the interests of the people should be clear to any right-thinking person, or true national. Those who fail to acknowledge such truths deserve to be treated with disrespect the way medieval heretics were abused when they questioned the "clear" truths of orthodox Christianity.

The Non-Dialogic Thesis

The absolutist strain encourages skepticism about the value of democratic deliberation. If what should be done is clear, why dialogue, debate, and compromise? Why engage in extensive, time-consuming deliberation across different ideologies, social classes, and interests? If extreme populists cite facts or evidence, it typically is to illustrate a prior, unmovable commitment to an opinion or perspective. Even where extreme populists call for referenda, it is not to encourage a broad-minded public discourse on an issue. It is to seek support for an opinion already formed. What is needed, then, are strong leaders willing to act.

For many extreme populists, democracy is irritating because of its commitment to pluralism, which requires open and prolonged debate. Their political views run up against inclusive, messy democratic processes such as taking votes; holding elections; appointing commissions of inquiry; challenging laws in courts; pursuing wide consultation with citizens; or forcing ideas to endure the scrutiny of Congress, scientific experts, and informed citizens. Extreme populists may think that the "truth"—their absolutist views—is so important as to override these mechanisms of democracy. Democracy is not a respectful dialogue about the common good, nor a search for compromise and common ground. Democracy is a clash of views where winner takes all. Persuasion and implementation, by whatever means, is the goal. According to this "inner logic," opposition to the will of the people, *as defined by the extreme populist*, is not legitimate. This way of thinking justifies personal attacks, manipulative rhetoric, a carelessness with fact, and the misrepresentation of other people as dangerous or unpatriotic.

The Nationalist Thesis

Extreme populism, especially over the past century, is almost invariably a strong, sometimes extreme nationalism that considers the nation as superior to other nations or regards the country as exceptional. The country's interests take automatic precedence over the interests of other countries. This is tribalism turned outward to foreign groups. I will have more to say about extreme patriotism and nationalism in chapter 6.

In summary, extreme populism is the antidemocratic, anti-egalitarian idea of the alleged *rightful dominance of a certain group of citizens, which comes to define the people.*

Examples of Extreme Populism

In recent times, political leaders who have been labeled extreme populists include Marine Le Pen of the National Front in France, Geert Wilders in The Netherlands, former far-right Austrian politician Jörg Haider of the Alliance for the Future of Austria, and Brexit promoter Nigel Farage in Britain. Among the extreme voices in Italy is Beppe Grillo, comedian, blogger, and activist, who in 2009 summed up his role this way: "Folks, it works like this: You let me know, and I play the amplifier."[25]

These leaders speak for groups that no longer lack popular support. In Germany, President Angela Merkel has struggled to contain right-wing groups, such as Alternative for Germany, which use the immigration crisis to sow popular dissent. In Italy, as noted, the Five Star Movement attracted a large share of the vote in the 2018 Italian election.

In Britain, Farage's Independence Party is a right-wing populist party. The party regards Brexit, the English vote to leave Europe, as an act of populism. The party used posters that read "BREAKING POINT: The EU has failed us all . . . and take back control of our borders." The posters showed images of thousands of refugees. The campaign was followed by a surge in hate crimes in the U.K., Germany, and other countries. On the left, Labour Party leader

Jeremy Corbyn has been called a left-wing demagogue given his strong positions on nuclear weapons and other issues.

Populism arose in Latin America in the late 1900s. A "pink tide," socialist and populist, spread over Latin America. Venezuelan president Hugo Chavez and regional allies used populist rhetoric to establish authoritarian regimes. In Latin America, of all fifteen presidents elected in Bolivia, Ecuador, Peru, and Venezuela between 1990 and 2012, five were outsiders and populists who eventually eroded democratic institutions in their countries: Alberto Fujimori, Hugo Chavez, Evo Morales, Lucio Gutierrez, and Rafael Correa.

Around the world, extreme populists, once elected and "inside the political system," have weakened democratic institutions in Hungary, Georgia, Russia, Peru, Chile, Argentina, Nicaragua, the Philippines, Poland, Sri Lanka, Turkey, and Ukraine. In India, Hindu nationalism and ethnic intolerance has grown under Prime Minister Narendra Modi and the Bharatiya Janata Party, which came to power in 2014. The government uses laws to curb free expression and to silence critics. For example, student leader Kanhaiya Kumar of Nehru University was charged with sedition in 2016 for allegedly shouting anti-India slogans. Human rights groups face harassment and intimidation.

In Turkey, President Recep Tayyip Erdogan and his Justice and Development Party have become authoritarian. As he rose to power, Erdogan, at party conferences, used a language of exclusion, saying, for example: "We are the people. Who are you?"[26] After a July 2016 attempted coup by factions within the armed forces, quickly suppressed, freedom of expression deteriorated. Many journalists and politicians face legal charges. After a declaration of emergency, 118 journalists were detained in jail and 184 media outlets were arbitrarily and permanently closed down by executive decree, damaging opposition media. People expressing dissent, especially on the Kurdish issue, were threatened with violence and criminal charges. Internet censorship increased. Nongovernmental organizations, from women's rights groups to humanitarian organizations, were shut down. Threats were directed at academics who signed a petition calling for peace and negotiations and recognition of the Kurdish political movement, and many were dismissed from their posts. Erdogan called the petition signers "a fifth column."[27]

In the Philippines, President Rodrigo Duterte decided to crack down on drugs. More than 6,000 people have been killed. Human rights defenders and journalists were killed by unidentified gunmen and armed militia. Duterte said in 2016: "Hitler massacred three million Jews. Now, there's three million drug addicts. I'd be happy to slaughter them."[28]

In Hungary, Prime Minister Viktor Orban is increasingly authoritarian. In 2016 and 2017, his government spent more than 20 million pounds on communication campaigns portraying immigrants and refugees as criminals and threats to national security. Orban spoke of migration as "poison, we don't need it and won't swallow it," and said that "every single migrant poses a public security and terror risk."[29]

In Austria, the Freedom Party, under Heinz-Christian Strache, used election campaign slogans such as "Homeland Instead of Islam: WE are for YOU," "Vienna Must Not Turn into Istanbul," and "More Courage for Our Viennese Blood." In France, Marine Le Pen of the National Front called immigration an "organized replacement of the population. This threatens our very survival." In The Netherlands, Party for Freedom politician Geert Wilders proposed a "head rag tax" of 1,000 euros, which he justified by saying he believes in the "polluter pays" principle.[30]

STRATEGIES OF EXTREME POPULISM

Extreme populists recruit members and gain popular support by employing strategies, techniques of persuasion, and methods of intimidation before and after gaining power.

Examples of Strategies

I Am the People

I have said that a typical claim of extreme demagogues is that they know the will of the people because they have a special, direct link with the people. They *alone* properly represent the people, or they speak for a "silent majority." This bond with the people, they claim, gives them political legitimacy and, sometimes, the right to flout laws, even constitutions. Like Marat in revolutionary France, the demagogue becomes the people, or claims to.

This is not a new idea. In India during the 1970s, supporters of Indira Gandhi used the slogan "Indira is India, India is Indira." Hugo Chavez liked to say to citizens that he was "a little of all of you." One of his slogans was "Chavez is the people!" and after his death, supporters used the phrase "Let's be like Chavez." Alabama governor George Wallace, in defending segregation, claimed to speak "in the name of the greatest people that have ever trod this earth." The "real America" was what he called "the Great Anglo-Saxon Southland."[31] As we saw, the idea that a leader embodies the nation originated in the medieval idea of God-appointed absolute monarchs.

Conspiracy Theories

Extreme populists have an affection for conspiracy theories.

A conspiracy theory is an explanation that posits an unusual or unlikely cause of an event without strong evidence. There exists some sinister conspiracy against the people, who are unaware of such machinations. In addition— and this is a crucial test for a conspiracy theory—people continue to believe and distribute it *against* strong counterevidence, even when less sensational and more obvious explanations are available. Moreover, the conspiracy theorist will use almost any type of "evidence" for his view, from astrology to phrenology. Some people continue to believe in a conspiracy of Jewish bankers against the Christian world, no matter what. Some people think Lyndon Johnson orchestrated the assassination of President Kennedy.

Extreme populists are attached to conspiracy theories because, if repeated frequently, they persuade some people. As an extreme populist, if I can damage an opponent—whom I regard as not legitimate or unpatriotic—by repeating and circulating a falsehood, why not do so? Another reason is that, lacking good evidence, the populist resorts to conspiracies. When people deal in conspiracies, they can avoid inconvenient facts, and there is no need to rigorously prove one's claims. One preaches to like-minded people. Counterevidence can be dismissed as the invention of political enemies. Another reason is psychological. The conspiracy may fit nicely with a person's beliefs and reinforce how they see the world. For all of these reasons, conspiracy theories are "irrefutable"—no citing of facts will change the conspirator's mind. If people intensely dislike Barack Obama for racial or political reasons, no amount of evidence will persuade them that he is not a Muslim or was truly born in the United States.

Finally, conspiracies help extreme populists explain why they are not in power. If they represent the people and the popular will is so clear, why are they not more successful politically? The answer is that it is the fault of conspiracies among the hated elites and news media, or unpatriotic citizens. The elites have "rigged" the political and electoral system against them, as Trump has said many times, although evidence of serious electoral fraud is weak.

Slogans as Code

Extreme populism has a strong emotive element—a capacity to stir emotions and release frustrations. This is one source of the emptiness *and* effectiveness of many populist slogans, such as "Make America Great Again." What, exactly, does such a slogan mean? Portend? All slogans are abbreviations and therefore empty of detail. But slogans have a special role to play in today's populist politics, which uses media to attract audiences with short attention spans. These slogans are not just mindless platitudes; they are political weapons. A populist's slogans contain a sort of hidden message for loyal supporters. The slogans are decoded or read by supporters as signaling support for certain policies, often politically controversial and not explicitly stated.

Too often, liberals and well-educated moderates shake their heads in disbelief. How could any rational person believe such simplistic slogans? They wonder why people don't see that the "arguments" that support the slogans use clearly fallacious forms of reasoning. For example, to attack a claim by attacking the person who expresses the claim is a case of the ad hominem fallacy, explained in introductory logic textbooks. The attack does nothing to show that the claim is actually true or false. Also, saying the media should stop asking a Republican leader about possible criminal activity by saying the news media should look at the Democrats is an example of the "red herring" fallacy—diverting attention away from oneself.

But in a polluted public sphere, these slogans and fallacious arguments are not advanced for the intelligentsia or for logic class. They are not advanced for the consideration of fair-minded citizens or to prompt reasonable debate. They are advanced for a strictly political purpose: to speak to people who are already invested heavily in a way of seeing the world (or an issue), who care for their version of the truth more than any critical assessment.

Working the System

For all their talk of communing directly with the people, extreme populists, once in power, do not always eliminate mediating institutions and forms of representative democracy. Many of them are content to work with an institutional framework, such as parliaments or court systems, as long as these institutions can be used to support their agenda.

One way of "working" the institutions is to politicize the state. Extreme populists appoint friends and cronies, without special merit or competency, to high state offices. Loyalty to the leader is demanded, and overt partisanship, even if it involves conflicts of interest, is acceptable. Extreme populists *politicize* the state's mechanisms and reduce the impartiality of the government bureaucracy. They fill courts with judges of their ilk and make parliaments subservient. They may close legitimate assemblies and construct another assembly more to their liking. They express frustration at political checks and balances where it thwarts their plans. They ignore the importance of the divisions of powers, interfering with the independent operations of justice and law-enforcement agencies.

Suppressing Critical Civil Society

Extreme populists who are in power seek to impair the operations of those parts of civil society that are critical of their actions, by attacking news media, threatening to withdraw publication licenses, reducing government funds for public broadcasting, intimidating or corrupting journalists, and eliminating funding for civic societies that oppose their policies.

Rewriting Basic Laws and Constitutions

To stay in power, or to ensure the long-term influence of their movement, populist leaders rewrite constitutions. They create their own political constraints with constitutions that do not recognize pluralism.

Seek Alliances for Legitimacy

One way to prevent extreme populists from eroding democracy is to keep them isolated and on the margins of power. This requires that politicians in power avoid making alliances with them, erroneously thinking they can control the extreme populist and, momentarily, use his popularity to revive their electoral fortunes. Demagogues from Hitler to Chavez have risen to power through such alliances. Often, the extreme populist cannot be controlled and will use the alliance to build his public profile and acquire political legitimacy. This entails that politicians must have the political courage to reject such alliances, even where an alliance might help their party in the polls.[32]

Extreme Populism and Democracy

Extreme populism is a danger to democracy on several levels.

First, its repeated attacks on institutions, from the news media to the courts, not to mention their portrayal of their country as an elite dictatorship, encourage public cynicism about democracy. Hence, in tough times, such as economic depression, citizens begin to wonder what could be so wrong with a strong populist leader with an authoritarian mind-set.

Second, as we explore in the next chapter, extreme populism undermines the idea of egalitarian democracy as a peaceful, fair way to govern plural democracies.[33] Its antipluralism rejects the view that we need to find fair terms of living together as free, equal, but diverse citizens. Its idea of the people as an authentic people with a single will is not only empirically false but a dangerous illusion. What constitutes the people of any nation is always changing, with people dying and new people arriving constantly. Exclusionary populism, if allowed to form governments and institute discriminatory policies, is likely to lead to civil violence.

As Cas Mudde and Cristóbal R. Kaltwasser write, extreme populists can sound democratic. They sound like Rousseau with their stress on the people's will.[34] This is an illusion. A regime that privileges a subgroup of citizens is not a democracy. It is an oligarchy of the favored group(s). Egalitarian democracy is rule by all citizens, with no arbitrary exclusions based on race, ethnicity, religion, language, gender, or sexual orientation. The only sane way to run a complex democracy is to acknowledge and utilize, not ignore or decry, pluralism.

Third, to think that respectful debate is not important opens the door to other types of government and rejects the ideal of participatory democracy. To the contrary, democracy should organize political life so that the best impulses of populism, e.g., the right of *all* of the people to have a say, are honored.

Extreme populism is not government of, for, and by the people at large. It is government by *some* of the people for their benefit, for their goals. The alleged mandate of extreme populists does not come from "the people." That idea is a concoction of their own minds and their *interpretation* of what the people need. The common good of democracy is not something known directly or intuitively by people calling themselves populists. The democratic common good is a temporal, discursive thing. It is the result of all citizens having a chance to inform themselves, compare beliefs, and amend ideas, together. Tomorrow, conditions may change and what is in the common good will have to be renegotiated and redefined. A democrat should make claims that are fallible hypotheses that can be empirically investigated, scientifically tested, and openly debated.

The epistemology of democracy is the epistemology of public inquiry put forward by American pragmatic philosophers.[35] Political claims should be put forward as claims that can be pragmatically debated as to possible consequences and compared with alternate policies. Political claims should be open to testing by all concerned in a fair, objective, and rational manner.[36] As Müller writes: "Most democratic politicians would concede that representation is temporary and fallible, that contrary opinions are legitimate, that society cannot be represented without remainder, and that it is impossible for one party or politicians permanently to represent an authentic people apart from democratic procedures and forms."[37]

Finally, populism is not necessarily democratic *or* nondemocratic. As we saw in chapter 2, populism can be democratic by opposing corrupt elites.[38] Or it can support a dictator "of the people." Mudde says that recent forms of populism, especially on the right, are an "illiberal democratic response to undemocratic liberalism"—a response to politics distant from the people.[39] I think a better description of these actions is an illiberal, populist response to problematic democracies. Kurt Weyland has argued that, as a strategy for winning state power, populism "inherently stands in tension with democracy and the value that it places upon pluralism, open debate, and fair competition."[40] After the 2017 constitutional crisis in Venezuela, an article in *The New York Times* argued that populism "is a path that, at its outset, can look and feel democratic. But followed to its logical conclusion, it can lead to democratic backsliding or even outright authoritarianism."[41] Here, the analysis mistakenly conflates populism with one form of populism in one region of the world—its capacity to be nondemocratic. That does not make populism "inherently" against democracy.

Extreme populists should be criticized for what they are: real dangers to democracy and not just to liberalism. As good democrats, committed to dialogue, we should try to engage them in debate, to take their problems or complaints seriously. But we should not resort to *their* tactics of manipulative persuasion, personal attacks, and emotive slogans. We should argue from rigorous facts and objective methods.

Populism, at its best, is a deep humanitarian impulse that insists that all citizens deserve equal recognition and concern. Complaints by populists can alert us to serious failures in our democratic institutions. Populism prompts us to rethink our basic political notions. The threat to democracy is not just external, e.g., some alternate ideology or powerful nondemocratic power bent on conquering democracies. The threat is, largely, internal. As Aristotle, Cicero, the Renaissance humanists, and Jefferson knew, you do not keep republics strong with armies or formal laws. Democracies depend on whether the public loves its constitution and way of life and is willing to explore the common good and defend its constitution against intolerant demagogues. We also need citizens who understand their political system deeply. They must be able to make sophisticated judgments on what form of populism is being advanced and where demagogues constitute a peril to the nation.

JOURNALISTIC GUIDELINES FOR EXTREME POPULISM

So far, this book has defined populism amid a polluted public sphere. It sought an overview of its history and its relationship with journalism. It has noted the ideas and strategies of extreme populism. At this point, let us stop and identify some general "lessons" for journalists when reporting on populists.[42] Here are some general ideas. I will expand on these points and provide more detailed guidelines in the following chapters.

Know Your Populism

Define populism carefully: Help citizens know the core ideas of populism. Be capable of defining extreme populism and recognizing examples of undemocratic demagoguery. Challenge the extreme populist's strategies to protect democracy.

Know your history: Know how populism arose in your culture and how it can take many forms. Do not define it as always a negative phenomenon.

Be Specific and Critical

Use populist language carefully: Do not overuse populist language; do not ascribe "populist" to almost anyone who appeals to the public or "fights" the establishment.

Be specific when you question people and movements who claim to be populist: Demand that populists explain their meaning of *populism* and what they think it entails for public policy.

Question their claim to be populist.

Cover Extreme Populists Where Necessary, but Carefully

There will be circumstances where coverage is required, e.g., when an extremist gains significant support in an election. Ignoring such developments will only give rise to the charge of an "elite media" censoring free speech and may even create public support for the leader. Yet coverage must provide "deep" context for such leaders and their views. Without context, audiences may regard the extreme populist as novel, provocative (in a stimulating way), and not that harmful. Also, as I will argue in chapter 5, extreme populist ideas should not simply be repeated, such that the reporter, seeking neutrality, becomes a mouthpiece for extreme claims. Media economist Robert Picard argues that not all political ideas are equivalent in democracies. Some ideas require journalists to be critical and engaged, and that means "ignoring, repudiating, or denouncing" some ideas and actions.[43]

Do Not Be Baited

Don't overreact to "elite" criticism: Extreme populists will almost inevitably seek to characterize journalists as untrustworthy elites. Where the journalist's reports are critical, extreme populists will dismiss them as "fake news" in service of a political party. Even if a reporter is not from a large media outlet, it is not productive to engage in a debate about who is or is not part of an elite. The best and perhaps only thing to do is for media outlets and their journalists to be transparent about their ownership, political perspectives, and editorial processes—and the firm factual basis for their reports.

Meet the populist on the high ground of ideas: Few people will win a name-calling dispute with an extreme populist. They are skilled at innuendo, stereotypes, and feeding the biases of their audiences. Journalists should not use the same demeaning forms of argumentation. Journalists need to challenge the extreme populist's ideas—will their ideas *really* resolve a problem? What is the evidence for this claim? Who wins or loses?

Stay calm and keep your powder dry: Journalists should not allow themselves to be baited into responding publicly in a manner that reinforces the extreme populist's negative view of media. For example, at a news conference, if Trump or some other leader makes fun of a journalist's question, or personally attacks the journalist as biased or stupid, do not reply in the same manner. Maintain your cool and keep asking factual questions (despite the incoming verbal "flak") or keep referring to your facts. Let your research do the talking.

Advance Egalitarian Democracy

Advance democratic dialogue across racial, ethnic, and economic divisions: Journalists have a duty to convene public fora and provide channels of information that allow for frank but respectful dialogue across divisions. They should seek to mend the tears in the fabric of the body politic.

Go deep politically. Explain democracy: Democracy-building conversations need to be well-informed. Journalism needs to devote major resources to an explanatory journalism that delves deeply into the political values, processes, and institutions of egalitarian democracy while challenging the myths and fears surrounding issues such as immigration, terrorism, and so on.

Detox the Public Sphere

Critically cover the scope and implications of global information disorder: Pay attention to groups that use global media to promote extreme populism. Refuse to amplify or give uncritical coverage of extreme populism on the Net.

Be part of society's overall response to the problem of global misinformation.

NOTES

1. For example, the mistaken identification of populism with undemocratic demagoguery is found in Steven Levitsky and Daniel Ziblatt, *How Democracies Die* (New York: Crown Publishing Group, 2018).

2. Walter Nugent, *The Tolerant Populists: Kansas Populism and Nativism* (Chicago: University of Chicago Press, 2013), xii.

3. For types of democracy, see David Held, *Models of Democracy*, 3rd ed. (Cambridge, UK: Polity Press, 2006).

4. Margaret Canovan, *Populism* (Chicago: Houghton Mifflin Harcourt, 1998), 5.

5. Steven Erlanger, "Eastern Europe, Populism Lives, Widening a Split in the E.U," *The New York Times*, November 29, 2017.

6. See, for example, Jason Horowitz, "Italy Election Gives Big Lift to Far Right and Populists," *The New York Times*, March 4, 2018.

7. Jan-Werner Müller, *What Is Populism?* (London: Penguin Random House, 2017), 1.

8. Stephen J. A. Ward, *Radical Media Ethics* (Malden, MA: Wiley Blackwell, 2015), 122–129.

9. Seymour Martin Lipset, *Political Man: The Social Basis of Politics* (Garden City, NY: Doubleday, 1963), 178.

10. Müller, *What Is Populism?*, 10.

11. On basic political concepts, e.g., freedom and equality, being fluid in meaning, see my *Radical Media Ethics*, 127–129.

12. Michael Freeden, Lyman Tower Sargent, and Marc Stears, ed., *The Oxford Handbook of Political Ideologies* (Oxford: Oxford University Press, 2013), Preface, v.

13. On ideology as interpreting political events, see Michael Freeden, *Ideology: A Very Short Introduction* (Oxford: Oxford University Press, 2003), 1–4.

14. Daniele Albertazzi and Duncan McDonnell, *Twenty-First Century Populism: The Spectre of Western European Democracy* (Basingstoke, UK: Palgrave MacMillan, 2008), 3.

15. Marx and Engels claimed that all written (or recorded) history has been a history of "class struggle" rooted in economic forces and inequalities. See Karl Marx and Friedrich Engels, *The Communist Manifesto* (Oxford: Oxford University Press, 2008), 3. This not completely true. Not *all* of history is class warfare, and there are factors in modern society that transcend class divisions. Large modern societies would not exist unless there were counterbalancing "unifying" forces such as patriotism, nationalism, national myths and symbols, national projects, social programs, and constitutions that assert common rights. Such factors can't be dismissed as just a false ideology for capitalism.

16. André Munro, "Populism," in *Encyclopedia Britannica*, last modified March 15, 2013, accessed November 13, 2017, https://www.britannica.com/topic/populism.

17. In Canada, senators are unelected. They are appointed by the prime minister. The Senate's role is to review laws passed by the elected House of Commons.

18. See Carlos de la Torre, *The Promise and Perils of Populism* (Lexington: University Press of Kentucky, 2015).

19. On the populist as "monster," see Nugent, *The Tolerant Populists*, 3–21.

20. James Fenimore Cooper, "On Demagogues," in *The American Democrat* (Cooperstown, NY: H. & E. Phinney, 1838), 98–104.

21. Reinhard H. Luthin, *American Demagogues* (Boston: Beacon Press, 1954), 3.

22. Aristotle, "Rhetoric," in *The Basic Works of Aristotle*, ed. Richard McKeon (New York: Modern Library, 2001), 1328–1329.

23. In politics, knowing what a person sincerely believes can be difficult to determine. A demagogue may sincerely or insincerely paint himself as a person "of the people." For definitional purposes, we do not need to restrict "demagogue" only to people we know are sincere in their populism.

24. See "CBS Weekend News," https://archive.org/details/KPIX_20160508_003000_CBS_Weekend_News, May 7, 2016.

25. Müller, *What Is Populism?*, 35.

26. Cited in Müller, *What Is Populism?*, 3.

27. Amnesty International, *Amnesty International Report 2016/17: The State of the World's Human Rights* (London: Amnesty International, 2017), 367–368, https://www.amnesty.org/download/Documents/POL1048002017ENGLISH.PDF.

28. Oliver Homes, "Rodgrigo Duterte Vows to Kill 3 Million Drug Addicts and Likens Himself to Hitler," *Guardian Online*, October 1, 2016.

29. "Hungarian Prime Minister Says Migrants Are 'Poison' and 'Not Needed,'" *Guardian Online*, July 27, 2016.

30. Michael Stern, "Intolerant Kingmaker Defies Dutch Cliches," *Financial Times Online*, February 26, 2010.

31. "The Inaugural Address of Governor George C. Wallace," January 14, 1963, Montgomery, Alabama, accessed March 8, 2018, http://digital.archives.alabama.gov/cdm/singleitem/collection/voices/id/2952/rec/1.

32. For examples of alliances with extreme populists, and how they go wrong, see chapter 1, "Fateful Alliances," in Levitsky and Ziblatt, *How Democracies Die.*

33. On how to construct a democracy for plural nations, see John Rawls, *Political Liberalism* (New York: Columbia University Press, 1993).

34. See Cas Mudde and Cristóbal R. Kaltwasser, "Populism," in *The Oxford Handbook of Political Ideologies,* ed. Michael Freeden, Lyman Tower Sargent, and Marc Stears (New York: Oxford University Press, 2013), 493–512.

35. On pragmatism, see James M. Albrecht, *Reconstructing Individualism: A Pragmatic Tradition from Emerson to Ellison* (New York: Fordham University, 2012).

36. See Michael Saward, "The Representative Claim," *Contemporary Political Theory,* vol. 5, no. 3 (2006): 297–318; and Paulina Ochoa-Espejo, "Power to Whom? The People between Procedure and Populism," in *The Promise and Perils of Populism: Global Perspectives,* ed. Carlos de la Torre (Lexington: University of Kentucky Press, 2015), 59–90.

37. Müller, *What Is Populism?* 40.

38. Cas Mudde, "The Populist Zeitgeist," *Government and Opposition,* vol. 38, no. 4 (2004): 560.

39. Cas Mudde, "The Problem with Populism," *The Guardian,* February 17, 2015.

40. Kurt Weyland, "Why Latin America Is Becoming Less Democratic," *The Atlantic,* July 15, 2013.

41. Max Fisher and Amanda Taub, "How Does Populism Turn Authoritarian? Venezuela Is a Case in Point," *The New York Times,* April 1, 2017.

42. Encouragingly, research into populism is increasing. For detailed studies, see the website of Team Populism at Brigham Young University (https://populism.byu. edu). Also, see the 2017 article "Political Journalism in a Populist Age" by Claes H. de Vreese, of the University of Amsterdam, available at https://shorensteincenter. org/political-populist-age.

43. Picard's comments are cited in Claes H. de Vreese's "Political Journalism in a Populist Age," 10.

DETOXING THE PUBLIC SPHERE

Democratically Engaged Journalism

The people "only appears in the plural."

—Jürgen Habermas[1]

For the rest of the book, I depart from history and context to examine the best practices of journalists in a global media era. The guiding question is: Beyond following the ideas at the end of chapter 3, what can journalists do to detox the public sphere and promote democracy?

In this chapter, I explain in more detail the ideal of dialogic democracy as the goal of journalism. I ask to what degree this ideal can be realized by surveying major obstacles. Then I consider what journalists can do to overcome these obstacles.

I suggest two avenues: One, journalists should reconceive themselves as democratically engaged public informers. I explore what democratically engaged journalism means. Two, I provide practical guidelines for journalists who wish to promote democracy. One of the guidelines is a litmus test for whether a leader or policy is undemocratic or would erode egalitarian democracy. The litmus test allows journalists to be a tocsin, or alarm bell, for democracy, alerting us to the erosion of democratic institutions and values. The second set of guidelines explain how journalists can advance the flourishing of citizens in democracy.

THE CULTURE OF DIALOGIC DEMOCRACY

Basic Ideas

Egalitarian, dialogic democracy is a form of political association realized by institutions and supported by a distinct political culture. The culture comprises a democratic mindset and shared norms for political conduct.

I begin with the long phrase "plural, egalitarian, dialogic democracy."[2] In chapter 3, I explained what *plural* and *pluralism* mean in this context. Egalitarian democracy seeks a "reasonable pluralism" where groups advance different but reasonable—i.e., rational and informed—perspectives combined with respect for other reasonable views.[3] This normative pluralism leads to egalitarianism. There should be a rough equality among the plurality of contending groups. Egalitarian democracy seeks equality among citizens on political, social, and economic levels. Equality is a supreme principle of democracy, no less fundamental than freedom. It is both a requirement of justice and a practical necessity for stable, peaceful government over the long term. As Ronald Dworkin states: "No government is legitimate that does not show equal concern for the fate of all those citizens over whom it claims dominion and from whom it claims allegiance." Equality is the "sovereign virtue" because, without it, "government is only tyranny," and when a nation's wealth is poorly distributed, "its equal concern is suspect."[4]

Equality, in turn, entails dialogue. Ideally, all citizens should be able to participate in public discussions on matters that affect themselves and their country. For dialogue to occur, participants must adopt two attitudes: First, participants hope that public discussion will *improve* our views and identify common ground. The goal is to arrive at better decisions about the common good for all, not to impose one's ideology on others or to use communication techniques to undermine other voices. Dialogue is not a monologue. Participants listen, learn, and improve their views in light of the discussion. Dialogue is ethical communication.

Second, the participants adopt an impartial stance toward issues.[5] Public dialogue is a cooperative inquiry into a topic from different standpoints, where we partially transcend our situations to listen. We put a critical distance between us and our beliefs. Knowing that social issues are complex, participants take on what John Rawls calls the "burdens of judgement": They acknowledge the possibility of other plausible views. They recognize that one's judgment may fail to fit the facts, or one's thinking is flawed, or one's view may be biased by past experience.

It is likely that, at some point, dialogue will bring up fundamental political principles such as appear in the nation's constitution, e.g., principles of free speech, freedom from discrimination, and equality before the law. Here, the dialogic approach is absolutely crucial. Intelligent and productive discussion of issues cannot take place unless groups agree on the principles that define their political association. This agreement is crucial even if they disagree on other matters, such as religious or metaphysical views about life. Democracy needs an "overlapping consensus" among groups on fundamental principles of justice and rights.[6] An intolerant approach to discourse about these fundamentals destroys hope of an overlapping consensus among reasonable views.

Dialogic democracy is a distinct form of democracy. It is not direct democracy and it is not expert democracy, where citizens let experts decide matters. It is not a populist government led by a popular "strong" man. Dialogic democracy is participatory democracy, but it wants the participation to take the form of reasonable discourse. Dialogic democracy is not a democracy where people have free speech but misuse that freedom to attack other groups.

Three Levels of Democracy

Democracy is a great political good. As John Dewey argued, democracy is a precondition for the richest kind of communal life and human flourishing.[7] Also, I would argue, dialogic democracy is the highest or fullest form of democracy. Nations must pass through three levels of political development to approach genuine dialogic democracy.

Level 1 is a nation with a minimal democracy in which denizens can consider themselves citizens and not just "subjects" of a king, tyrant, or military junta. Citizens have limited rights to free speech, association, and political participation. The list of rights is meager, and the list of duties and restrictive laws is long. Inequalities are obvious and entrenched, and institutions often unjust, tainted by power and conflicts of interest. Such nations have citizens, but the citizens do not form a true public.

Level 2 is a further development of democracy. The list of liberties is longer and better protected, including constitutional protections for both the liberties and the rights of minorities. Inequalities are less evident and reforms seek to bring about egalitarian society. Institutions are more independent and seek to honor principles of justice. Citizens can be called a public since they are effective, to a significant extent, in holding government accountable and, through their interactions, influencing decisions. At its best, Level 2 democracy is a participatory democracy where citizens can speak out publicly and take common action. As mentioned in chapter 1, it is mistakenly thought that participatory democracy, e.g., through the Internet, is the best form of democracy. It ignores the importance of *how* people communicate.

Level 3 is a participatory democracy that is egalitarian and dialogic. Much of the participation is tolerant and cooperative. In addition, the society exemplifies democratic community. Institutions and groups are organized around the democratic principles of inclusivity, transparency, and equal participation.

Countries must create Level 1 and Level 2 democracies before they can aspire to Level 3. Most democracies in the world exist somewhere between Level 1 and Level 2 and move toward or away from Level 1 and Level 2 over time. Every day, people around the world fight to be members of minimal democratic publics. Achieving and maintaining democracy is a constant struggle. Among nations approaching Level 3, I would name the countries at the top of the surveys that measure democracy, such as Norway, Sweden, and Canada. Using the criteria for measuring democracy in Chapter 1, we can ask about our own nation's level of democracy.

Political Culture

Unwritten Norms

Steven Levitsky and Daniel Ziblatt argue rightly that, when it comes down to maintaining democracy, unwritten democratic norms are as important as the written rules.[8]

The "written rules" are the laws and formal procedures of institutions necessary for democratic governance, such as rules for legislatures and judicial proceedings. The unwritten rules govern something that is more intangible—people's attitudes and norms. The norms shape how people act toward each other in the political sphere: how they talk to each other, how they reciprocate, how they restrain their desire for power. At question is conduct that goes beyond what the law requires yet is crucial for good governance. It is a matter of political morality.

These unwritten norms shape a country's political culture in the same way that unwritten norms shape our social culture, i.e., how we interact with families, friends, and colleagues. A pickup game of "road hockey" in Canada needs no referees and no written list of rules. There is unwritten agreement on what constitutes overly aggressive play, what happens when an automobile rumbles down the road, and so on. We *expect* others to honor these norms so cooperation is possible. The same holds when we participate in our political culture.

The informal norms of democracy breathe humanity, compassion, and life into the "hard," formal aspects of democratic structures. Agreement on these norms helps institutions work better. Without them, we experience a hollowing out of democracy, until all that is left is an empty shell of public buildings and formal rules. What are the main norms of dialogic democracy? We have already touched on them here and there. So it may be useful to bring them together in a list.

The Main Norms

Treat each other as free and equal citizens: Joshua Cohen wrote that democracy is a "political society of equals, in which the justification of institutions—as well as laws and policies addressed to consequential problems—involves public argument based on the common reason of members, who regard one another as equals."[9] Laws protect individuals from overt discrimination. But laws alone cannot force people to be respectful and cooperative in everyday life. Even when laws are in place, democratic culture can lag well behind. Recall, for instance, how difficult it was for black Americans to secure the right to vote across the nineteenth and twentieth centuries, despite formal laws that supported universal suffrage. Or, in Canada, recall that it was not until 1929, in a famous high court decision, that women were declared to be persons and could serve as senators. Women in Quebec could not vote until 1940.

Act as partners in self-government: Citizens do not regard political opponents as sworn enemies in the running of our country, but as partners in advancing the common good, despite their differences.

Value democratic processes: Citizens understand and support the messy, time-consuming process of representational democracy and regard public deliberation as intrinsically valuable.

Adopt the objective stance: Citizens are willing to step back and critique their views, seek rigorous evidence, and fairly compare rival positions.

Develop a deep understanding of one's democracy: Citizens understand their governing political principles and challenge misinterpretations.

Display political courage and responsibility: Citizens, including politicians, need courage to oppose extreme measures and to isolate demagogues.

Expand democratic culture beyond politics: Where possible, citizens introduce democratic attitudes and processes to the running of schools and civic meetings, to the governance of corporations and institutions, and so on.

CAN WE BE CIVIL?

Is this ideal of dialogic democracy so unrealistic as to be utopian? Is it psychologically unrealistic because it expects a level of civility and tolerance that is beyond what most people can practice? Does it ignore certain facts about humans and the world that constitute unsurmountable obstacles to the ideal? Is the ideal of dialogic democracy just a comforting oversimplification like the democrat's dream of chapter 1?

The answer, I believe, is no, although I understand the skepticism. It is a tough world in which to preach ideals. The problem is not that democracy or dialogic democracy are ideals. Ideals are an important, and inescapable, part of thinking and being human. Our lives would be immeasurably impoverished if humans were to give up any attempt to pursue the ideals of truth, justice, fairness, tolerance, dialogue, human rights, and the flourishing of humanity. The real issue is how we think about ideals, and how we use them. Ideals are unrealistic if that is *all* they are to us—just a rosy idea in my mind that comforts me. These ideas are fantasies, disconnected from any reality. What is crucial is that we *use* ideals to guide action. Otherwise they truly are useless, and can be obstacles to progress. We should use carefully defined ideals as a target at which to aim, and by which we evaluate our progress. We must be grounded in the real world, constantly aware of facts about humans and their social conditions so as to identify obstacles to our ideals. We should be pragmatic, identifying concrete ways to pursue our goals. There should be, at the basis of ideal theorizing, an almost brutal honesty, or realism, about ourselves as imperfect humans, acknowledging the reality of human aggression, power-seeking, ruthless ambition, and antisocial instincts. Only then can we seek to improve society with both of our feet planted on the proverbial ground.

This is why, before going any further, I discuss, in broad terms, the psychological, economic, and social obstacles to dialogic journalism.

Why So Nasty?

The nasty nature of public discourse in the United States and elsewhere has prompted dozens of books, to which I cannot do justice. For example, Josina Makau and Debian Marty argue that substantial harm has been done to the American body politic—and the country's ability to respond to urgent issues—because of a simplistic individualism that creates an intolerant, non-listening "argument culture." Canadian philosopher Mark Kingwell argues that civility and dialogue are important for democracy. It is not just about being "nice" to others. When taken to extremes, incivility is "a creeping nihilism here, a disregard for the very idea of reason."[10] In search of solutions, some writers recommend that debaters accept certain general principles. Dworkin, for example, thinks that the first step is for all citizens to refuse to violate human dignity through scurrilous conduct or untruthful debate.[11] Others, like Amy Gutmann and Dennis Thompson, develop a theory of deliberative democracy.[12] Some propose new ways to make political deliberation more inclusive and representational, while others see "digital citizenship" as the key to better dialogue.[13] Still others, like Christopher McMahon, argue, realistically, that a "zone of reasonable disagreement" will always surround political morality.[14]

These books are valuable contributions, but the nastiness continues and thwarts the realization of the books' many fine proposals. What is missing is not ideas. We have many ideas. What is missing is the pragmatic side: the ability to make practical proposals combined with the political will (and advocacy skill) to realize proposals. The key practical issue is: How can we implement the best of our ideas? How go beyond moral suasion—urging combatants to be more reasonable? What are the concrete ways to make actual changes to political culture, such as refashioning how we teach civics and media literacy? And, equally important, how can society create incentives for politicians and political groups to be more civil? Perhaps progress will only occur when it is no longer a good electoral strategy for political leaders to play the ideological "card" and treat opponents as unpatriotic. Here the public must turn against undemocratic demagogues, whether they are politicians or media commentators. It will require many other types of citizens—beyond academics and philosophers—to take effective political action and to concentrate pressure on the right politicians in the right way.

Moreover, some of the writing against uncivility underestimates the forces aligned against civility. We seem to be reduced to asking (or begging), in a plaintive voice: Why can't we be more civil?

Material Conditions

Whether people are motivated to dialogue or, instead, to join in the hot, intolerant discourse depends a good deal on the basic "material conditions" of the world in which they live. By material conditions I mean the economic conditions of society and how groups fare differently under those conditions. I also mean social conditions, such as which groups dominate society and the general level of economic, social, and political equality in a nation.

One does not have to be a Marxist to agree that these material conditions affect almost everything else that happens in society, and the world. In chapter 1, I noted how "externalists" think such conditions decide whether a democracy is stable. In the competition for goods and social status, distrust and fear can undermine dialogic norms. For example, in America today, many middle- and upper-class citizens who are predominately white and Christian prefer to listen to ideologically strident media voices that feed their fear that the country they once knew—i.e., the country they once dominated as a majority—is changing, watering down their power and values. Much of the attraction of right-wing voices in the Republican Party in the United States is due to what Richard Hofstadter once called "status anxiety," which leads to a desperate attempt to retain power and a politics that is "overheated, over-suspicious, and over-aggressive."[15]

On the other hand, deep inequalities can undermine the people's belief in the desirability of democracy. Citizens near the bottom of society, or citizens who belong to nonwhite, non-Christian minorities, experience status anxiety in reverse: How can they protect what they have against hostile (if dwindling) majorities? Citizens who feel alienated from a society, e.g., where a minority of people enjoy power and great wealth, see their government's rhetoric about equal concern as "suspect," as Dworkin has said. We have the unedifying spectacle of a public coming apart at the seams, each group suspicious of each other. Under such conditions, why dialogue? Better to fight, viciously, for what you have. Therefore, the call for civility will not be heard until society addresses inequality. That is a daunting challenge far beyond the control of journalists.

Also, damaging events, such as famine, disasters, terrorist attacks, war, job losses due to globalization, and the incapacity of democracies to fix burning economic problems, can alter people's attitudes about the value of democracy and dialogue.

The attitudes of different generations within society may play a role in support for democracy. Canadian political scientist Paul Howe has studied how a large percentage of young people, including "Millennials," are lukewarm about democracy. Global surveys suggest that they might be "open" to other forms of government. Howe attributes the lukewarm support to the narcissism and strong individualism of these generations, which creates an aversion to "traditional politics" and anything having to do with established social structures. If this is true, there is no straightforward political solution to such worrisome attitudes, such as encouraging more people to vote. Again, society needs to create greater social equality and, Howe adds, somehow making alienated people feel they "belong" to the political culture.[16]

Another factor is the manner in which citizens communicate, and the overall media ecology—the complex system of media in which we are immersed. Since I discuss media and democracy throughout this book, I only note it here to remind readers that media is part of the material conditions.

Psychological Conditions

By psychological conditions I mean something broader than how people, as individuals, tend to think about democracy. I include facts about human nature.

We should start with a frank realism: The norms of democratic culture are demanding and do not come naturally to many people. Human self-interest, greed, ambition, wealth and fame, love of the exercise of power over others, arrogance and feelings of superiority, elitist indifference, tribalism and the fear of the stranger—all work against democratic culture and the desire to dialogue. Human nature and psychology is not foursquare in support of democracy. *Democracy is an imperfect and difficult-to-maintain human construction, a social experiment in whether humans can govern themselves rationally, fairly, and collectively—despite themselves.*

Democracy brings into the open the good and the bad elements of our psychology, the reasonable and the unreasonable impulses within us, the rational and the irrational faculties, the cooperative and noncooperative tendencies; and it pits our ability to trust (and even love) against our equally robust capacity to fear and hate. Moreover, these psychological elements are affected by the society in which they are formed and operate.

Authoritarian Mind-set

If I had to choose the psychological force that poses the strongest obstacle to developing dialogic democracy, it would be the authoritarian mind-set. This mind-set is hostile to the democratic mind-set at almost every turn. It is also, in its negative view of human nature, set against a more positive liberal view of humans. In the history of populism, we saw examples of thinkers who supported authoritarian views of political power. Augustine and Luther thought that sinful mankind needed strong rulers; kings claimed a divine right to govern; and Hobbes argued that society needs a leviathan. Authoritarian impulses are also at the bottom of current extreme populism.

Authoritarianism is not the belief that some people must have authority in society. It is the belief that citizens need to be firmly ruled by powerful leaders allowing limited individual freedoms. Order, law, and stability is all. Why do some adults seem to want or need leadership by strong, authoritative figures, whether a parent, a hockey coach, a teacher, a military officer, or a president? Many great minds have sought to answer this question. Freud explained it as a "herd instinct," long part of human evolution. In 1915, Freud explained the First World War's descent into barbarism as the expression of deep desires and instincts that civilization normally represses and sublimates through the teaching of moral self-restraint and the observance of social rules. Among these unconscious impulses is a "herd instinct" that leaders can stimulate and use for their own purposes. Freud wrote that people should not be "disillusioned" that humans in the war had sunk to a "new low" because humans were never that "high" to begin with. The instincts and emotions unleashed by mass warfare, group pressure, and fierce nationalism lift, temporarily, the moral pressure of civilization and allows the satisfaction of turbulent instincts hitherto held in check.[17] Authoritarianism is obedience to a "primal horde"—a tendency innate to the human mind. Freud describes the instinct as such: "The leader of the group is still the dreaded primal father; the group still wishes to be governed by unrestricted force; it has an extreme passion for authority; in Le Bon's phrase, it has a thirst for obedience. The primal father is the group ideal, which governs the ego in place of the ego ideal."[18]

Later, Erich Fromm defined the authoritarian attitude as the personality of someone who "affirms, seeks out and enjoys the subjugation of men under a higher, external power" whether this power is a state, a leader, natural law, the past, or God. He attributed modern authoritarianism to the desire of individuals to "escape from freedom," which can be frightening and demanding. Modern life is isolating, and it lacks absolute certainties to assuage doubtful minds. "This isolation is unbearable," writes Fromm, and encourages humans to "escape from the burden of his freedom into new dependencies and submission."[19] Similarly, psychoanalyst Rollo May thought that modern man's "age of anxiety," which is an era of "hollow people" lonely and anxious, is caused by the deep changes and confusions caused by modern life.[20]

Fromm viewed the authoritarian person as a sadomasochist who feels pleasure in submission to authority and the subjection of underdogs. Authoritarian personalities show a lack of sympathy for others and aggression against the defenseless. Hannah Arendt, who delved into the causes of Nazi totalitarianism, saw the latter as an authoritarian assault on the individual conscience and sense of responsibility. The moral person—an individual capable of making choices on principle—is replaced by the follower of an authoritarian leader.[21]

Theodor Adorno and others, in *The Authoritarian Personality* of 1950, asked what makes up a "fascistic individual" and what constitutes "anti-democratic thought." The study surveyed American citizens, supplemented by in-depth interviews. The study found that the authoritarian personality comprises nine dimensions, including submission to authorities; belief in rigid categories and stereotypes; belief in the power and toughness of good leaders; and hostility in general toward humans and strangers. Recently, Christian Fuchs used the work of Fromm and Adorno, among others, to construct a model of right-wing authoritarianism. It has four dimensions:[22]

1. *Authoritarianism in leadership:* A belief in strong authorities and hierarchical leadership.
2. *Nationalism and ethnocentrism:* A belief in the superiority of a particular community as a nation or ethnicity. Strong nationalists create a homogeneous "fictive" *Volk* or ethnicity for the nation.

3. *The friend-enemy scheme:* The national community is defined in opposition to out-groups within and without the nation that are portrayed as dangerous enemies. The hostility is combined with an idealization of one's own preferred group.
4. *Conservative patriarchy:* A belief in conservative values, e.g., traditional gender roles, sexism, and the heroism of soldiers who fight outsiders.

Fuchs's four features are reflected in my earlier definition of extreme populism and extreme speech.

When authoritarianism joins forces with tribalism, we have extreme nationalism, with scant respect for the subtleties of egalitarian democracy or human rights. In *Moral Tribes*, Joshua Greene argues that the world, divided into conflicting "tribes," needs a global meta-ethic that finds common ground among the tribes, a role Greene thinks is best fulfilled by utilitarianism. Psychologist Jonathan Haidt, in *The Righteous Mind*, blames political and religious divisions on the certainty we have in our own moral intuitions and emotions, plus our "groupish" nature.[23]

Am I taking a too negative view of our world? Stephen Pinker, in *The Better Angels of Our Nature*, argues that, in the past, human violence and insecurity was much worse than in modern times. In fact, violence has been diminishing for "long stretches of time," and we may be living in "the most peaceable era" in human existence.[24] Pinker fails to persuade me that human violence and authoritarian politics are not still enormous problems. We should place recent horrific episodes into perspective. But our ever evolving technology means that greater violence may occur in the future.

The authoritarian mind-set taps into reservoirs of resentment, hate, and fear. The phrase "politics as warfare" is not just a metaphor. For the authoritarian, it is literally true. The mind-set of authoritarian citizens is that of the warrior following a leader in whom they place too much trust. The "combat" of words and ideology requires participants to become desensitized to the dignity of people who have opposing views. The latter are enemies, traitors, dangerous foreigners, liberals, liars, communists, socialists, ungodly atheists, and so on. Name-calling is central to supporting false beliefs and hatred. Add all of these words together, and the "other" begins to appear as less than human, and less than a full citizen with equal rights.

Desensitization is a well-known phenomenon allowing, for example, soldiers to slaughter and torture. The central moral restraints in life are what Jonathan Glover calls the "human responses." These are restraints we impose on ourselves because we are capable of seeing others as human, like us.[25] We are capable of having sympathy and respect for other people. These moral restraints can be "neutralized or anaesthetized." Our capacity for empathy and "fellow feeling" can be deadened by distance, by coming to see other people as lacking rationality, or by rationalizing horrific violence as justified by war. Further, our moral identity can fail to operate in times of conflict where responsibility is diffused across many people over time. Desensitizing is a main psychological feature of authoritarianism. It has been a contributor to the Holocaust, the mass killings of Stalin and Mao Zedong, the Rwandan genocide, and today's global violence.

Educating the Political Emotions

What does this awareness of the material and psychological conditions tell us about the future of democracy? Should we be despondent, thinking that the obstacles are unsurmountable? No, we should not. I have stressed these obstacles so we start from a realistic view of the task. It is not a counsel of despair. To balance your thinking, remember that humans have other instincts, noble desires, and rational capacities that lead them to be social and cooperative. The fact that many of us live in stable democracies shows that the negative forces do not always win. Moreover, the most antisocial and antidemocratic instincts do not, of necessity, express themselves in full. Rather, as Freud knew, societies typically are successful in channeling these instincts into socially cooperative behavior.

Rather than argue in the abstract whether humans are basically good or evil, we should talk, practically, about how to organize our social life to bring out the best in us. How, for example, can journalism support the positive forces? How can we educate people to fully adopt the democratic mind-set? Philosopher Martha Nussbaum is one source of ideas. She believes that we need to set up our educational system and civic life to foster the "right" political emotions of democracy. Nussbaum defines the political emotions as those which "take as their object the nation, the nation's goals, its institutions and leaders, its geography, and one's fellow citizens." These emotions express love for a nation as "one's own."[26] For Nussbaum, political emotions and principles need to work together. Abstract principles, such as a love of humanity or equality for all, often fail to move us to action or concern. Principles are psychologically inert unless supported by emotions. We need to *care* about equality and freedom.

Nussbaum thinks liberal societies need to imagine ways in which emotions can support the principles of a Rawlsian overlapping consensus on liberal principles. Nussbaum discusses two ways: (1) by teaching a critical patriotism in schools and in the public sphere and (2) by learning from those who have practiced humanistic patriotism across history. In schools, we should teach critical thinking early and keep teaching it. We should use "positional imagination" that asks students to imagine cultural differences, such as imagining the experience of minorities. Schools should teach the reasons for past wars without demonizing cultures and teach a love of historical truth and methods for evaluating historical evidence. Patriots too often dislike reality and want a glorified version of past and present. This teaching should be supported by institutional measures such as protection of constitutional rights, an independent judiciary, and an emphasis on free speech and a free press. We should teach the patriotic rhetoric of Abraham Lincoln, Martin Luther King Jr., and Mohandas Gandhi.[27]

WHAT JOURNALISTS CAN DO

In the rest of the chapter, I explain what journalists can do to support dialogic democracy. They should begin by adopting the philosophy of democratically engaged journalism.

What is that?

Agency in Society

"Engagement" has three senses: being occupied with something; being committed to something, and finding something interesting or entertaining.

We are occupied or engaged when we perform a role or job. Teachers are engaged in classrooms; the police are engaged in directing traffic; seventeenth-century European explorers engaged in colonization. Being occupied can also mean being engrossed or absorbed in some activity, e.g., learning to paint watercolors or to play chess. Engagement is commitment when we undertake some serious course of action or pursue some complex, difficult-to-reach goal. One gets "involved" or entangled with someone or some process where withdrawal is difficult, e.g., to engage in combat, to get married, to devote one's life to helping street people. One is occupied and committed. We are engaged with something as entertaining when something grabs our attention, such as when we say it was an engaging play.

What the three senses have in common is human agency and intentional action.

Engagement presupposes our capacity as agents to pursue and evaluate goals. In being engaged, we express our values and life plans. To be not engaged, or disengaged, means that one's agency is diminished or less active than in the past, or diminished relative to some goal. We are not taken up in the pursuit of a practical goal that demands a commitment. This disengagement can take two forms, global and local. Global disengagement is an overall withdrawal from agency, often caused by a decline in interest in the world. One can take little interest in the plans of others or in the issues that roil social life. One can withdraw to one's study, become an ironic spectator on life's passing show, or become a hermit. Seriously depressed people experience a nihilism about the world and the value of acting in it. Local disengagement means that a person is not engaged in *this* issue, or *that* activity, or *these* groups, at *this* time. I may temporarily become detached from some of my beliefs and my agency to critically reflect on my views or develop a theory.

In this book, engagement is social commitment. It means agency in the development and reform of society. Engagement includes performing an important social practice, protesting government policy, using the arts to explore problems, being an activist for a new law, or being an official who, for example, protects the environment from corporate polluters. Depending on the cause, the people engaged, and the methods employed, engagement can have a positive or negative meaning for the public.

We have names for some of these engaged people. We call them partisans or ideologues; some we call advocates; some we call activists. How close these terms are in meaning is shown by consulting their dictionary meanings. For example, a partisan is usually associated with a party: "a strong supporter of a party, cause, or person" and "prejudiced in favor of a particular cause." An advocate is defined as "a person who publicly supports or recommends a particular cause or policy." On this score, the difference between a partisan and an advocate is the former's allegiance to a party. Further, an activist is a person who uses "vigorous campaigning to bring about political or social change." Does the introduction of "campaigning" distinguish the activist from partisan or advocate? Clearly not, since both the partisan and advocate may campaign.

We should not expect precise definitions. Rather, we should think of these social activities as differing in the degree of some property, e.g., adherence to party or campaigning. They are different (yet similar) forms of political engagement. What these people have in common is a rejection of disengagement as a mode of being in society. They actively support some *thing* (person, party, idea, cause, law, or reform). All are "partial" in preferring certain goals and activities. All are "ready to act" by voicing concerns, recruiting supporters, or marching in protests. They differ on what they support, the degree to which they are willing to act, and the methods they are prepared to use—as extremists, fanatics, moderates, or democrats.

Journalists as Engaged

Journalists have many goals. They can be engaged in ways that are positive or negative, responsible or irresponsible. So we face a choice in forms of engagement.

In the past, engaged journalism was more likely to be called advocacy or activist journalism. We have seen how advocacy journalism, as reformist or revolutionary, goes back to the origins of modern journalism. Today, advocacy journalism could be a gay newspaper in Vancouver that advocates against discriminatory marriage laws. Or it could be an online site in New York that supports the Jewish community. Advocacy journalism includes "adversarial journalism," where the journalists see themselves as watchdogs on and, in many cases, opponents of government and other sources of power.

Advocacy journalism gets a bad press in some quarters of journalism, particularly from the supporters of neutral, professional reporting. The latter complain that advocates produce journalism that is biased, that twists or ignores facts, and that unfairly represents the views of opposing groups. It is true that engagement may cause bias. But so can many other things. Almost any form of journalism can be biased or misused, including neutral fact-reporting. The issue is not what forms of journalism to avoid, but what constitutes good and bad practice in each category of journalism. The central question is: journalistic engagement for what and for whom? I contend: *Journalism should pro-*

mote plural, egalitarian, dialogic democracy, locally and globally, since dialogic democracy is intimately related to human freedom, justice, and flourishing.[28]

Democratically engaged journalists are advocates because to protect and advance anything is, by definition, to advocate. But they practice an important advocacy of a certain kind. They are *objective advocates* of democracy as a whole. They practice an informed and fair advocacy for the common good. Journalists are not stenographers of alleged fact, but they are avid investigators into fact. This advocacy is different from the partisan advocacy for a group or ideology. It is opposed to an extreme partisanship that would use any manipulative means of persuasion. Democratic journalists see their methods as means to a larger political goal—providing accurate, verified, and well-evidenced interpretations of events and policies as the necessary informational base for democracy. Democratic journalists seek to be rational, reasonable, and objective public informers and dialogue generators *within* an overarching commitment to liberal democracy.

Neutrality and Engagement

How is democratically engaged journalism compatible with objective journalism?

Objectivity and engagement are compatible because there is a difference between methods and goals. Goals are the aims of engagement in life and society. We are partial about our goals, favoring them over others. But our methods of achieving goals can be objective and impartial. The norms that help us report impartially, e.g., accuracy and verification, help us to be properly engaged, to achieve certain goals or perform certain functions. Scientists follow objective methods to create new technology to solve a problem. Judges follow the objective methods of law to pursue their goal of justice.

Democratically engaged journalists have a dual commitment: They are committed to impartial methods as a means to their partial commitment to plural democracy. They commit themselves to rational and objective methods for deciding what to publish and how to persuade. Their desire for objective belief is part of a desire for reason-based democratic processes. In contrast, there are engaged citizens, such as extreme partisans, who use partial methods for partial goals. They do whatever it takes to advance their cause. Their manipulative strategies exploit the sources of subjective belief such as fears, biases, and stereotypes.

Objectively engaged journalists are impartial (or disinterested) because their do not let their partialities or interests undermine objective judgment and inquiry. Impartiality of method means that not only do journalists use accurate methods for verifying stories, but they approach topics and evidence with an open and unprejudiced mind, willing to follow where inquiry leads. Impartiality and neutrality are not self-sufficient stances. They make sense relative to a larger set of purposes, a nonneutral engagement with the world.

Objective engagement does not require an all-encompassing neutrality that precludes expressing a view or coming to a conclusion. Objectivity is not a value-free zone. Both scientists and judges are impartial in method, but they reach conclusions. Following where inquiry leads means stating the conclusions at which one arrives. Impartial journalists are free to express an informed judgment or evaluation just as an impartial judge passes judgment. This view should not surprise anyone. It has been the approach of investigative journalism for decades.

Neutrality is an entrenched misunderstanding of modern journalism ethics. Historically, journalists have never been able to practice strict neutrality with any consistency. Also, among the best examples of journalism are nonneutral investigations. Were the editors of the *Washington Post* neutral when they opposed Nixon as he tried to prevent the publication of the *Pentagon Papers*? Many codes of ethics appeal to the social goals of journalism: to serve a public, to give voice to the powerless, to reveal wrongdoing and injustice, to unearth the truth about some person or agency who lies and conceals facts. When journalism societies give out awards for excellence, the judges stress how the journalists gave voice to the voiceless, or stopped injustice, or enhanced democracy. Neutrality is not stressed. A studied neutrality is a luxury we cannot afford today when powerful groups practice journalism, often through manipulative means. Being a neutral stenographer of alleged facts is not the goal of journalism. Impartiality in service of democratic engagement is the correct goal.

What Does the Public Need?

In deciding which approaches to journalism deserve our allegiance, we should reflect back on what the democratic public needs from its journalists. The public needs many types of information and communication beyond straight factual reporting. Consider the types of information in Figure 4.1. I

Dialogic Needs
Participatory Needs
Advoca⁼onal and Reform Needs
'Perspectival Enrichment' Needs
Explanatory Needs
Need For ꞍReporting and Investigations

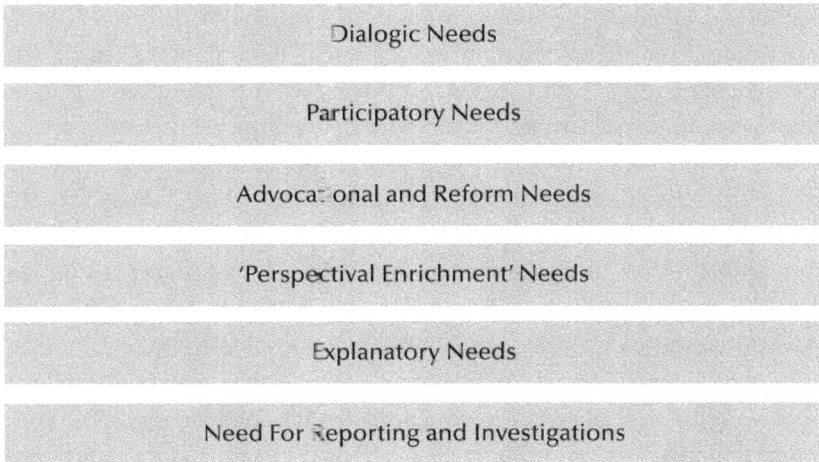

FIGURE 4.1.
Democracy and Plural Media Needs

identify six kinds of "media needs" in a democracy: (1) factual reporting and in-depth investigations; (2) explanatory journalism, such as we find in science journalism; (3) exposure to a wide variety of informed perspectives to enhance perspectives; (4) reform and advocacy journalism; (5) a media system where citizens can participate in doing journalism and in media discussions; and (6) dialogic forms of media discussion, not ranting.

Traditionally, the professional model of neutral journalism has privileged one of those needs—the bottom square, representing factual information needs. But once you admit the other five needs, you introduce ways of doing journalism that go beyond fact stating. You place value on a journalism that involves explicit interpretation, the reasoned sharing of views, historical and causal explanations, and knowledge of the values of one's society and their links to global issues.

Avoiding Dualisms in Journalism

To develop democratically engaged journalism requires rethinking journalism ethics from the ground up. We will have to spell out the principles, methods, and advantages of democratically engaged journalism. In so doing we will encounter resistance from journalists (and others) who remain committed to the neutral, facts-only professional ethic in journalism.

Traditional journalism ethics is a dualistic way of thinking about journalism. Journalists are either neutral or biased, neutral or engaged, and journalists either report just the facts or propagate subjective opinion. The development of mainstream journalism ethics, beginning in the early 1900s, underplayed the crucial role of engagement in journalism. In fact, many of the principles that populated the codes of journalism ethics, like objectivity, were based on a view of the professional journalist as a neutral, nonengaged stenographer of facts. It did *not* support the idea of journalists as active, interpretive, value-laden, and advocational. To be active, interpretive, and goal-driven was to be biased in one's news reports. Objectivity required the repression of subjectivity, i.e., repression of journalistic viewpoints, values, and goals. Reporters chronicle events from a detached perspective. They report on the clash of views among engaged groups in the public sphere, but journalists are not themselves engaged. They report on advocates; they do not advocate. To be engaged or to advocate is to go beyond the facts.[29]

This framework of professional objectivity still influences journalism practice and debate despite widespread skepticism about objectivity. The influence is mainly negative. As a rigid and outdated conception, it limits our capacity to think creatively about alternatives. It has become a tradition to be overcome by spelling out an alternative conception of journalism.

Attachments and Emotions

To make its case, democratically engaged journalism needs to have a plausible view of attachments, values, and emotions in journalism, since it is committed to *not* excluding them from practice. What is that view?

To ask journalists to repress all attachments and value judgments places them in an impossible position. Journalism is replete with value judgments. The daily news is full of tales of winners and losers, good guys and bad guys. Reporters cannot avoid evaluative language in reporting on unfair bosses, brutal massacres, vicious murders, notorious pedophiles, and dangerous terrorists. Journalists employ evaluations in selecting credible sources or displaying skepticism toward a new scientific theory. To enter journalism is to enter a value-laden craft.

What journalism theory needs is not a demand to repress values and emotions but a way for journalists to assess their values and emotions in many situations. I do not have such a detailed theory, but we do have ways to evaluate values and emotions, contrary to popular belief. We do it every day. We ask: Do the facts of the case support the value judgment? Does the value judgment cohere with my other values and goals? Have I come to my judgment with a sufficient degree of critical distance? Do I provide reasons for pursuing such goals that are acceptable, or at least understandable, to other rational agents? A report is not subjective just because it contains evaluative language. What matters is whether such language has support in logic, facts, and rational argument.

But what about journalistic attachments to groups? Doesn't this create bias or conflicts of interest? I have already suggested what my answer will be: All journalists have attachments, just as all journalists have values and goals. So, ethically, everything depends on what those attachments are and how they influence their reports. Advocacy and activist journalism are ethically responsible so long as they report on their favored groups and causes in a manner consistent with the larger goal of dialogic democracy. Democratically engaged journalism requires that journalists make their attachment to democratic publics *primary*. It regulates and trumps their attachments to more specific groups.

In journalism, there has always been the danger that bias toward a specific group may override one's fundamental duty to inform the general public. Partisan and extreme activist journalists may twist the truth where it advances their specific cause or group. Journalists may become so close to groups that they fail to report negative facts about the group. From my view, when serving a particular group clashes with serving the public, the latter must prevail. If it is in the public interest to inform society about problems within a minority or marginalized group, it is the ethical duty of any journalist to report these facts. If the advocacy takes the form of cheap rhetoric, blatant bias, partisan propaganda, or the denial of inconvenient facts, then it is unethical journalism. At its worst, attached journalism is irresponsible, noncredible journalism. However, when well practiced, attached journalism provides new evidence, sharp arguments, and new perspectives.

Meanwhile, democratically engaged journalism has a more positive view of emotions in journalism than the traditional professional model. Emotions are important forms of access to the world. They help us know the world and pay attention to aspects we might ignore. Feelings of injustice can motivate courageous journalism, and empathy can prompt journalists to pay attention to people in distress. The issue is to be attentive to the emotions we have as journalists. There should be no call to repress emotions in general. Better discussions of emotion are much needed in journalism ethics.

The best journalism is a judicious blend of two fundamental impulses: (1) the passion for important stories for the democratic public and (2) an objective impulse to make sure this passion results in accurate and well-verified stories. Reason and passion cooperate.

JOURNALISTIC GUIDELINES

In addition to adopting a new philosophy, what can journalists do to help democracy?

Below are practical guidelines.

The Litmus Test

Journalists (and citizens) should have a litmus test for detecting undemocratic leaders, dangerous demagogues, and the erosion of democracy. Below is my democratic index. The idea of a table for testing authoritarian leaders was put forward by Levitsky and Ziblatt.[30] I develop a more comprehensive, "thick" index of eight major tests, posed as questions to ask about a leader. I do not limit the test to a person's respect for the constitution and civil liberties. I include a leader's attitudes about pluralism, nationalism, violence, authoritarian regimes, and the impact of their actions on political culture. This reflects my emphasis on unwritten political culture.

The index is not a precise tool for quantifying threats to democracy. There is no strict formula for judging to what degree leaders and their political parties are a danger to democracy or for predicting how they will act in the future. However, the index highlights the propensities of authoritarian-minded leaders. Few leaders will violate all criteria, but as we apply the tests we should get a sense of where the person stands on key democratic values, how worried we should be, and where we should concentrate our attention. I leave it to the reader to judge specific leaders, parties, and movements, but it should be clear that leaders such as Trump and Putin would fare badly on the tests.

WARD'S DEMOCRACY INDEX: DETECTING THREATS TO DEMOCRACY

Test 1: Constitutional Basics

1. *Questions or rejects democratic principles and institutional structure?*
   - Rejects constitution, or willing to violate it?
   - Questions the need for checks and balances among executive, judiciary, and legislative powers?
   - Misinterprets basic principles such as freedom of speech, association, and so on?
   - Complains that democratic institutions, e.g., courts, are an illegitimate restraint on "what must be done"? Critical of the role of independent judiciary?
2. *Need for constitutional change for their benefit?*
   - Suggests that conditions, e.g., economic problems, civil strife, or ineffective legislature, require extraconstitutional acts to change government, e.g., insurrections, mass protests?
   - Claims that conditions require a "new" constitution and/or the dissolution of democratic assemblies or agencies?
   - Questions limits on how many terms a leader can serve as head of state?
   - Threatens to curtail the civil liberties of groups participating in democracy, such as protesters, journalists, rival parties, outspoken academics, and critical civil society groups?

Test 2: Procedures and Opponents

1. *Questions (or denies) the legitimacy of procedures and political opponents?*
   - Questions the legitimacy of elections as "rigged" or riddled with fraudulent voting?
   - Refuses to say if will accept the results of an election or vote in legislature?
   - Rejects rival leaders as legitimate voices? Suggests they are a threat to the nation's existence and may work with foreign powers?
2. *Exclusive notion of the good citizen?*
   - Questions the patriotism and character of critics and suggests they are not "real" citizens?

- Suggests, baselessly, that opponents are criminals and should be investigated and punished?
- Implies or states that a subgroup of citizens are the true members of the democracy? Implies their group has a claim to rightful domination of society?

Test 3: Populist Legitimacy

1. *Claims a special political status and legitimacy from the people?*
   - Claims "I am the people" with an alleged, intuitive "link" to the populace?
   - Claims to be the sole, legitimate representative of "the people"?
   - Claims to be indispensable to the fate of the nation, a political "savior"?
2. *Uses populist language uncritically?*
   - Employs populist slogans that simplify and falsify issues, or slogans decoded by supporters as support for racist or other controversial views?

Test 4: Strategies for "Working the System"

1. *Alters how institutions work to achieve ambitions and goals?*
   - Politicizes government and bureaucracy: fills key offices with family and cronies?
2. *Loyalty above all?*
   - Loyalty to leader the key attitude of advisors and officials?
3. *Seeks alliances with establishment leaders?*

Test 5: Attitude to Violence and Authoritarianism

1. *Has links to violent groups?*
   - Ties to gangs, militias, or organized crime that engage in violence and intimidation against citizens?
   - Suggests (or fails to condemn) violence against party leaders or opposition movements?
2. *Appears to have a positive or tolerant attitude to authoritarian regimes and leaders?*

- Refuses to condemn far-right groups, violations of human rights, and actions of authoritarian regimes in the world, and in the past?
- Lacks commitment to advancing democracy across borders?
3. *Advances tribalism and extreme nationalism?*
    - Regards foreign nations as the dangerous "other"? Promotes a fictional view of the nation as made up of a homogeneous and superior group, and the nation as superior to other nations?

Test 6: Attitude to Egalitarian Democracy

1. *Skeptical about value of pluralism?*
    - Rarely speaks of pluralism or egalitarianism?
2. *Favors the powerful?*
    - Portrays lower classes or less fortunate people as lazy, stupid, or violent?
    - Favors economic policies that benefit the most wealthy and powerful?
3. *Dismissive of rights claims?*
    - Disrespectful to women, minority religions, immigrants, and other groups as they attempt to secure or expand their protections and rights?

Test 7: Attitude to Democratic Dialogue

1. *Regards dialogue as nonessential?*
    - Sees no intrinsic value in extended, inclusive discussion in coming to decisions?
    - Regards their political beliefs as absolute or self-evident, not revisable ideas that need inquiry, discussion, and improvement?
2. *Prefers the politics of division?*
    - Fails to talk much about common ground, compromise, and dialogue; seldom acts magnanimously to bring groups together?

Test 8: Impact on Political Culture

1. *Weakens political culture by:*
    - treating politics as unrestrained "warfare," using extreme language, tactics, and decrees?

- lying, bullying, belittling, adopting arrogant postures, and ignoring common decencies?
2. *Empathy-challenged?*
   - Has trouble showing empathy and compassion for the troubled or downtrodden?
3. *Shows little concern about lying, fairness, and exaggeration?*
   - Dismisses criticism as fake news?
   - Trades in conspiracy theories, falsehoods about opponents, and stereotypes?

Doing Good: Flourishing

Engaged journalists fight the erosion of democracy by employing their knowledge of populism and by using the democratic index. Yet this is not the whole story, by far. Such activities put journalism (and democracy) in a defensive crouch, fending off threats. Are there positive actions that journalists should take to "do good" and advance egalitarian democracy?

There are. Engaged journalists have positive duties to perform for egalitarian, dialogic democracy. The duties stem from a commitment to human flourishing in society, a flourishing that includes but goes beyond participation in democratic politics.

In previous books, I provided a theory of human flourishing as the ultimate goal of global news media.[31] Here is a summary: Flourishing means the exercise of one's intellectual, emotional, and other capacities to a high degree in a supportive social context. Ideally, flourishing is the fullest expression of human development under favorable conditions. In reality, humans flourish in varying degrees. Few people flourish fully. Life often goes badly; many live in desperate conditions where flourishing is a remote ideal. Nevertheless, the ideal of flourishing is important for evaluating social and political systems.

Four Primary Goods

Flourishing is a composite of primary goods. To identify such goods, we need to consider what needs must be met and what capacities must be developed to (1) establish the basis for a decent human life and, after that, (2) lead, hopefully, to a flourishing life. These goods are "primary goods" because they allow us to pursue other goods. There are four kinds of, or levels of, primary goods: individual, social, and political goods, and the goods of justice. To achieve the goods of each level is to achieve a corresponding form of human dignity.

By individual goods, I mean the goods that come from the development of each individual's capacities. This level includes the "physical" goods that allow physical dignity. All persons need food, shelter, and security to live a normal length of life in health. This level also contains the rational and moral goods that allow physical capacity to flower into distinct human traits. A person enjoys the rational and moral goods when she develops her capacities to observe and think as a critical individual and to carry out a rational plan of life. In this manner, a person achieves individual dignity. The social goods arise when we use our rational and moral capacities to participate in society. Among the social goods are the freedom to enter into and benefit from economic association, the goods of love and friendship, and the need for mutual recognition and respect. In this manner, we achieve social dignity. By political goods, I mean the goods that accrue to us as citizens living in a just political association that is plural, egalitarian, and dialogic, as discussed. A citizen who enjoys these goods has political dignity, and citizens in general acquire political dignity, through collaborative self-government. By the goods of justice, I mean the goods that come from living among persons and institutions that are just and ethical in character. We can rely on them to act ethically.

How are the four goods to be related? Ideally, the four levels are realized simultaneously for most citizens to some tolerable degree. But human flourishing will spiral down unless the goods of justice (and equality) restrain the pursuit of the rest of the goods. Without the restraint of principles of justice, the pursuit of goods by individuals and groups becomes the pursuit of my freedoms and goods at the expense of other people's freedoms and goods. We should pursue our goods within the bounds of justice. We seek a congruence between the good and justice.

What has this to do with politics and democracy? The best chance for a congruence of the good and the right, of the good and of justice, is egalitarian, dialogic democracy.

Journalism and the Four Goods

Journalists promote democracy positively by seeking to promote the individual, social, and political dignity of citizens, plus the dignity that comes from justice realized. Practically speaking, how can journalism promote something as abstract as "justice" and "primary goods"? Here are some ways:

Individual Goods

Journalism can promote the individual goods by monitoring basic levels of physical and individual dignity in their own country and around the world in at least three ways:

1. *Provide accurate, timely, contextualized information:* Reliable information is the basis for the deliberation of autonomous citizens in any nation.
2. *Monitor basic levels of physical, individual, and social dignity:* Debate the fairness of existing physical, social, and educational opportunities within countries and also globally.
3. *Investigate inequality:* Conduct in-depth investigative stories on people and groups who have been denied any of the four dignities. Journalists should reveal whether gender, ethnicity, and other differences account for inequalities. By exploring below the surface of society, journalism promotes citizens' awareness of how egalitarian their society is.

Social Goods

Journalists should report on and critique the ways in which citizens interact and create associations so as to enjoy the goods of social cooperation in at least four ways:

1. *Report critically on economic associations:* Analyze how societies allow citizens to participate and benefit from various forms of economic association, including fair economic competition. Monitor society's use of economic power.
2. *Assess the quality of social life:* Report on social and technological trends and social possibilities available for citizens. Do the trends nurture caring relationships, meaningful collective activity, and flourishing communities?
3. *Assist social bridging:* Act as a bridge of understanding between diverse classes, ethnic groups, religions, and cultures within and among countries. Explain cultures and practices. Encourage tolerant but frank cross-cultural discussion of issues.

4. *Assist media literacy and the evaluation of media:* Inquire into the impact of journalism, media, and communication technology on the global public sphere and on society, and how new communication technology can help minorities represent themselves to the public.

Political Goods and Goods of Justice

Journalism can promote political goods and the goods of justice by helping to nurture a climate of reasonable debate, and to nurture a society where the pursuit of goods is restrained within principles of justice. Journalism can promote the political goods in at least five ways:

1. *Critique the basic structure:* Pursue inquiry into fundamental justice. Journalism should report on the basic institutional structures of societies and how well the principles of justice and international law are embodied by institutions, political processes, and legal systems.
2. *Monitor the basic liberties:* Promote and defend basic liberties around the world. Are citizens able to exercise these freedoms for self-development?
3. *Encourage participation:* Monitor (and help to make possible) citizen participation in public life and in their own media so they have a meaningful influence on decisions.
4. *Report on diversity and representation:* Help to make possible a diverse public forum within and across borders, with accurate representation of nondominant groups.
5. *Support the exercise of public reason through dialogic media:* At the core of the media system should be deliberative spaces where reasonable citizens can robustly but respectfully exchange views.

NOTES

1. Jürgen Habermas, *Between Facts and Norms*, trans. William Rehg (Cambridge, MA: MIT Press, 1998), 469.

2. An extended argument for dialogic democracy exceeds the boundaries of this book. I provide a detailed description in *Global Journalism Ethics* (Montreal: McGill-Queen's University Press, 2010) and *Radical Media Ethics* (Malden, MA: Wiley Blackwell, 2015).

3. John Rawls, *Political Liberalism* (New York: Columbia University Press, 1993), 36–37.

4. Rawls's claim that justice, as fairness, is the "first virtue of social institutions, as truth is of systems of thought" is similar in spirit to Dworkin's primacy of equality. Ronald Dworkin, *Sovereign Virtue: The Theory and Practice of Equality* (Cambridge, MA: Harvard University Press, 2000), 1–3; and John Rawls, *A Theory of Justice*, 12th Impression (Oxford: Oxford University Press, 1992), 3.

5. I explain this impartial stance in chapter 6, as "pragmatic objectivity." See my *The Invention of Journalism Ethics*, 2nd ed. (Montreal: McGill-Queen's University Press, 2015), 299–301.

6. Rawls, *Political Liberalism*, 150–154.

7. Dewey, *Democracy and Education*, 16.

8. Steven Levitsky and Daniel Ziblatt, *How Democracies Die* (New York: Crown Publishing Group, 2018), 8.

9. Joshua Cohen, *The Arc of the Moral Universe and Other Essays*, 1.

10. Mark Kingwell, *Unruly Voices*, 13.

11. Ronald Dworkin, *Is Democracy Possible Here? Principles for a New Political Debate* (Princeton, NJ: Princeton University Press, 2006), 1, 9–17.

12. See Amy Gutmann and Dennis Thompson, *Why Deliberative Democracy?* (Princeton, NJ: Princeton University Press, 2004).

13. See Kevin O'Leary, *Saving Democracy: A Plan for Real Representation in America* (Stanford, CA: Stanford University Press, 2006); and Karen Mossberger, Caroline Tolbert, and Ramona McNeal, *Digital Citizenship: The Internet, Society and Participation* (Cambridge, MA: MIT Press, 2008).

14. See Christopher McMahon, *Reasonable Disagreement: A Theory of Political Morality* (Cambridge, UK: Cambridge University Press, 2009).

15. Richard Hofstadter, *The Paranoid Style in American Politics and Other Essays* (New York: Vintage, 1967), 4.

16. See Paul Howe, "Eroding Norms and Democratic Deconsolidation."

17. Sigmund Freud, "The Disillusionment of the War," in *Civilization, Society, and Religion*, Vol. 12, ed. Albert Dickson, 72–74.

18. Sigmund Freud, "The Herd Instinct," in *Civilization, Society, and Religion*, Vol. 12, 160.

19. Erich Fromm, *Escape from Freedom* (New York: Avon Books, 1972), viii.

20. Rollo May, *Man's Search for Himself* (New York: Delta Publishing, 1953), 7.

21. Hannah Arendt, *The Origins of Totalitarianism* (New York: Harcourt, 1976), 451.

22. Christian Fuchs, *Digital Demagogue: Authoritarian Capitalism in the Age of Trump and Twitter* (Chicago: Pluto Press, 2018), 53, 57.

23. Jonathan Haidt, *The Righteous Mind*, 190.

24. Steven Pinker, *The Better Angels of Our Nature* (New York: Viking, 2011), xxi.

25. Jonathan Glover, *Humanity: A Moral History of the 20th Century* (New Haven, CT: Yale University Press, 2012), xix.

26. Martha C. Nussbaum, *Political Emotions: Why Love Matters for Justice* (Cambridge, MA: Harvard University Press, 2013), 2, 208.

27. Nussbaum, *Political Emotions*, 250–256.

28. This civic sense of engagement is different from a current and popular use of journalism engagement as an economic and audience-building concern—of how to attract readers to your online publication. See Jake Batsell, *Engaged Journalism: Connecting with Digitally Empowered News Audiences* (New York: Columbia University Press, 2015).

29. On the history of professional journalism ethics, see my *The Invention of Journalism Ethics*.

30. Levitsky and Ziblatt, *How Democracies Die*, 23–24.

31. See my *Radical Media Ethics* and *Global Journalism Ethics*.

Extremism

Hate Speech and Media Harm

No man by deed, word, countenance, or gesture, declare Hatred, or
Contempt of another.

—*Thomas Hobbes*[1]

We must not content ourselves with the narrow measures of bare justice;
charity, bounty, and liberality must be added to it.

—*John Locke*[2]

In the next two chapters, I explain how the idea of democratically engaged
journalism applies to practical issues for journalism, especially in a time of
Net-powered extremism and disinformation. I show (1) that democratically
engaged journalism entails ethically attractive approaches to these issues and
(2) that these approaches lead to guidelines for practice.

In this chapter, I look at questions attached to the issue of hate speech,
causing offense, and freedom of expression. Should extreme populists, and
others, enjoy the full protections of a free society, despite the odious nature
and consequences of many of their comments? How should responsible
journalists deal with their public actions? How should journalists understand
these issues and then design new guidelines?

The guidelines below will apply to both extreme and hate speech. As I said in
chapter 1, the difference between strong, extreme, and hate speech is a matter of

degree. Hate speech, properly speaking, is the deliberate, virulent, and sustained attempt to attack, demean, or dehumanize groups based on racial, ethnic, religious, or other grounds, often attended by a lurking or explicit threat of violence. In law, hate speech is usually associated with speech that is likely to incite violent or discriminatory actions against some group. Hate speech is a form of extreme speech. It is an extreme form of extreme speech. Hate speech includes much more than verbal communication. It includes images, texts, sounds, signs and symbols, banners, and dramatic actions such as burning crosses. The speech may not be "loud," created by shouting. It can be relatively calm and rational-sounding yet still induce social alienation.

For brevity, I will use "hate speech" to cover both extreme speech and hate speech since both raise similar problems. Both are based on hatred toward some group. My guidelines apply to both forms of speech

In the past, we may have thought of extreme speech and hate speech as the infrequent actions of a "crazed" minor group on the fringes of society, such as neo-Nazis. Things have changed dramatically. Today, extreme and hate speech is used frequently by extreme populists, strong right-wing candidates, and intolerant citizens on social media. Moreover, the extreme groups are no longer "minor" but have gained popular support. Journalists in a populist era need guidelines on how to report extreme speech, especially where it becomes hate speech.

Be forewarned: These issues are complex. The problem of extreme speech by demagogues and intolerant groups is hardly new, as our history has shown. But the problem is especially acute (and transformed) as a result of Net populism. There are better or worse positions, but no simple answers. In fact, one of the problems is that people think there are unequivocal answers that can be easily formulated. For instance, some people in the United States appear to think that free speech is an absolute right, with almost no valid restrictions. In this view, hate speech is a regrettable fact of life that free societies must endure.

The issues are complex because they involve a tension among central values and beliefs, each of which has some merit. Free speech is a great value, but so is living without hate speech. Does your belief in democracy entail unrestricted freedom of speech, or does your belief system make room for equality and civility? Such tensions are a feature of all ethical and political thought. But the tensions are especially difficult when dealing with fundamental, emotional questions such as free speech and the protection of minorities. Hate speech prompts dark mental images for many people in an era that remembers the Holocaust and has witnessed, in recent years, genocides by hate-speaking, weapon-wielding groups.

The best I can do is to put forward a plausible view of how these tensions should be balanced by ethical news media. I proceed by explaining my ethical perspective. Then I provide practical guidelines.

PHILOSOPHICAL FUNDAMENTALS

Let me state my position from the start: Hate speech, or what used to be called calumny, is a serious moral wrong. It is a pernicious obstacle to creating and maintaining a tolerant democratic society. Citizens and the state have a negative duty to refrain from (and condemn) hate speech. Groups are not to be persecuted or maligned, physically or verbally, to the point where the conduct becomes hate speech, and a hate crime. The absence of persecution and violence is a necessary condition for tolerant democracy.

But it is not sufficient.

Citizens and the state have a positive duty to take steps to develop a society marked by a thoroughgoing tolerance and respect for others, in deed and in word. We have a positive duty to interact in open and generous ways with groups who have different beliefs and practices. Therefore, I support hate speech laws. Carefully constructed, they are not a threat to a society that values free speech *and* flourishing for all citizens.

The Idea of Hate Speech

Here are two examples of hate speech, the first from legal scholar Jeremy Waldron.

> A man out walking with his seven-year-son and his ten-year-old daughter turns a corner on a city street in New Jersey and is confronted by a sign. It says: "Muslims and 9/11! Don't serve them, don't speak to them, and don't let them in." The daughter says, "What does it mean, papa?" Her father, who is a Muslim—the whole family is Muslim—doesn't know what to say. He hurries the children on, hoping they will not come across any more of the signs. Other days he has seen them on the streets: a large photograph of Muslim children with the slogan "They are all called Osama," and a poster on the outside wall of a mosque which reads "Jihad Central."[3]

Now imagine a small town in Alberta, Canada, where the local newspaper starts an antigay campaign on its front page, in its news stories, and in its images. The paper declares that gays violate God's commands, that they endanger society, that they will sexually attack children. The paper starts to name the gays and to publish their home addresses. It publishes photos of people on the list. For the town's gay minority, such stories do more than profoundly offend them. The stories cause them harm and set back their interests. The publicity creates a climate of fear and intimidation. It causes extreme anxiety with physical effects on their health. Some gays stop going to public events. They are passed over for jobs, and their children are shunned in school.

What are the messages of the communicators in the two examples? For the groups under attack, the messages are twofold:

1. *Permanent, social exclusion:* You do not belong in this community; you will never be accepted; and you will never be assured of a place in this society like the rest of us.
2. *Denial of social (and political) dignity:* You will never be treated as free and equal citizens. We will make it difficult for you to pursue your own lives freely, without discrimination, or without menace. We do not recognize your right to pursue your goals, to raise your family, to fairly compete for jobs, to have equal access to education, or to practice your religion.

The message for the public is this: Those of you who agree with our messaging—you are not alone. Your frustrations and views are shared by a potentially powerful group.

These messages are an intentional, calculated attempt to deny the four levels of the human good explained in chapter 4, especially the social and political goods. Hate speech is toxic, a polluting of the social environment, encouraging scapegoating, shunning, and restrictions on liberties. It undermines democratic, dialogic political culture. It is an *authoritarian* use of the freedom of speech: to use such freedom to deny full life and liberty to others, to keep minority groups and religions in their place or, by opposing immigration, out of the country.

Waldron argues that this denial of dignity, and its many negative consequences for the attacked groups, is the harm in hate speech. It is the use of public communication and media to deny a great public good: the right to enjoy a social reputation that allows citizens to be treated as equals in the "ordinary operations of society."[4] I agree. The consequences of hate speech are the issue, and it is a deep moral and political wrong.

Many Western nations, committed to free speech, have come to recognize the danger of hate speech at work among plural populations. Canada, Denmark, Germany, New Zealand, and the United Kingdom, among others, have hate crime laws. In Canada, hate speech provisions of the Criminal Code, Section 319(1), prohibit public statements that "incite hatred against any identifiable group where such incitement is likely to lead to a breach of the peace." Denmark's Criminal Code (Article 266b) opposes statements by which "a group of people are threatened, insulted or degraded on account of their race, colour, national or ethnic origin, religion, or sexual inclination." In Germany, the penal code [Section 130(1)] prohibits speech that "assaults the human dignity of others by insulting, maliciously maligning" groups or individuals. New Zealand's Human Rights Act [Section 61(1)] prohibits "matter or words likely to excite hostility against or bring into contempt any group of persons in or who may be coming to New Zealand on the ground of the colour, race, or ethnic or national origins of that group of persons."

These laws cannot be dismissed as anti–free speech measures imposed by a number of narrow-minded bureaucrats. The laws have general support in these countries and were instituted after serious examples of hate speech arose in the public sphere. The laws reflect two valid concerns: (1) that hate speech can incite violence and public disorder; and, more positively, (2) that restrictions on hate speech express a social commitment to human dignity, respect, and the right of all citizens to flourish. Supporters of hate speech laws can ask critics this question: Why does the freedom to say whatever you like, in any manner or context, always trump the right of the person demeaned to live freely and without fear? How can you not take into consideration the very real consequences of hate speech?

Emergence of Tolerance

To appreciate the fragility of tolerance, we only have to consult history. In Europe, until about the seventeenth century, it seemed natural to think about society as intolerant toward minority groups, beliefs, and new religions. Groups at the top of hierarchical society practiced a self-interested intolerance against minority groups, such as new Christian sects. For example,

England set up a state-protected "established" Church of England that was part of society-wide discrimination against Puritans, Catholics, and other religions. Even John Locke, in his famous *Letter Concerning Toleration*, did not extend toleration to Catholics, because he believed they were loyal to a foreign power, the Pope.[5] High court jurists judged cases as to whether the matters that came before them were consistent with their Christian religion. There was no "wall" between church and state.[6]

The idea that society should tolerate different religious groups only emerged after European countries had worn themselves out in bloody wars of religion. The endless religious hatreds and competition between sects, promoted by fiery and intolerant "hate speech" from the pulpits, prompted Locke, Pierre Bayle, Denis Diderot, Voltaire, and other Enlightenment figures to write about the need for toleration in religion. These works are the ground for modern writings on the need for toleration beyond religious differences, such as race, ethnicity, and ideology.

To get a sense of what an intolerant society in Enlightenment Europe was like, consider a case from England: In 1732, someone identified in law reports as Osborne published a broadsheet claiming that the Jews, newly arrived from Portugal, were guilty of the infamous "blood crime" of Jews, perhaps Western society's oldest conspiracy theory. The broadsheet claimed the Jews burnt to death a woman and an infant because the infant's father was not Jewish. Even worse, this crime was being committed regularly. The report inflamed anti-Semitic sentiments in London. Law reports tell us that "Jews were attacked by the multitudes in several parts of the city, barbarously treated and threatened with death, in case they were found abroad anymore." When a Jewish prosecutor laid a libel charge against Osborne, the former was mercilessly beaten within an inch of his life.[7] The public can surely be a mob seething with hate when fueled by "fake news."

The use of untruthful hate speech to attack Jews carried on. It was on display in Nazi Germany, inciting street fights, attacks on shops, and eventually the "final solution." In recent history, the Rwandan genocide of 1994 saw Hutu gangs, stirred by hate speech on radio (among other factors), slaughter more than 500,000 Tutsi. Reports of hate crimes have increased of late in North America, Europe, Africa, and elsewhere. In America, the Anti-Defamation League has reported an upswing in the use of large highway banners to spread racist messages against Muslims.[8] The United States has a long history of hate speech and violence, from lynching and state-enforced racial segregation to firebombings and mass murder attacks on churches. President Trump during the 2016 election campaign refused to explicitly disavow support from the KKK and neo-Nazis groups. One could also say much the same about the hate speech record of other countries. To use a phrase from John Stuart Mill, there is no guarantee whether our attempt at free and tolerant societies, this "experiment in living," will prevail or decline.[9]

On Not Intervening: Misunderstandings

Many people in Western democracies become upset, or intensely worried, when there is any mention of restraining hate speech. Some people will say they dislike and are offended by hate speech but disapprove of restrictions on the right to express oneself. One source of this attitude is the aforementioned idea that the right to freedom of expression is absolute. Restraints constitute odious censorship and are contrary to democratic society. I will set aside the rejoinder that, in fact, freedom of expression is not absolute in the United States, or in any country of which I am aware. There are many reasonable restrictions, such as prohibitions of "fighting words" that incite violence and laws that require advertisements to be truthful. I am interested not in the particulars of law but in the attitude that opposes doing anything significant about hate speech aside from complaining about it.

There are a number of misunderstandings that support this reticence about intervention:

It's about Worldly Consequences, Not What's inside Your Mind

Restraining hate speech is not about mind control by Big Brother or any other entity. It is not about somehow "reaching" into people minds and changing their beliefs. Part of the problem is the term *hate speech*, which suggests that hate speech is something mental or internal, and therefore negligible in impact. After all, *hate* is a mental attitude, and *speech* suggests that hate speech is "only" about words or what I happen to say. Neither my mental attitudes nor my words can harm you the way fists, boots, and guns can harm. Recall that childhood bravado when we dismissed someone calling us names by saying, "Sticks and stones may break my bones, but words will never hurt me."

But speech is a form of action that affects others vitally. It is false that the public use of extreme words cannot cause serious harm. Just consider the two examples above. I *hate* hate speech; I literally hate such demeaning thoughts and their expression. But my main objection to hate speech is not what is in someone's mind. My objection is based on the nonmental, and very real, social consequences for the groups maligned.[10]

A Slippery Slope to Censored Society

Another misunderstanding is that extreme speech restraints are (necessarily?) the first step down a slippery slope to an unfree society, a highly censored polity. The slippery slope argument is so abused in political argument that no one should accept uncritically any such claim. People exaggerate the negative effects of policies they dislike. Therefore, the free speech advocate who wishes to claim a slippery slope must show a strong cause-and-effect linkage between free speech restraints and a spiral downward to censored society. Empirically, the claim is false. There are many nations, some of them named above, that have had speech restrictions for many years and have not spiraled downward to censored society. True, hate speech restrictions need to be carefully worded so as to not impinge unduly on robust free speech. But that can be said of many laws. The idea that we must fight, with our First Amendment backs to the proverbial wall, any attempt to restrain hate speech or we are doomed to be censored citizens is a false dilemma. There is a much room between totally free and totally censored public spheres. Moreover, although it sounds paradoxical, less free speech can mean more free speech overall and in the long run. It has long been recognized that, without some restraints, loud and powerful voices shut down citizens from less powerful and vulnerable groups. The public sphere is too fearful a place to go toe-to-toe verbally with media-savvy members of the majority.

Hate Speech Restraint Is Not Political Correctness

The restraints I support do not amount to political correctness. Since the 1980s, the charge of political correctness has been so abused that I cringe when I hear anyone base their argument on the scornful phrase "Well, that's just political correctness." The phrase simply registers disagreement with some idea. Political correctness has been "weaponized" so that people (and leaders) of different ideologies can quickly reject the views of others without bothering to argue seriously or fairly.

Yet there is one valid sense of political correctness. Some people are so leg-islative and sensitive about what words people use, or beliefs they hold, that it restricts frank discussion. For example, in academia, the attempt to set up "safe" places is valid if this means spaces where people are safe from assault or discrimination. But it is not valid if it is used to apply to rational debate, especially in universities, and if it attempts to prevent discussion of certain ideas. Fortunately, hate speech resistance is *not* about protecting you from ideas and attitudes, even if they are controversial. The goal is to restrain hate speech within a society whose public debate is robust, honest, and, to a large degree, unrestrained. Hate speech is about reducing the actual harm caused by truly extreme speech.

We should not let our frustration with overzealous, politically correct peo-ple blind us to the importance of improving the language we use to describe others, and the progress that has occurred in this area. For example, it is al-together beneficial that many citizens, especially members of the news media, no longer describe American blacks as "niggers," the Japanese as "Japs," and so on for Native Americans and other minorities. This is not political cor-rectness; it is the avoidance of demeaning (and inaccurate) stereotypes. The capacity of words to act as a slur on a group is evident, for example, in the long and disgraceful history of war propaganda, using dehumanizing images, speech, and stereotypes to stoke warmongering among the public.

It's about Harm, Not Taking Offense

Hate speech should not be identified with any public communication that offends someone, for whatever reason. Hate speech is about harm to groups, not individual responses. The idea of not causing offense should *not* be a liberty-restricting principle in a free and democratic society. What offends people can be trivial, fleeting, and subjective. I have a friend who is so homo-phobic that seeing gays kiss on television offends him terribly. He would like to see such images restricted from broadcasts. That is why liberal and legal philosophers such as Mill and Joel Feinberg[11] think that causing harm to oth-ers is a reason to restrict liberty. But they do not make causing offense a harm. Instead, they wisely define harm more narrowly. Harm is defined as a serious setback to someone's interests over the long term. If I pinch you on the arm, I cause an unpleasant sensation but it does not amount to harm. If I offend you by swearing when I stub my toe, I do not harm you. However, if I drink and drive my car and hit a pedestrian, then I cause harm. If the pedestrian is a young baseball pitcher with a great professional career ahead of him, and I break his pitching arm, then I have seriously set back his interests.

Just Get Used to It?

Another justification for not actively opposing hate speech is to reduce it to the status of an irritant that one should accept. The advice to the demeaned is: Just get used to it. We should develop a thicker skin to insults and negative attitudes. The best remedy, if we wish to do anything, is "more speech"—rebut the claims in public. This is the old liberal idea that a free "marketplace of ideas" where views clash can sort out most issues. Eventually someone will quote the most famous line that Voltaire never wrote—"I disapprove of what you say, but I will defend to the death your right to say it."[12] The focus is on the rights of the hate speech perpetrator, not the victim.

The problems with this response are several: To begin with, who is the "we" in the preceding paragraph? When wealthy people, liberal professors like myself, and other elites provide this advice, the response from demeaned groups is typically this: It is all too easy for such people to counsel stoicism when stoicism costs them so little. They are not the ones under attack, and they have power and influence to deflect criticism directed at them. When it comes to hate speech, we must consider power. The worst victims of hate speech around the world tend to be women, immigrants, refugees, and vulnerable minorities. Should the Muslim father mentioned above, trying to explain to his children the hatred directed at them, be told that there is not much that can be done. Just get used to it? Is this an adequate response to the fear instilled into the gays of that small Alberta town by its newspaper? Easy for us—the non-attacked majority—to say so. It is true that for ordinary, robust public exchanges we need to put up with sharp comments. But when people use hate speech to vehemently attack certain groups and threaten their welfare, such advice sounds callous, arrogant, and out of touch.

Further, the idea of "more speech," by itself, is not a sufficient remedy for the social degradation of hate speech. The tactic of "more speech" does help to challenge errors, and there are benefits in putting ideas to the test in a marketplace of ideas. But this testing only makes sense, and is only fair, where the rival voices are approximately equal in social status and/or the capacity to use media. Too often the playing field for public debate in the media is slanted against poor or neglected populations.

Those who challenge hate speech restrainers, like myself, fail to meet our arguments head-on by worrying about mind control or focusing on political correctness. What they must explain is this: Why are valid concerns about the social harm of hate speech not something society should attempt to mitigate? Also, why should society not be as concerned about the rights of targets of hate speech as it is concerned about the rights of hate speech perpetrators?

The Best Reason to Restrain Hate Speech

Before I turn to hate speech and journalism, I want to deepen my position. I provide what I consider to be the best reason for opposing extreme and hate speech.

The duty to create a tolerant, nontoxic social environment—a duty of special importance to journalists—goes to the very foundations of human morality: the right of all humans to flourish and to realize the four levels of the human good, unrestricted by grave intolerance, discrimination, and hate. As I said earlier, the moral injunction against intolerant communication is not only a negative injunction to not do something—to not disparage or threaten another person and their social standing. We also have an obligation to act in positive and charitable ways toward our fellow human beings, while avoiding unjustified harm.

This duty to cooperate and respect others, rather than harm them, is a central teaching of major ethical systems and religions. It is not possible to place one's political speech in one compartment and one's ethical and religious views in another compartment. The hostile and derogatory verbal treatment of others does not occur in some realm where morality does not apply. Speech matters, crucially, in all domains of life. Ironically, some people who use social media to maliciously attack the character of other people or to spread conspiracy theories about Jews or Muslims are violating the Christian (or other) values they hold. Somehow, this dissonance is ignored.

The idea that ethics is central to communication takes its inspiration from Renaissance and Enlightenment thinkers who ushered in a new thinking about tolerance and peaceful republics. Machiavelli, who was personally acquainted with the nastiness of factions, believed that "detestable calumnies"—false accusations circulated in an irresponsible way—should be prohibited to maintain order in a republic.[13] Hobbes, who watched the English Civil War play havoc with his country, knew well the link between words and violence, warning that "all signs of hatred, or contempt, provoke a fight."[14]

For Locke and the French philosophes, a "minimalist" view of a tolerant society is not enough. It is not enough that people not be persecuted, i.e., that people refrain from violence and threats against religious groups. Citizens must also refrain from *expressions* of hatred and loathing. We do not need to love everyone in society, and we can disagree with other people's beliefs or practices. But we do need to interact with people in a civil manner. Waldron provides a good description: "The guarantee of dignity is what enables a person to walk down the street without fear of insult or humiliation, to find the shops and exchanges open to him, and to proceed with an implicit assurance of being able to interact with others without being treated as a pariah."[15]

Locke, in *A Letter Concerning Toleration*, writes about clergy and churches that punish "heretics" and force individuals to affirm their religious beliefs— nominally, and paternalistically, to save their souls. Locke will have none of this hypocrisy, pointedly saying that this zealotry is intolerance for the sake of dominion over others. He decries the "burning zeal" of religious leaders to use "fire and faggot" to harass, intimidate, torture, and even kill others in the name of a Christian religion that presumably requires utmost charity and meekness.[16] Any true Christian church, government, or public has a *duty of toleration* to others.[17] Citizens are bound by a duty to "charity, bounty, and liberality" due to that "natural fellowship" that exists between all humans, regardless of their faith. Even when a church excommunicates a member, Locke insists they use no "rough usage of word of action" to attack the person or their estate. Locke's treatment of tolerance presumes a Christian foundation, but it can be applied to non-Christian contexts.

Similarly, Bayle's *Philosophical Commentary on These Words of the Gospel, Luke 14:23* in 1686, published a few years before Locke's *Letter*, argues that intolerant speech causes serious harm.[18] Bayle says religious authorities condemn other sects by "smiting and slaying Men, blackening 'em by all manner of Calumny, betraying 'em by false Oaths," which are the signs of members of a false church. Slander is "that Pest of Civil Society," and its use is never justified to convert people to one's religion. Similarly, Diderot, in "Intolerance"—one of his entries in the famous *Encyclopedia*, a principal work of the Enlightenment—describes intolerance as a "savage passion that leads us to hate and persecute those in error." If we adopt the views of these writers, then the ranting and vicious attacks in today's social and partisan media are a morally objectionable (and socially toxic) intolerance of others.

We can summarize the ethics of hate speech by noting Locke's three features of a tolerant society: (1) public expressions of hatred and vilification are typical of intolerant societies, and tolerant societies lack them, in large part; (2) there is a specific duty to refrain from "rough usage" of words and actions if calculated to damage a person or a group; and (3) there is a duty of toleration bound up with a duty to charity, civility, and good fellowship. A country's political morality is incomplete if it thinks it should only restrain violence and coercion but does not deal with hatred and social exclusion.

MEDIA HARM AND EXTREMISM

I have been arguing against a laissez-faire attitude toward hate speech and for a duty of toleration. So far, I have spoken of citizens publishing hate speech. But what about journalists? Let us assume there are journalists who are not extremists and do not wish to spread hate speech, nor assist far-right or far-left groups. They want to practice a fair, accurate, and responsible journalism that assists democracy as a whole, not divides it. Two major questions confront such journalists: (1) Should they avoid coverage of all extreme speech or actions? Or should they not cover, selectively, particular cases of extreme speech? (2) If they cover extreme speech, how should they report it?

Don't Cover?

One might say that news media should *never* publish any hate speech because news media should avoid causing harm and not give publicity to extremists. But that position is too sweeping. The premise that journalists should never cause harm is not credible. News media do harm every day, and a good deal of it is justifiable.[19] The types of harm that journalists do include physical harm (my report on malpractice causes a doctor to commit suicide, or I fail to protect the identity of a source on biker gangs who is then attacked by bikers); financial harm (my report accuses a hamburger chain of unsanitary conditions, prompting lower sales); psychological harm (my images of a soldier killed in war cause pain for the soldier's family); and social harm (my biased reporting about some vulnerable group leads to violence).

These forms of media harm are justified ethically if the reports are truthful and accurate and are part of journalism's social role in democracy, e.g., to inform the public about the abuse of power or the reality of war. Also, it may be argued, in utilitarian fashion, that the harm that is done is less than the overall good of reporting stories of that type. In the same way, we justify harmful acts by other professionals, such as the judge who sends a criminal to prison for life, the policeman who physically overwhelms a shooter at a shopping mall, or the teacher who must give a student a fair but low grade on an important exam. However, even where journalists are justified in reporting, this does not give them the right to report in any manner. Journalism ethics requires journalists to *minimize* the harm of reporting, especially for children, innocent people, and vulnerable groups. In so many cases, journalism ethics is about *how* one reports.

So journalists can cause harm that is justifiable under certain conditions. But this reasoning does not justify journalists who themselves publish hate speech. The harm caused by maliciously attacking groups is *not* part of journalism's role in society. But what about non-extreme journalists who cover hate speech? They are justified in reporting on hate speech if the speech is significant enough that it is the journalist's duty to cover. However, journalists should cover the event in a manner that minimizes harms and gives the public a full and accurate idea of the meaning of the event. Journalists violate the duties of tolerance and of informing the public if they uncritically repeat what extreme groups say, and then compound the problem by giving them a prominence undeserved because of the sensational nature of their statements.

However, someone might raise a different objection. In covering the event are you not being manipulated or "used" by obnoxious groups? Are you not giving them "free" publicity? Are you *complicit* in the harm of publishing hateful views? Tough questions. The straightforward reply is that news media are "used" every day by groups for publicity and to promote their causes and interests. News media, in a manner of speaking, give "free" publicity to everyone they cover in the news, every day. But this does not by itself amount to improper manipulation *if* journalists can ethically justify shining the news spotlight on an event and they cover the event critically and contextually. If Canadian aboriginals stage a protest outside a meeting of the federal cabinet to pressure government to provide more assistance to poor members of their tribes, this event is staged for the media. Should the media feel manipulated?

Should they ignore these "media attention seekers"? No, because the protest is a valid form of drawing public attention to a serious issue. Everything hangs on whether the event is socially and politically significant and should not be ignored. For example, news media should report that a leading politician spoke at a KKK rally; that a prominent right-wing evangelist has announced that his church will mount a campaign against gays and lesbians, who are, he says, perverted "devils" who should be denied certain rights, such as adopting a child; and that a far-right group received substantial popular support in a federal election.

Cover Everything, or Inform?

The opposite of the "don't cover" argument is the "cover everything" counterargument that supports reporting on all, or almost all, controversial people and events, an argument popular among some journalists. At first, the argument strikes one as clear and plausible. The journalist's job is (at least) to chronicle events in the world and then let the public draw their own conclusions. As a newsroom editor used to tell me: "Report and let the chips fall where they may." To act otherwise is to restrict a free press and not inform the people.

How to respond to this argument? By pointing out that chronicling and informing are not the same thing. Also, given the power of the media, the decision on what to chronicle needs to be guided by ethical principles. Chronicling, in a journalistic context, means description, i.e., reporting what happens in front of you without much testing of the data, images, or statements provided. Chronicling resembles the stenographer in a court who records what is said and done without judgment. Informing, however, is judgmental. It is normative, selective, and tests the data. Journalists have a duty to inform *according to the standards and guidelines of good journalism*, that is, to inform in a manner that is truthful, accurate, and verifiable. Informing cannot ignore questions of journalism ethics: of truth or falsity, of the evidence for statements, of the motivation and credibility of sources, of the harmful consequences of publishing and the need to minimize harm, and of being accountable. Journalists are *not* informing the public if they echo the extremist's remarks or cause people to believe in conspiracy theories or false depictions of issues. Journalists are not informing the public if they simply provide for public consumption an extremist's view of some issue that departs from reality or ignores our best available knowledge. The duty to inform does not require journalists to cover something because someone may be interested in it or it may boost ratings. The impulse to report an event because it is dramatic, or audience-grabbing, is a commercial imperative.

Moreover, when it comes to speech about religious, ethnic, or other groups, there is no duty to repeat people's calumny, slander, or libel; misrepresentations of minorities; or provocative statements calculated to make headlines or inflame tensions within communities. In fact, the duty is the opposite: to *not* simply repeat and circulate such materials. The duty to inform obliges journalists to consider the impact on the peace, tolerance, and civility of a democracy. Journalists have a prima facie duty to report on events in the world. But this duty is not absolute, or unrestrained, especially in a world where facts are manufactured and journalists are the target of the greatest manipulators on the planet. Hence we arrive at the following principle: *Journalists should honor their duty to inform in a manner that is truthful, accurate, verifiable, and responsible in its depiction of groups so as to promote democratic tolerance.*

So, honoring this general principle, how should journalists cover hate speech? What are the best practices and guidelines?

GUIDELINES FOR HATE SPEECH REPORTING

When journalists decide to cover events or groups that use hate speech, they should consider the questions and recommended actions in the six areas below.

Six Areas for Hate Speech Reporting
Area 1: Who Is the Speaker or Actor?

Journalists should always consider the credibility of sources and spokespersons when reporting an event, even more so when they cover strong statements that affect relations among groups. Reports should include information on the speakers and their backgrounds:

- Who is the speaker and what is his political biography? Has the person been associated with groups that have expressed bigoted or extreme views? What has this person said and done in the past? How credible and reliable has he been? Has he ever suggested (or clearly advocated) discriminatory or violent actions?

- Do the speaker's statements show a pattern of extreme speech and dis-criminatory language, or was his strong statement a one-time, emotional reaction? If it was a one-time reaction, will the speaker be willing to retract or moderate the statement?
- How media-savvy, powerful, and manipulative is the speaker?

Area 2: What Is the Aim of the Speech?
By considering the statements and context, seek to determine:

- Is the primary (or only) aim of the speech to demean others and attack the rights and dignity of certain groups? Is the aim to stir up racist or other passions in a tense setting? If the aim is primarily to stir hatreds, and the speaker is not influential or reliable, journalists should consider not cover-ing the event.
- Are other aims present, such as recruiting followers or pressuring govern-ment to enact certain policies, such as restricting immigrants?

Area 3: Affiliation and Sources of Support
Journalists should report on the speaker's group:

- What is the group's history, aims, and attitude toward other groups?
- Why is this event occurring, here and now?
- What are the group's financial and political sources of support?
- What is their political significance? For example, in polls and elections, what level of public support do they receive? What level of coverage is justified?

Area 4: Content of Statements and Coverage
What is the content and style of the speech?

- What degree of extremism is indicated by what is stated? Consider the kinds and degrees of extremism in chapter 1. Consider the forms of expres-sion, e.g., dehumanizing a group by comparing members to an insect, or mocking a group with nicknames and racial slurs.
- What content from the event should go into the reports? Should reports use racist or inaccurate representations of a group? Should reports use offensive

gestures or symbols that could inflame community tensions? Should one report that offensive remarks were made but avoid direct quotations?

- How much media play does the story warrant; what prominence should it have on the newscast, in the newspaper, or on the news website? How often will the images and audio of the event be repeated? How should journalists maintain proportionality in coverage?
- Should the news outlet explain why and how they reported the event and refer to the outlet's editorial guidelines?

Area 5: Testing of Facts and for Evidence

For stories on hate speech, journalists incur an extra duty to test dubious claims and question any allegedly "scientific" studies cited. Fact-check vigorously.

- Does the report assess the alleged facts cited by the newsmaker, such as numbers that would exaggerate a problem?
- Do journalists seek out independent experts to analyze or rebut claims?
- Be aware of techniques familiar to propaganda and hate speech, such as the use of emotional language and name-calling, scapegoating, and stereotyping.
- If an extreme group increases its popular support in polls, journalists should maintain a critical, vigilant stance. They should not let down their critical guard to appear neutral.

Area 6: Consequences for Political Culture

To promote a tolerant society, journalists should ask these questions:

- What will be the impact of this story, and stories like it, on the groups maligned and how they are represented in society? Will the stories increase the likelihood of discrimination or violence or the denial of social dignity? What is the impact, in the long run, on future relations among social groups?
- Will such stories help to undermine the norms of reasonable political culture and negate a willingness to cooperate and engage in dialogue?
- Has the journalist considered ways of minimizing harm by not publishing highly inflammatory statements or images?
- Are the groups attacked or misrepresented given an opportunity to reply to the claims?

Table 5.1.   Review Worksheet
Hate Speech Reporting

Review six areas:
1. *Who is the speaker?*
   • Bio and affiliation of speaker
2. *Aim of speech*
   • To stir trouble?
   • To attack specific groups?
3. *Affiliation*
   • History of speaker's group
   • Sources of financial and political support
4. *Content of speech and coverage choices*
   • Levels of extremity
   • Manner in which groups are maligned (beliefs, practices, moral character?)
   • What to report directly?
   • Prominence and proportionality
5. *Testing of facts and for evidence*
   • Factual representation of others
   • Validity of claimed empirical facts
   • Factuality of portrayal of issues
   • Check techniques of persuasion
6. *Context, impact, and culture*
   • Harm to maligned groups?
   • Harm to political culture and tolerance?
   • Accountability and transparency for the report?

Given these six areas, we can construct a review worksheet for coverage of hate speech:

Overall, the questions in the six areas convey a strong and unwavering message to journalists with regard to hate speech: *If you must cover it, then you have a duty to do so critically, self-consciously, and contextually.* Remember that you are not simply a chronicler or stenographer; you are a member of a democratic institution that informs critically and promotes tolerance so that a dialogic democracy can be sustained.

Extreme Speech and Extreme Offense

As we approach the end of the chapter, I want to return to an issue mentioned earlier: the idea that news media may offend people. More needs to be said.

I have explained why Mill and Feinberg use a narrow definition of harm that does not regard trivial offenses as harms that should be legally prohibited. The trouble is that not all cases of being offended are trivial. People, and news media, can cause profound offense. Conduct that causes profound offense is more than a nuisance or a momentary attack on one's sensibilities. It offends people's most profound values, symbols, and sources of identity. Examples of profound offense include hateful speech about someone's religious beliefs, race, gender, or sexual orientation. The Alberta paper caused profound offense. Profound offense occurs when a neo-Nazi group decides to march through a community of Jewish survivors of the Holocaust.

Here is an anecdote from my family history. When my father converted to Catholicism to marry my Catholic mother, some of my father's Protestant family and friends were upset. When my family visited their homes, they would mock, in front of us, Catholic beliefs and practices, such as the belief that the host becomes the body of Christ during mass, the confessionals, the Pope, the incense, and other rituals. My family stopped visiting these people. It created a lasting rift between families. My parents were profoundly offended. Something similar happens when, today, media commentators mock Muslim beliefs and practices. The offense is so personal that some people believe it should be classified as a serious harm, in Mill's sense, and they would like to see legal penalties for this class of offense.

My view is that profound offense can be a form of extreme speech that rises to the level of harm. It is a moral wrong to be criticized. Moreover, some acts of profound offense, such as the Alberta newspaper's actions, are socially alienating forms of hate speech. Not only do they cause harm, but society has the right to consider legally restraining such conduct. However, I do insist that only the most egregious forms of profound offense be considered as harms requiring legal remedy. In a free society, we want to leave plenty of room for robust, strong, and even insulting criticism of beliefs and practices. There should be a large zone in the public sphere where people can disagree strenuously about ideas, beliefs, and practices without descending into attacks on the integrity, intelligence, or moral character of the people with whom we disagree. If broad laws restricting criticism of beliefs were instituted, journalists and citizens would be tightly confined in what they could say or publish about controversial issues. Coverage would be confined to a rather small and safe zone of inoffensive stories. But I draw the line where the debate turns into sustained and virulent hate speech, especially where the groups attacked are vulnerable. In such cases, I favor the application of hate speech laws, although

I would hope other measures, such as education, moral suasion, ethical condemnation, and dialogue across divides, might address the problem.

Discussion of provocative stories that deeply offend would not be complete unless some reference was made to the famous publication of cartoons of Mohammed by a Danish newspaper, the *Jyllands-Posten*. Although it occurred over a decade ago, it still is a good test for a theory of profoundly offensive media.

On September 30, 2005, the paper published twelve editorial cartoons, some of which depicted the Islamic prophet. The newspaper announced that this publication was an attempt to test the limits of free speech in Denmark. The cartoons were reprinted in newspapers in more than fifty other countries. The visual depiction of Mohammed—at times seemingly as a terrorist—was profoundly offensive to Muslims and sparked protests and violence.

The cartoons were not consistent with journalism ethics. They were legally permissible but ethically wrong. They were irresponsible. The publication amounted to unjustified profound offense. If news media wish to explore limits of free speech involving a plurality of groups with different views, the ethical approach is to foster frank but respectful dialogue, not to prompt religious anger. This was the point that Locke and the other Enlightenment writers insisted on, knowing how religious disagreement can turn violent. The publication of the cartoons was almost certain to provoke protest and violent reactions. Some journalists have said the offended Muslims failed to see that the cartoons contained elements of social humor or satire. But it is unreasonable to expect that many Muslims would pick up on these nuances. Nor are these nuances relevant to the ethical analysis. What is relevant is that the publication of the cartoons represented the equivalent of sticking a finger in someone's eye to see if they recoil in pain and anger.

The cartoons were a reckless and clumsy attempt to stir up debate. It downplayed (or ignored) the consequences of publication and made no attempt to minimize harm. The cartoons did not attempt to promote deliberation on cultural differences and free speech. If the paper wanted to test views or start a dialogue, almost *any* other method would have been better than publishing the cartoons. It could have published a series of stories presenting views from the main parties to the problem, accompanied by informed analysis of Islam and its views on free speech. Instead, it resorted to images that would only increase fears and social tensions. Nothing justified the violent reaction to the cartoons; but neither is the publication of the cartoons an example of responsible journalism. Lastly, other news organizations were under no ethical obligation to reprint the cartoons. News organizations had a right to come to the legal defense of the Danish paper and to argue against censorship. But they were not compelled to republish the cartoons if they regarded them as ethically questionable material.

Global Offense and Attention-Seekers

Consider another type of case: profound offense generated by someone who seeks media attention.

In the summer of 2010, the minister of a small Florida church warned that his church members would burn copies of the Koran as America approached the ninth anniversary of the 9/11 terrorist attack. Rev. Terry Jones and his Dove World Outreach Center announced in July 2010 that the burnings would proclaim the evil of Islam. By August the pastor bathed in a global media spotlight. His unholy plan was top of the news around the world, sparking riots and prompting widespread criticism. On one day alone in late August, Jones's blatant media manipulation garnered front-page coverage in more than fifty U.S. daily papers.

The questions asked repeatedly on media programs were: How did this little-known pastor get so much news coverage? Should the media have given him a global platform for his questionable views and potentially harmful actions? From the view of media ethics, the question is: What guidelines can help newsrooms respond responsibly to a Terry Jones? How should journalists deal with media attention-seekers?

In the Jones story, the question of responsible news selection involved two different time periods: in the summer, when the plan was first announced, and in late August, when the story had gone viral. In the early weeks, newsrooms should have ignored Jones's plan. There was no justification for selecting Jones's announcement as an important news story. At the very most, the announcement merited an initial item on the controversial pastor from Gainesville, Florida.

What should responsible editors do when the media system turns the story into an ugly global incident, with the news story starting to cause riots in many countries? Caught inside a media maelstrom, responsible editors may feel they cannot completely ignore the story. There are no easy answers. But media ethics does counsel that news organizations should minimize harm and exert their editorial independence by not playing media games such as that initiated by Jones.

Here are guidelines on how to exert that editorial independence:

Democracy needs intelligent news selection: A democracy whose media is distracted by sensational events is headed for trouble. A news media that does not—or will not—distinguish between trivial and essential news, or between genuine newsmakers and media manipulators, creates a society that is underinformed on the crucial issues that define its future. It is to embrace the "cover all" argument and report on whatever pleases the audience or the whims of the journalists. Journalists should base their news selection on a sober assessment of what really is important—developments in the political, economic, legal, and social arenas of the body politic. When a Terry Jones gets too much air time, or when an actor's latest personal faux pas trends on Twitter—and the blogosphere is abuzz—this is exactly the time when journalists must push back in the opposite direction. They must question a news selection that feeds this media circus. Media should cover pop culture and the merely novel or amusing, but the media's news selection should not be hostage to manipulators or entertainment values.

Go hard on manipulators: News selection should be guided by who is seeking media attention and why. Jones guessed correctly that a book burning would get attention. He loved appearing before the cameras and toying with reporters. Editors have every right to work against a manipulator's media strategy by providing critical coverage. It is not the job of journalists to provide unthinking coverage of events that are gratuitously manufactured to provoke and cause harm.

Swim against the flow by doing good journalism: Even if a story is too big to ignore, journalists and newsrooms are not helpless victims of a faceless media world. When confronted by a Terry Jones, they can avoid the drama or practice proportionality, i.e., reduce the quantity of coverage and reduce the prominence of the story. For example, in the lead-up to September 11, the Associated Press announced that it would reduce the number of stories it would do on the Jones affair and would not distribute images or audio that showed Korans being burned.

Relentlessly provide context: Widen the story by avoiding a narrow focus on the event in question. For example, in the case of a Terry Jones, media should not follow his every move or gather outside his church. Media need to explain who the provocateur is. In the case of Jones, this meant noting the small size of his following. It meant noting Jones's previous attempts to get media attention and questioning whether his views are affirmed by many Americans. On a number of days, *The New York Times* reduced the impact of the Jones story by folding the event into larger explanatory stories of how Americans were approaching the 9/11 anniversary.

Be a catalyst for informed discussion: When manipulators arise, journalists can water down their impact by expanding and deepening the sources of the story. In the case of Jones, some news media included other voices, such as moderate Muslim leaders and interfaith associations that were rallying against Jones. Use the moment to bring intolerant views about Islam out into the open for rigorous review. Rather than try to pretend that people like Jones don't exist, use this shabby affair as an opportunity to spark a more reasoned and intelligent discussion of religion. Meet intolerant, uninformed speech with tolerant, informed speech. Here, the "more speech" strategy can help.

Trump Tweets

Let us fast-forward from Reverend Jones to President Trump communicating his thoughts and policy decisions on Twitter and other social media. Trump, like Jones, wants (and perhaps craves) media attention, despite his harsh criticism of the media.

Like Jones, Trump hopes to manipulate not only public opinion but the mainstream news media. Trump knows that, because he is president, the mainstream media will not ignore his remarks on social media. And he knows that by constantly creating controversy and chaos through strong statements and unpredictable decisions, he will control much of the news agenda each day.

In terms of numbers, the strategy appears to have worked well. His Twitter feed is read by millions. Moreover, speaking through social media is less risky than defending one's views in situations where journalists can ask tough questions, such as at news conferences.

This leadership-through-Twitter strategy is an authoritarian, top-down method for telling the masses what you think. It presumes, dogmatically, that one already knows the answers. Trump's leadership-through-Twitter uses extreme speech to get attention, simplify issues, and fire up his right-wing political base. The president can portray issues and groups in racist, near-racist, and stereotypical terms. He can lie, exaggerate, and not care about the truth—all that matters is that the speech in question have the intended political effect. When maligned groups respond negatively, the president dismisses their views as fake news.

Therefore, news media should respond to this strategy, exerting their editorial independence. Since a president's public assertions cannot be ignored easily, what can the media do? Journalists can combine my recommendations on combating hate speech and media attention-seekers, as follows:

- As much as possible, reduce the number of stories on the tweets, reporting on significantly *new* comments or positions. Do not simply use the stream of tweets as a source of endless news stories and online alerts.
- Where possible, place the tweets within larger stories on the issue, pushing back on Trump's manipulative intent to be the sole voice driving the daily news agenda.
- Avoid self-promotional tweets, or avoid the parts of those messages that amount to boasting or self-aggrandizement. Do not cover tweets in which the president simply wants to say how great he is as a person or as a politician.
- Do not be baited by presidential taunts about the dishonest media. Keep your powder dry and let your factual reports and professionalism do your talking.
- Where the president uses extreme speech, e.g., attacking the character of Muslims or Mexicans, journalists should include the group's reply in the same story, or shortly thereafter.
- Point out errors, lies, and exaggerations. Go hard on manipulators.
- Place the tweets in context, sharing with citizens the best knowledge on the topic.
- Balance coverage of tweets with accurate, important investigations. Investigate without fear or favor allegations of Russian connections, election

interference, conflicts of interest, or any other serious matter involving the presidency.

- Use dialogic media approaches to discuss issues in informed, reasonable, and respectful ways. Show how democratic debate should be carried out.
- Report on the global impact of the tweets and the decision-making style of the president, such as the confidence of allies in the presidency. Report on the impact of decisions on international initiatives such as attempts to strengthen democracy worldwide.

NOTES

1. Thomas Hobbes, *Leviathan* (London: Penguin Books, 1968), chapter 15, 210–211.

2. John Locke, *A Letter Concerning Toleration* (Mineola, NY: Dover Publications, 2002), 124.

3. Jeremy Waldron, *The Harm in Hate Speech* (Cambridge, MA: Harvard University Press, 2012), 1.

4. Waldron, *The Harm in Hate Speech*, 5.

5. Locke, *A Letter Concerning Toleration*, 145.

6. Thomas Jefferson popularized the phrase, but English theologian Richard Hooker used the term in *Of the Laws of Ecclesiastical Polity* of 1594, a founding document of Anglicism and a critique of Puritanism. Hooker opposed a wall.

7. See Waldron's account, *The Harm of Hate Speech*, 204–205.

8. See the League's report, "New White Supremist Tactic: Banners of Hate," March 14, 2018, accessed March 27, 2018, https://www.adl.org/blog/new-white-supremacist-tactic-banners-of-hate.

9. Mill speaks approvingly of forms of societies as "experiments in living" in *On Liberty and the Subjection of Women* (London: Penguin Classics, 2006), 65.

10. Author Anthony Lewis made the same mistake when he called his otherwise erudite book in 2007 *Freedom for the Thought That We Hate*. It is not the thought that we hate so much as the harmful consequences of hate speech.

11. See Mill, *On Liberty*; and Joel Feinberg, *Offence to Others: The Moral Limits of the Criminal Law* (Oxford: Oxford University Press, 1987).

12. Voltaire supported the freedom to publish, but this line was written in 1906 by Evelyn Beatrice Hall (pseud. S. G. Tallentyre) in the biography *The Friends of Voltaire*. The author did not attribute the words to Voltaire. She used it to sum up Voltaire's attitude on free speech.

13. Cited in Waldron, *The Harm in Hate Speech*, 277.

14. Hobbes, *Leviathan*, chapter 15, 210.

15. Waldron, *The Harm in Hate Speech*, 220.

16. Locke, *A Letter Concerning Toleration*, 116.

17. Locke, *A Letter Concerning Toleration*, 123.

18. Luke 14:23, in the King James Version of the Bible, says: "And the lord said unto the servant, Go out into the highways and hedges, and compel them to come in, that my house may be filled " Locke's *Letter* was composed in about 1667 but was not published for political reasons until 1689. Bayle's *Historical and Critical Dictionary* of 1697, a huge and incredible collection of topics from skepticism to obscenity, made Bayle one of the most widely read philosophers of his era. See Bayle, *Historical and Critical Dictionary: Selections*, trans. Richard Popkin (Indianapolis, IN: Hackett Publishing, 1991).

19. For an extended treatment of media harm, see my *Ethics and the Media: An Introduction* (Cambridge, UK: Cambridge University Press, 2011), chapter 5, 161–206.

Serving the Republic

Patriotism, Fake News, and Objectivity

Nothing then is unchangeable but the inherent and inalienable rights of man.

—*Thomas Jefferson*[1]

In this final chapter, I explore how my democratically engaged approach to journalism deals with two controversial issues raised by extreme populism and nationalism—serving the public, patriotically; and serving the public through objective information, not fake news.

What does patriotism require of democratically engaged journalists? By what method can journalists assess claims that may be fake news?

FORMS OF PATRIOTISM

Patriotism as Master Norm

Patriotism is a serious and long-standing problem for journalism ethics. The problem is serious because patriotism is an emotion-laden loyalty that may prompt journalists to practice their craft unethically. It may cause journalists to promote extreme nationalism or violate their duties of truth-telling when reporting on issues affecting their nation. Acting as "patriots first, journalists second," journalists may misinform the public, maintain public support for an unjust war, or reduce their criticism of leaders.

The problem is long-standing because the conditions that prompt journalists to report in questionable patriotic ways are as old and permanent as journalism itself—the desire of leaders to have a compliant news media; the emotional commitment of journalists to their country; and the expectation of many citizens that journalists will act as patriotic reporters when their country comes into conflict or competition with other nations. Group loyalties, such as extreme nationalism, are notorious for causing bias. In an era of Net populism, the means of spreading a narrow patriotism are multiplied and strengthened.

We might dismiss patriotism as a secondary issue causing a lapse in journalists' ethical conduct only here and there if it were not for two unfortunate facts: First, the ethical aberrations caused by patriotism are not "here and there" but plentiful and recurring. The history of modern journalism contains many examples of how the pressure to act as a patriotic citizen compromised the principles of truth-telling, objectivity, and verification. For instance, the history of war reporting is largely a history of uncritical patriotic journalism.[2]

Second, patriotism has been, since the advent of modern news publication, the *master norm* of journalism ethics. By master norm, I mean that, in practice, patriotism is fundamental among the values of journalism. Patriotism trumps other values where they conflict. Patriotism should not be understood as the intrusion into journalism of an external social value. Patriotism, from the beginning, has been part of the very idea of public journalism.

A commitment to patriotism is an implied premise of many codes of journalism ethics. As noted earlier, in the early 1900s, the first explicit codes justified the practice of journalism in terms of serving the public through information and investigation. But the codes, then and today, do not make explicit that serving the public means serving only, or primarily, a *specific* public, the public of a nation. Canadian journalists serve the Canadian public. Australian journalists serve Australians. Such service is done for love of country, or patriotism. In journalism codes, the master norm of patriotism to country lies just below the surface—below the high-minded appeals to objective reporting and impartial truth-telling. In times of social division or threat, journalism's commitment to the master norm of patriotism reveals itself.

An objective analysis of patriotism is challenging because of the many forms of patriotism and because of disagreement over the value of patriotism. Some writers argue that patriotism is an emotional attachment to concrete and parochial objects, such as one's native soil and customs. Others argue that patriotism is (or should be) a rational affirmation of broad political principles, such as liberty and equality. Others say it is time to move away from national patriotism toward a cosmopolitan loyalty to humanity.[3]

Moreover, patriotism is a contested value.

Some praise patriotism as a primary civic virtue that binds a society together. Critics reply that patriotism can be aggressive and xenophobic. More than 100 million people were killed in patriotic wars during the last century. Tolstoy wrote: "Seas of blood have been shed over this passion [of patriotism] and will yet be shed for it, unless the people free themselves of this obsolete relic of antiquity."[4] Therefore, is patriotism an unruly emotion or an essential civic attitude? Do appeals to patriotism carry ethical weight, and if so, how much?

Yet despite its importance, there is not a lot of systematic writing on patriotism in journalism ethics.[5] Public debate is sparked by, and confined to, specific controversies. Journalists are accused of acting unpatriotically when they question their country's participation in a particular war or when they publish classified state documents leaked by whistleblowers. Discussion can be unenlightening. Whether someone condemns or praises a report or a leak often depends on whether the report helps that person's political party or not. The discussion fails to probe deeper questions, such as what type of patriotism is appropriate for journalists in a democracy?

I have said that journalists should promote egalitarian democracy. Is this a form of patriotism? Yes, but a moderate form of patriotism. Since media is a prime method for making patriotic claims, journalists need a broad and consistent view of how they serve their country. Also, they need an ethical "calculus" that uses standards to assess claims that journalists should do x or y to be patriotic.

In this chapter, I address both needs. I explain what form of patriotism is compatible with democratic journalism and I provide a calculus for judging patriotic claims. I also show how practicing the method of pragmatic objectivity can block the dissemination of fake news. I conclude the book by arguing that detoxing the public sphere will require the cross-border "macroresistance" of many groups, and a global redefinition of journalism ethics.

Patriotism is a group loyalty. It is a loyalty to, and love of, one's country or nation. Patriotism is parochial. It is a love of country as *my* country. In drawing a line between what belongs to *us* (co-nationals) and what belongs to foreigners, I draw a political boundary between nations.

Stephen Nathanson defines patriotism as "a special affection for, identification with, and a concern for one's own nation and a willingness to act on its behalf." It is "positive commitment to act on one's country's behalf in ways that one would not normally act for other countries."[6] For instance, one is ready to die for one's country but not for another country. As noted in chapter 4, Martha Nussbaum defines the political emotions as emotions that "take as their object the nation, the nation's goals, its institutions and leaders, its geography, and one's fellow citizens."[7] Patriotism is a political emotion par excellence. My nation and its interests are more important to me than other nations and their interests. It is one reason citizens in a country can be less concerned about distressed foreigners than distressed co-nationals.

Patriotism: Object and Strength

One way to categorize forms of patriotism is to distinguish them according to the object of their loyalty and according to the strength of that loyalty.

The main object of patriotism has been communal or political. Communal patriotism is love of nonpolitical or communal aspects of a society: a loyalty to one's country because of its beautiful land, peoples, languages, and customs. Communal patriotism is concrete, emotive, and folksy, based on direct personal ties to specific peoples and places. Communal patriotism existed before the modern nation-state and nationalism. Political patriotism is the love of one's country's political leader, the state, or its political values and institutions, such as democracy. One loves one's country because it realizes certain political values. Political patriotism is usually more abstract, symbolic, and rational. It is an attachment to principles, laws, and ideals. Political patriotism is expressed in many ways, such as swearing allegiance to a political constitution. Political patriots may support an authoritarian, socialist, or democratic form of government.

Pure forms of political and communal patriotism are rare. Across the centuries, forms of communal and political patriotism have evolved and mingled.[8] The difference between communal and political patriotism is a matter of degree. It depends on which aspect receives the most emphasis. Jürgen Habermas has argued that, after the Holocaust, only a noncommunal, political form of patriotism could be valid in Germany since communal forms had supported Hitler's fanaticism. It must be a "patriotism of the Constitution" based on universal political principles of liberty and democracy embodied in the constitution of the Federal Republic of Germany.[9] Maurizio Viroli and Nussbaum have replied that the concrete emotions of communal patriotism cannot be ignored. These emotions should be social, cultivated to support non-fanatical forms of patriotism.

Forms of patriotism also differ according to the strength of the attachment to their object. We can place the kinds of patriotism on a continuum with extreme patriotism on one end and weak patriotism on the other end. Moderate patriotism lies between these extremes.

Extreme patriotism includes (1) a special affection for one's country as *superior* to others, (2) an *exclusive* concern for one's country's well-being and few constraints on the pursuit of one's country's interests, and (3) automatic or *uncritical support* for one's country's actions. Extreme patriotism takes a narrow or often prejudicial attitude toward other nations and cultures. It prepares the ground for extreme nationalism until both are barely distinguishable. Weak patriotism maintains that patriotism is not an important value.

Moderate patriotism is a moderate loyalty to one's country. It consists of (1) a special affection for one's country, (2) a desire that one's country flourishes and prospers, (3) a special but not exclusive concern for one's country, (4) support for a morally constrained pursuit of national goals, and (5) conditional and critical support of one's country's actions.[10] In other words, moderate patriotism seeks to affirm a love of country but in a way that avoids superiority, exclusivity, and pressure to support one's country uncritically. The loyalty is genuine but limited. Moderate patriots have an inclusive attitude toward other nations. They eschew exaggerating the uniqueness and superiority of their country.

The strength of the emotional attachment is, for most people, conversely related to the distance or abstractness of the object in question. We struggle to be emotionally attached to distant people and abstract philosophical principles. Emotional appeals for foreign aid for strangers may have a temporary and wavering effect. Empathy, compassion, and care "start at home," and unfortunately, they often stay at home, ignoring those beyond our borders.

Democratic Patriotism

The ethically preferred form of nation-based patriotism is a moderate, inclusive patriotism. I believe this moderate love of country should be mainly political: love of one's country insofar as it embodies the features of egalitarian, dialogic democracy. For brevity, I call this democratic patriotism. Democratic patriotism is not identical to love of a leader or the state. It is love of a society dedicated to the flourishing of citizens under liberal democratic principles and institutions. Democratic patriotism makes principles primary. Moral principles are the ultimate, rational restraints on our communal attachments to a *Volk*, a fatherland, a "dear" leader, or a race.

Democratic patriotism has three main components, which draw upon the ideas in chapters 4 and 5: first, a love of democratic political structure, i.e., the principles, institutions, and laws that secure liberties and self-government for citizens; second, a love of dialogic democracy, i.e., meaningful political participation by informed and deliberative citizens; and third, a love of the diffusion of liberal democratic values into the nonpolitical areas of society. Freedom, equality, transparency, and openness characterize the manner in which citizens associate in the many domains of society, from scientific inquiry to the professions. The values of moderate, democratic patriotism run directly against the values of extreme patriotism. Moderate, democratic patriotism stresses tolerance for other cultures and an openness to criticism. It agrees with Spanish philosopher José Ortega y Gasset that, in a democracy, "criticism is patriotism."[11]

Why prioritize the political? Because as Tolstoy and Habermas warn, a purely emotive, communal love of one's country is a potentially dangerous loyalty, vulnerable to excess and the rhetoric of undemocratic demagogues. As a war reporter, I witnessed, and grew to fear, a communal, nationalistic patriotism of "blood and belonging" that is not restrained by principle and rationality.[12] Moreover, an extreme patriotism, in time, undermines the liberal principles of equality and tolerance, leading to an illiberal populist democracy, a tyranny of the powerful or the majority. To be a democratic patriot, it is not necessary to deny personal affection for one's country. But it is important to constantly subject that affection to scrutiny.

The application of this approach to journalism is straightforward. We make moderate, democratic patriotism the form of patriotism appropriate to journalism and critically resist patriotic claims that violate it. Assume that, as a citizen, I commit myself to democratic patriotism. Also, assume that I am a journalist committed to ethical standards. How compatible are these two commitments? They are largely compatible *if* journalists subscribe to moderate, democratic patriotism as a political principle. The principles of democratic journalism are largely compatible with the principles of moderate, democratic patriotism because both share the goal of democratic community. An individual can be both a democratic journalist and a patriot of democratic community, although the journalist may serve democratic community in distinct ways. Democratic journalism and democratic patriotism share a substantial overlap of values such as freedom, openness, and tolerance. The democratic patriot and the democratic journalist will be on the same side of a number of public issues: Both will support accurate, unbiased information; free speech; a critical news media; and a public sphere with diverse perspectives. Both will favor the protection of liberties, transparency in public affairs, and the evaluation of appeals to patriotism. Strong or extreme patriotism is largely incompatible with democratic journalism because it tends to support editorial limits on the press or it exerts pressure on journalists to be uncritical, partisan, or economical with the truth.

EVALUATING PATRIOTISM: A CALCULUS

Moderate, democratic patriotism is my proposal for a broad and consistent view of how journalists should view patriotism. Now I develop a more fine-grained "calculus" that will help journalists evaluate specific claims of patriotism as they arise in practice.

In evaluating patriotism, we examine a partiality, a partiality toward my country. Partialities enter into ethics when they influence our judgments about what is morally right or good. Partialities can be good or bad. Partialities can motivate praiseworthy actions, such as acting generously toward a friend. However, some partialities motivate dubious conduct. A narrow loyalty to Canada may cause me to be callous toward an epidemic in Africa.

More precisely, we are evaluating a claim of patriotism. People claim that, in situation s or t, patriots should do x or y, or the government should do m or n. Examples of claims of patriotism are that patriots should not allow fellow citizens to burn the national flag, patriots must defend the constitution, patriotism means discouraging criticism of the nation's decision to go to war, and officials who leak confidential state documents to the media are traitors.

Journalists need a method for evaluating these claims. How? They evaluate a claim to patriotism by using the values consistent with morality, democracy, and good journalism. There are four general criteria for evaluating any claim of patriotism:

Compatibility with General Morality

A claim to patriotism should be compatible with widely accepted ethical principles, what Bernard Gert calls the "common morality."[13] The common morality expresses society's social and political values. I have already mentioned some of these principles: truth-telling, promise-keeping, not causing unnecessary harm to others, not cheating or lying, not killing, not assaulting or intimidating, and benevolence—helping others in distress. Also, a claim of patriotism should "fit" the political morality of egalitarian liberal democracy, such as respecting equality before the law, the freedom to criticize officials, and so on. On these grounds, a claim that journalists should not tell the truth, or not the whole truth, about some event—so as not to embarrass their country—would conflict with the principle of truth-telling in general, and the principle of truth-telling in journalism. If a claim to patriotism violates ethical principles with no persuasive, extenuating reasons, then it is open to severe criticism and rejection. Exceptions to ethical principles should be limited and require rigorous justifications.

Compatibility with Three Themes of Ethics

A claim of patriotism should be tested by the three great themes of ethics: the good, the right and the dutiful, and the virtuous.

With regard to the good, we ask about the good or bad consequences of being patriotic to x in situation y by doing z. For example, what are the consequences of patriotically supporting this war? We also ask about the implications of certain notions of patriotism. For instance, is it a consequence of your view of patriotism that officials, as patriots, may conceal facts about why a government is going to war? If so, this notion of patriotism could be used to justify the actions of several presidents who lied to Americans about the Vietnam War, as revealed by the publication of the *Pentagon Papers* in the early 1970s. Also, this notion of patriotism would condemn the newspapers that published the papers.

With regard to rights and duties, does a patriotic claim violate the human rights of citizens or ask an official to not fulfill a duty? For example, does patriotism mean that soldiers are not accountable to any legal body if, in the heart of battle, they run amok and start killing innocent women and children? And does it mean that journalists, out of patriotism, turn a blind eye to such violations of human rights?[14] As for virtue, we need to consider the impact of certain patriotic claims on the moral character of citizens. For instance, does the notion that patriotism means "my country right or wrong" encourage citizens to not deliberate carefully about issues and to be too obedient to government?

Compatibility with global values: As our global world has developed, the idea of "common morality" has expanded to include global values such as advancing global democracy, reducing global poverty, and respect for human rights anywhere in the world. Claims of patriotism should be compatible with global ethical principles.

Compatibility with Journalism Codes of Ethics

A claim of patriotism should be compatible with the principles of democratic journalism, as discussed in chapters 4 and 5. Journalists have special democratic roles that must be taken into account when citizens demand that journalists act in certain patriotic ways. For instance, asking journalists to not question a government's decision to enter a war violates the watchdog function of journalism.

Compatibility with Democratic Patriotism

Finally, a claim to patriotism must be compatible with moderate, democratic patriotism.

The claim of patriotism is moderate and democratic: Is the claim of patriotism a form of extreme or moderate patriotism? What is the object of this patriotism? Is it allegiance to the commands of a charismatic leader or is it love of democratic society?

The claim of patriotism is inclusive: It respects the rights and freedoms of all citizens in a nation. Patriotism has no moral force when it supports actions that favor a subsection of citizens or the repression of a subsection of citizens.

The claim of patriotism is restrained: It is not xenophobic about other peoples. It lacks the aggressiveness associated with robust nationalism and extreme forms of patriotism. The policy must be consistent with fair relations among countries and respect principles of international law and human rights.

The claim of patriotism is evidentially strong: The claim is supported by strong empirical evidence and logical argument, not merely emotion and group pressure. The evidence should include a careful analysis of consequences. The facts upon which the claim is based must indeed be facts, not convenient myths, stereotypes, and unsubstantiated generalizations. Patriotism should be what Thomas Scanlon calls a "judgment-sensitive attitude," i.e., an attitude in which we can ask for facts and reasons.[15]

The claim of patriotism must survive sustained public scrutiny and investigation: Such evaluation can only be made in a public sphere that is informed by a free press.

By using these tests, journalists erect an ethical barrier against immoderate claims of patriotism. Yet honoring the standards will require independence and courage. Journalism's democratic values come under severe test when a country decides to go to war, to deny civil liberties for security reasons, or to ignore the constitution in order to quell domestic unrest. The duty of journalists to critique a country's leadership may be very unpopular among some citizens in times of war. The publication of a government's human and civil rights abuses may lead to accusations that the press is aiding the enemy. Officials and citizens may condemn journalists who report illegal or unethical actions in foreign countries by the nation's military or intelligence communities. Nevertheless, the public journalist is still duty-bound to resist such pressures and not fear social condemnation.

In times of uncertainty, journalists have a duty to continue to provide news, investigations, controversial analysis, and multiple perspectives. They should not mute their criticisms, and they should maintain skepticism toward all sources. Journalists need to unearth and explain the roots of their country's problems and assess alleged threats. The political morality of democratic patriotism ascribes to journalism the duty to publicly analyze and question patriotic assertions by leaders and groups. Journalists need to fact-check and verify patriotic claims like any other important political claim in the public sphere. And they need to robustly defend the freedom to question such claims. If journalists abandon their democratic role, they will fail to help the public to rationally assess public policy.

In summary, a claim of patriotism upon journalists (and citizens) is reasonable and has ethical weight if and only if it can pass these tests.

The tests are summarized in Table 6.1.

Table 6.1. Evaluating Claims of Patriotism

Type of Test	Sample Principles
Test 1: Compatible with General Morality	*Social values:* Truth-telling, promise-keeping, harm reduction *Political values:* Freedom, equality under law, right to criticize officials, uncorrupt institutions, respectful political culture
Test 2: Compatible with Three Themes of Ethics	Consequences, rights and duties, virtues (and global values)
Test 3: Compatible with Journalism Ethics	Truth-telling, editorial independence, minimizing harm, transparency, accountability
Test 4: Compatible with Democratic Patriotism	Moderate and democratic, inclusive, restrained, evidentially strong, open to scrutiny

Extreme Patriotism and Journalism

Today, the abuse of patriotic feelings is widespread. Media coverage of the Brexit referendum in Britain in 2016, the continuing refugee crisis in Europe, and the Trump campaign for the presidency of the United States provided examples of extreme groups and journalists reporting in ways that mixed patriotism and strong nationalism. The result was inaccurate and fearmongering coverage of issues such as immigration. With the advent of global news media and its power to frame issues, the influence of patriotism on practice is problematic.

Narrow, immoderate patriotism also arises as nations and leaders become more authoritarian. Authoritarian leaders in China, Hungary, Turkey, Russia, Iran, Poland, and elsewhere introduce new restrictions on critical voices on the grounds that criticism is unpatriotic. Patriotism, crudely defined and enforced, is a weapon for maintaining social order and political power. Now, with Net populism, the means for ensuring conformity are strengthened. When journalists stray from a narrow patriotic path, they are hounded by social media, e-mail campaigns, and trolls as unpatriotic. These campaigns do not go unnoticed by media owners, who fear a loss of audience.

Strong appeals to patriotic feelings are not limited to non-democracies. In the United States, for example, expressions of patriotism are more overt than in countries such as Canada. Patriotic ceremonies and emotional renditions of the national anthem at events abound. Yet these patriotic feelings can be whipped up by demagogues, resulting in intolerance. At major sports events, a particular form of patriotism is advanced by media, sports leagues, and other groups: a militaristic patriotism that features air force flyovers; marching bands and flag "parties"; and unstinting reverence for the military, police, and all law enforcement agencies. The underlying message can become authoritarian, implying that protest or criticism is somehow unpatriotic. For those who know the history of nationalism, it is understandable if these patriotic moments are tinged with nervousness at such massive displays of devotion to the fatherland. Nervousness is not out of place. Consider the bitter response in 2017, from sports announcers to the president, to professional football players who dared to "take a knee" when the national anthem was played, to call attention to how police treat black citizens. In a time of Trump, it is imperative for both citizens and journalists to define patriotism carefully and to avoid a tribalism of Us versus Them. Ask yourself: Who will do more harm than good for the republic (and the world) in the long run: advocates of tribalism or advocates of moderate patriotism and openness to foreigners?

SERVING THE TRUTH, NOT FAKE NEWS

Journalists serve the public by telling stories that are as accurate and objective as possible, given the restraints of daily journalism. Objectivity comes into the picture as a means to truthful reports. Objectivity is a method for testing reports.

A method is necessary because journalists face many obstacles to determining what is true or false. They may lack the specialized knowledge necessary to cover a complex topic. They labor under deadlines, powerful publishers, and finite newsroom resources. Their investigations begin with a jumble of unconfirmed reports from which good journalists ferret out the most plausible accounts through a gradual accumulation of facts and verified claims. Even where facts are available, the journalist faces an abundance of interpretations of the facts. Many stories deal with matters where no consensus exists and where controversy, bias, and conflict surround the issues. That truth in journalism is a work in progress is evident to foreign reporters. In conflict zones, the fog of war severely hampers journalists' search for truth.

Obstacles include lack of access to conflict areas, a plethora of dubious atrocity stories, a dearth of hard evidence, and many well-orchestrated efforts to mislead the media.

What Is Fake News?

Now, on top of all of these obstacles, journalists face the fake news of extreme populists, authoritarian leaders, and anonymous agents of disinformation.

Fake news can have three meanings:

1. *Unintentional falsehood:* A story is false because a journalist makes errors for any number of reasons, such as misunderstanding a set of numbers.
2. *Intentional falsehood:* A journalist intentionally reports falsehoods or misleading descriptions of some event. A journalist may spin the facts to make the story more sensational than it is. Or a journalist may fabricate sources. Or a journalist reports negatively about some person because she dislikes the person.
3. *Intentional political falsehood:* A journalist may report falsehoods intentionally about events, parties, and leaders for political reasons. The journalist seeks to support an ideology by maligning other views or publishing badly sourced stories (or rumors) that damage opponents. This is the primary sense in which "fake news" and "fake facts" are used today.

The idea that journalists make honest mistakes is not fake news, since "fake" means intentionally produced. And the second sense, that journalists intentionally report inaccurately, is nothing new. What is distinct about "fake news" is the claim that some report is false because of the journalist's political bias or strong ideological perspective.

The idea of fake news, as politically inspired news, is so general that it is easily misused and overused in the political sphere by members of the left, center, and right wing, although it appears to be more popular among the right wing. Like "politically correct," the charge of fake news becomes weaponized to dismiss any report that is unfavorable to one's political ideology or political party. You can make a fake news charge without caring about the facts. You simply claim that the report is politically motivated. Strangely, the charge of fake news becomes one more piece of fake news.

Objectivity as Testing

How can being objective restrain fake news? To answer that question, we first have to answer two questions: What does it mean to be objective, and why be objective?

Since philosophy in antiquity, objectivity has been an ideal of inquiry. Objectivity in this long tradition is ontological; i.e., it is knowledge of the world as it exists independent of mind. Objective beliefs map the world. Subjective beliefs fail to map. To be concerned about objectivity is to ask: Which beliefs, reports, and theories are reliable representations of the world? Humans err. The sources of error are well-known. Among them are our desires, prejudices, faulty logic, and careless methodologies.

How to decide which beliefs map the world? There is only one way. We examine how the belief was formed. We evaluate its reasons and its methods. Objectivity becomes epistemological. Objective belief is defined as belief supported by evidence. Subjective belief lacks support. Objectivity comes down to testing beliefs by the methods of good inquiry. For example, we test beliefs to see if they follow valid statistical methods. The most familiar modes of testing are the methods of science. But criteria for objective inquiry populate philosophy, logic, critical thinking, social science, law, and journalism. Being objective is not easy. It requires mental discipline and a willingness to critique one's views. So "Why be objective?" becomes "Why value well-evidenced belief?" For two reasons. We need objective beliefs to guide actions. And we need objective methods for adjudication.

Too much time has been wasted of late on the flabby, unfocused question as to whether objectivity exists. Of course objectivity exists, if we mean there are people capable of reasonably objective judgments. That happens every day, among teachers, judges, scholarship committees, journalism awards panels, job hiring committees, sports referees, members of human rights agencies, and so on. Endlessly. The real issue is what type of objective testing is appropriate for journalism.

Pragmatic Objectivity as Method

Given their corrupted informational environment, journalists can contribute to a healthier public sphere by following a method that I call pragmatic objectivity. Pragmatic objectivity is, I believe, the appropriate epistemology for engaged journalism.[16] It guides the difficult search for verified truths, and it restrains partiality. Journalists and their reports are objective to the degree that they (1) adapt an objective stance and (2) follow appropriate standards of evaluation on two levels. On the first level, reports must satisfy, to some tolerable degree, the requirements of objectivity in general, that is, generic standards that define any rational inquiry. On the second level, reports must satisfy, to some tolerable degree, standards specific to journalism. Journalists are objective to the degree that they adopt the objective stance and adhere to the two levels of objective standards in composing their stories.

The Objective Stance

Journalists adopt the objective stance by displaying a number of cognitive virtues—dispositions that help inquiry. They define the mind-set that helps us to know the world in a rigorous manner, where the influence of our biases is reduced. The main virtues are four in number: open rationality, partial transcendence, a desire for disinterested truth, and integrity.

Objective journalists practice open rationality in their domain of inquiry by accepting the aforementioned burdens of rationality—to listen to all sides, to learn from criticism, and to be accountable to the public for the content of their reports. Objective journalists exhibit partial transcendence by putting aside, at least temporarily, their biases and parochial preferences. They put a critical distance between themselves and approach stories with a healthy skepticism. The objective journalist is disposed toward disinterested truth if he or she refuses to prejudge a story and follows the facts to the truth, wherever the facts lead. The disinterested journalist does not allow personal interests to overwhelm the passion for truth. She is willing to correct errors. She is willing to admit that a story idea is wrongheaded. By following these and other virtues, the objective journalist acts with integrity.

Standards of Evaluation

Adopting the objective stance is not sufficient for pragmatic objectivity. Objective journalists must put these virtues to work by applying the two levels of evaluative standards to stories. On the first level, of generic standards, they should base any report on sufficient evidence derived from reliable observations and, where possible, from solid empirical studies. A report should not contain logical inconsistencies, manipulative rhetoric, or fallacies. If claims violate well-known facts and established knowledge, the objective journalist investigates this incoherence.

Pragmatic objectivity also requires reports to satisfy, to a tolerable degree, standards specific to journalism in the same way that health researchers apply their specific standards to evaluate drug trials. These rules and standards interpret the meaning of objectivity for the domain of journalism. Many of them exist as informal rules of practice in newsrooms or occur in journalism codes of ethics.

Pragmatic objectivity provides a list of journalism standards in five categories:

Standards of empirical validity: Accuracy, verification, and completeness are prime empirical standards in journalism. Accuracy calls for accurate quotations and paraphrases of statements and correct numbers. It forbids manipulation of news images and use of misleading dramatizations and "reconstructions" of events. What is the empirical evidence for the story? Are the facts carefully collected? Are counter-facts treated seriously? Verification calls on reporters to cross-check claims of potential whistleblowers against original documents. Its standards include rules on the number (and quality) of anonymous sources. The standard of completeness means that stories should be substantially complete by including the essential facts, main consequences, and major viewpoints. Good newsrooms have standards for recurring stories, such as the reporting of opinion polls. The standards demand that reporters check the poll sponsors, the polling agency, the sample size, the margin of error, the wording of questions, and the dates when the poll was taken.

Standards of clarity, logic, and coherence: Beyond the checking of facts, pragmatic objectivity requires additional tests. Does the story cohere with existing knowledge in the field? Is the newsmaker's interpretation logically consistent? Are their concepts clear? Are fallacious arguments or manipulative techniques used?

Codes of ethics for journalism typically do not spell out standards of coherence. They do not contain directives to "be logical" or "test your claim against other beliefs." But quality journalism tests for coherence at every turn. Any journalist who has tried to construct a complex story knows that the coherence of evidence from many sources is a prime consideration. Any journalist who has tried to report on an alleged scientific breakthrough knows how important it is to evaluate the claim by comparing it with existing scientific knowledge.

Standards of diverse and trusted sources: The quality and diversity of sources are center stage when journalists attempt to weigh perspectives on a controversial issue. Journalists cannot avoid selecting and evaluating viewpoints. Journalists need to make sure their sources are reliable and, if they claim to be experts, are truly experts in their field as judged by their work. On diversity, they should ask questions such as: Are all important sources taken into account and fairly assessed? Journalists need to make sure that their sources are not drawn only from elite institutions but include ordinary people, minorities, and the people who are most affected by some event. This is not the idea of a quantitative balance, where two rival spokespersons are quoted at equal length. It is "appropriate diversity," which differs depending on the story. For example, equal balance does not apply to all stories, such as sexual assault cases. There is no need to quote someone who favors sex with children to report on child sex abuse in an orphanage. The aim is to represent fairly the views of all relevant groups.

Standards of self-consciousness: Journalists need to reflect on themselves. In constructing a story, are they conscious of the frame they use to understand the topic? Are there other frames from which to report the event? What are the assumptions they make in approaching the story in this manner? What is their role in reporting this event? Does their use of language reflect a bias?

Standards of open, public scrutiny: This category reflects the discussion on dialogic democracy in previous chapters. Have journalists subjected their opinions to the views of others? Are they prepared to alter their views? Does this report contribute to informing people in respectful ways or is it likely to spark social tensions or aid extremists?

Table 6.2 summarizes the method of pragmatic objectivity.

In summary, a report is objective to the degree that it derives from an objective stance and satisfies these generic and domain-specific standards.

Table 6.2. Tests of Pragmatic Objectivity

Type of Standards	Sample Standards
Standards of Empirical Validity	Accuracy, verification, completeness of fact
Standards of Clarity, Logic, and Coherence	Coherence among beliefs, well-defined terms
Standards of Diverse and Trusted Sources	Appropriate range of sources, less powerful voices, "real" experts
Standards of Self-Consciousness	Question approach to story, alternate frames, assumptions, language used
Standards of Open Scrutiny	Rational arguments, respectful disagreement, informed positions, avoidance of ranting and extreme emotion

The standards apply to many forms of journalism, from "straight" reporting to editorial commentary and advocacy journalism. It is a flexible, platform-neutral method.

Pragmatic objectivity is a powerful tool for combating biased reporting and fake news. Most fake news will be identified if one applies the method rigorously. Reports will not be "politically inspired reports" if journalists adopt the objective stance and apply its standards to themselves. There is no better antidote to fake news than real news, objectively tested. Fake news and alternate facts are just other terms for non-objective news.

Journalism beyond Facts

I now state something that may sound like heresy to objective journalists. While fact-checking is important to good journalism, we need a journalism beyond facts. Not journalism *without* facts; rather, interpretive journalism that is informed, but not reducible to facts. We need journalistic sherpas helping citizens navigate through a miasma of shock talk, trolls, and partisan diatribe by analyzing the meaning of events and the motivations of the political players. We need journalists with the cultural knowledge and critical skills to create credible interpretations of events *and* critique other people's views. A journalism beyond facts displays a healthy respect and appetite for empirical fact and our best empirical theories. But it does not seek to be neutral or to reduce narratives to facts scrubbed clean of all interpretation.

Journalism needs a revolution in journalism education. We need a new generation of journalists who can mount a resistance to the "mind warfare" of ideological fanatics. We need to educate journalists who can place isolated facts into meaningful context. We need journalists who are at home in the world of policy, culture, and global affairs—cosmopolitan journalists of broad mind.

In many cases, the problem is not that the public have the wrong facts but that they have the wrong principles—or, to be precise, the wrong understanding of principles. They misunderstand the political principles involved in the debate. Many disputes involve someone's dubious interpretation of principle. In the United States, citizens may misunderstand the importance of the First Amendment when a president threatens to remove the license of a major broadcaster because of critical stories; or the public may uncritically accept the National Rifle Association's interpretation of the Second Amendment to oppose gun laws. Journalists create informed citizens not only by supplying them with facts. They inform them by "going deep" politically—by discussing the meaning and scope of the political principles that apply to current disputes. Pragmatic objectivity is flexible enough to provide standards that help journalists test not only facts but interpretations of principle.

SERVING HUMANITY

For most of this book, I have tried to sort out problems from within a parochial viewpoint—of what journalists in various nations need to do to improve their news media. I conclude the book by challenging that nation-based viewpoint. Journalists need to take a more global perspective. I believe that detoxing the public sphere needs collaboration across borders. It requires what I call macro-resistance. Moreover, I propose that journalists become global patriots for humanity and redefine journalism ethics from this global perspective. I have delved into these ideas at length elsewhere, so I will be brief.[17]

Macro-Resistance

To reduce the stream of polluted media information washing over us, we need to organize a macro-resistance—a global collaboration of diverse organizations and publics who are concerned about their media and their world. Only macro-resistance can counter macro-corruption. It is time to create, at the center of our media system, a networked core of groups that care about responsible communication for democratic community. We need to *con-nect* across many boundaries. Journalists, scientists, librarians, data workers, community advocates, and others need to join in macro-resistance to fakery, harassment, ideology, and manipulation.

Here are a few ways to collaborate and to detox the media sphere. I start with the United States, but what I say applies to other democracies.

A National Coalition

Journalists, with academics and media foundations, should build a na-tional coalition for media accountability in the United States. I envisage a system of online, networked centers, independent of government or any one media organization, and plural—open to many approaches to media. Univer-sities, journalism organizations, media ethicists, nongovernmental organiza-tions, media websites, news councils, and citizens would create a high-quality resource for daily media discourse, evaluation, and promotion of excellence. It would be global in outlook, linked to coalitions in other countries, and learning from other media systems.

The coalition would focus not only on the work of mainstream journal-ists. It would pay attention to the media content and practices of citizens, advocacy groups, and the so-called fifth estate—online critics of mainstream media. No one has a "get out of jail" pass when it comes to media ethics. The coalition's functions would include fact-checking, exposure of dubious sources, debate on media ethics, and the coverage of events, and all of this based on our best scientific and community knowledge. Crucial to the coali-tion is that it be *high-profile*—well-known to the public as a trusted place to check a media source and debate media policy. The hub of this network could be a school of journalism or a multidisciplinary center for democracy. Perhaps there should be several coalitions. Whatever its structure, it would be a place for macro-resistance, a center of gravity amid the information wars that engulf us.

Building the coalition would take imagination, leadership, and resources. Turf wars will flare. But there *are* resources out there. In North America, the Association for Education in Journalism and Mass Communication has thousands of members—instructors and students of media at dozens of uni-versities and colleges. There are numerous journalism societies and media foundations, and many civil society groups concerned about information, in the United States and abroad. Their macro-resistance would be greater if they joined in common cause.

Macro-resistance will require a better understanding of why citizens believe some media sources and not others. I believe that most polls on public confidence in news media are measuring the wrong thing—trust. Trust should be reserved for one's partner, spouse, close friends, and colleagues. Trust is personal and intense. I don't think our relations with media and other impersonal institutions amount to trust.[18] Further, I don't think we should trust any institution. We should grant them a temporary and earned credibility. We should try to understand and measure what I call "media reliance"—how people come to rely on certain media as more reliable than others. The public has a right to rely on journalists to provide accurate reports. Journalism must earn the public's reliance every day. The judgment that media sources are worthy of our reliance is tentative, fallible, and dependent on media performance over time.

We need to rethink *how* citizens evaluate media. No longer is it believing what one news anchor or one newspaper tells us, a passive, top-down form of trusting. Today, media evaluation is active and plural, as we compare stories from many sources and we share stories among us. We need a digital *epistemology* of media reliance grounded in actual media use. We should look at how people actually weigh claims from many sources. Then we can find ways to teach the critical assessment of information in a contested media environment, where no claim is published without challenge. If media literacy is defense from manipulation, then today we need more sophisticated means of defense.[19]

Media Ethics for Everyone

Macro-resistance will falter unless we make journalism ethics a more inclusive, important civic enterprise than debating decisions in newsrooms or teaching ethical case studies in journalism schools.

In a world where citizens create and absorb information and participate in news coverage, media ethics is, or should be, a media ethics for everyone. We need to start teaching about media early in public education. This includes information on who owns the media, how content is produced, and how to evaluate online data. We also need to teach a broad communication ethics that addresses cyberbullying and other issues beyond journalism. To this end, educators should design curricula for teaching media literacy and ethics, perhaps an international template sponsored by the United Nations. Meanwhile, in universities, we should end the segregation of ethics in schools of journalism; and within the journalism schools, end the further segregation of ethics into one course in the program. We should teach media ethics across faculties.

Macro-resistance entails better forms of public accountability for all who use media and have public impact. Accountability is usually defined in terms of professional journalism. Newsrooms are urged to articulate their media values, avoid conflicts of interest, provide accessible methods for public queries, explain controversial decisions, and follow firm correction policies with unstinting apologies and corrective action—showing how the problem will be avoided in the future. Over time, I think some of these features should become part of anyone's media use, not just big news media, and not just in journalism. If you are communicating with the public, you—whoever *you* are—owe concrete and effective accountability methods to your audience. Today, citizens cannot just blame professional journalists for bad media, since citizens are now players in the media sphere. They have responsibilities to support good media and adopt good media practices. They should expose themselves online to many viewpoints. They can, for example, use diversity-encouraging sites such as http://www.readacross theaisle.com.

Also, we need a public revolution in media ethics—the participation of publics in the formulation of standards and in the monitoring of media performance. Rather than talk of media "self-regulation," we should think about a public-directed "regulation" of media ethics. By regulation I mean not laws but ethical norms and processes that give the public a meaningful place in code revisions and debate on media issues. Maybe we should call it public-participatory ethics.

However, neither individuals nor professional journalists alone can detox the media sphere. For citizens, there is no individualistic, technological fix to the problem of macro-pollution, e.g., to simply download a better software. Government and society must take steps to address problems beyond what journalists can fix. Macro-resistance requires action from society in general. Technology experts need to protect electoral systems from hacks; our education system needs to prepare digital citizens. Governments can pressure social media to identify fake news, refuse accounts to racists, and be transparent about who pays for ads.

Global Patriots

I have done what I can to make love of country and objective journalism compatible. But this approach to patriotism is incomplete. Journalists who look inward to their nation's self-interest are less able to help the world address urgent global problems, from immigration to terrorism. Journalists need to transcend, to a significant degree, their reliance on tribal ways of thinking. Yet the latter is precisely the stance that extremists and nationalists shout from the rooftops: a suspicion of "them" and an aggressive desire to put one's country "first." This dog-eat-dog tribalism made some sense in the past, but now it may wipe our species off the face of this blue planet. We need a global ethics that helps us resolve disputes between nations and groups.

If this is true, we have reason to question the master-norm status of nation-based patriotism. Journalists should regard themselves as global patriots first, and national patriots second.

A global patriot bases her ethics on what I call moral globalism. Her primary values are cross-border principles of human flourishing and human rights, including the promotion of democratic institutions globally and working in good faith on global issues. Journalists see themselves as public communicators to the world, to a global public sphere. Global patriotism, then, is loyalty to the largest group possible—humanity. The global claim of patriotism is the claim that humanity makes on all of us. Globalism does not deny that people can have legitimate feelings of concern for their country or compatriots; it only insists that such feelings must not violate the nonparochial principles of human rights and other global values.

Global Identity

If journalists adopted moral globalism, they would alter their self-identity and alter their notion of who they serve. They would embrace three imperatives:

Act as global agents: Journalists should see themselves as agents of a global public sphere. The goal of their collective actions is a well-informed, diverse, and tolerant global "infosphere" that challenges the distortions of tyrants, the abuse of human rights, and the manipulation of information by special interests.

Serve the citizens of the world: The global journalist's primary loyalty is to the information needs of world citizens. Journalists should refuse to define themselves as attached primarily to factions, regions, or even countries. Serving the public means serving more than one's local readership or audience, or even the public of one's country.

Promote nonparochial understandings: The global journalist frames issues broadly and uses a diversity of sources and perspectives to promote a nuanced understanding of issues from an international perspective. Journalism should work against a narrow ethnocentrism or patriotism.

These imperatives have revolutionary import for journalism ethics. They change the journalist's self-conception from that of a citizen of one country to that of a global citizen serving humanity. They make the serving of humanity the primary allegiance of journalists. Journalists owe credible journalism to all potential readers of a global public sphere. Loyalty to humanity trumps other loyalties where they conflict. In addition, the aim of journalism becomes to promote the four levels of primary goods on a global scale. Journalists, as global citizens, seek the individual, social, political, and ethical dignity for humanity at large.

A global journalism ethic would alter basic concepts and ways of practice. In a global public sphere, if global journalism has a social contract, it is not with a particular public or society; instead, it seems to be something much more diffuse—a multi-society contract. The cosmopolitan journalist is a transnational public communicator who seeks the trust and credence of a global audience. Also, the ideal of objectivity in news coverage takes on an international sense. Traditionally, news objectivity asks journalists to avoid bias toward groups within one's own country. Global objectivity would discourage allowing bias toward one's country as a whole to distort reports on international issues. The ideas of accuracy and balance become enlarged to include reports with international sources and cross-cultural perspectives. Global journalism ethics asks journalists to be more conscious of how they frame major stories, how they set the international news agenda, and how they can spark violence in tense societies.

Global journalism ethics holds that transnational principles of human rights and social justice take precedence over personal interests and national interests when they conflict. When my country embarks on an unjust war against another country, I, as a journalist (or citizen), should say so. If I am a Canadian journalist and I learn that Canada is engaged in trading practices that condemn citizens of an African country to continuing, abject poverty, I should not hesitate to report the injustice. It is not a violation of any reasonable form of patriotism or citizenship to hold one's country to higher standards.

Finally, a global media ethics rethinks the role of patriotism. In a global world, nation-based patriotism should play a decreasing role in ethical reasoning about media issues. At best, nation-based forms of patriotism remain ethically permissible if they do not conflict with the demands of a global ethical flourishing.

A global ethics attitude limits parochial attachments in journalism by drawing a ring of broader ethical principles around them. When there is no conflict with global principles, journalists can report in ways that support local and national communities. They can practice their craft parochially. What is at issue is a gradual widening of basic editorial attitudes and standards—a widening of journalists' vision of their responsibilities.

Global journalism ethics is already an established area of inquiry, with books, conferences, and projects aimed at broadening journalism ethics.[20] For example, the Ethical Journalist Network (EJN) in London is helping journalists in different countries combat common problems. EJN has partnered with media organizations in different parts of the world to launch a campaign called "Turning the Page on Hate." It helped stage a meeting of African journalists in Kigali in April 2014 on the twentieth anniversary of the Rwandan genocide to educate journalists on how to avoid spreading hate speech. Subsequent workshops and training have been held in South Africa, Tanzania, Kenya, Nigeria and, Uganda. In June 2016, journalists and academics from China, Japan, South Korea, and the Hong Kong Baptist University met in Hong Kong to create an East Asia Media Forum. The forum produced a glossary of hate speech terms to avoid in reporting. The forum seeks to promote dialogue and media cooperation in a region where the media of each country attack each other, raising political tensions.

Conclusion

I hope that our troubled Internet-based media system will lead to a more reliable, better-protected, public communication system, although I lack the technical expertise to imagine its shape. Until such a system arrives, we should not simply complain about a polluted public sphere, extreme populists, or fake news. The situation is complex, but not hopeless.

Digital citizens can act in common cause. Do not be despondent. We are not powerless. But we will accomplish little unless we collaborate in moving both media and society in the direction of egalitarian democracy with healthier channels of communication.

Despite the daunting problems, it is possible to work together in social resistance to the corruption of our public sphere. We can, together, be digital, democratic citizens.

NOTES

1. Founders Online, "Letter from Thomas Jefferson to John Cartwright, 5 June 1824," https://founders.archives.gov/documents/Jefferson/98-01-02-4313.

2. See my *Invention of Journalism Ethics*, 2nd ed. (Montreal: McGill-Queen's University Press, 2015), 224–226.

3. Martha C. Nussbaum, "Patriotism and Cosmopolitanism," in *For Love of Country*, ed. Joshua Cohen (Boston: Beacon Press, 1996), 3–17.

4. Leo Tolstoy, *Writings on Civil Disobedience and Nonviolence* (Philadelphia: New Society), 142.

5. However, see Mitja Sardoc, ed., *Handbook of Patriotism* (Basel, Switzerland: Springer International Publishing, 2019).

6. Stephen Nathanson, *Patriotism, Morality, and Peace* (Lanham, MD: Rowman and Littlefield, 1993), 12.

7. Martha C. Nussbaum, *Political Emotions: Why Love Matters for Justice* (Cambridge, MA: Harvard University Press, 2013), 2, 208.

8. See Maurizio Viroli, *For Love of Country: An Essay on Patriotism and Nationalism* (Oxford: Clarendon Press, 1996).

9. Viroli, *For Love of Country*, 169.

10. Nathanson, *Patriotism, Morality and Peace*, 37–38.

11. José Ortega y Gasset, *Meditations on Quixote* (Urbana: University of Illinois Press, 2000), 105.

12. The phrase "blood and belonging" is from Michael Ignatieff, *Blood and Belonging: Journeys into the New Nationalism* (New York: Farrar, Straus and Giroux, 1993).

13. See Bernard Gert, *Common Morality* (Oxford: Oxford University Press, 2004).

14. For example, consider the disgraceful lack of justice handed out to the American soldiers who carried out the My Lai massacre of civilians in South Vietnam in 1968. Charges were laid against only one soldier, Col. William Calley, who, due to an intervention by President Nixon, spent only a few years in detention. Also, opinion polls at the time showed that many Americans thought that such actions were in some sense acceptable or part of war. Others resented the journalists who brought the murders to light. What concept of patriotism can justify such unpunished atrocities? None that could be justified by a moderate, democratic patriotism.

15. Thomas Scanlon, *What We Owe to Each Other* (Cambridge, MA: Harvard University Press, 1998), 20.

16. For a history of the epistemologies of journalism, see my "Epistemologies of Journalism," in *Handbook of Communication Science*, ed. Tim P. Vos (Berlin: Mouton de Gruyter, 2018), Vol. 19, 61–77.

17. I redefined journalism ethics globally in *Global Journalism Ethics* (Montreal: McGill-Queen's University Press, 2010) and *Radical Media Ethics* (Malden, MA: Wiley Blackwell, 2015).

18. See my "Digital Reliance: Public Confidence in Media in a Digital Era," *Georgetown Journal of International Affairs*, vol. 18, no. 3 (Fall 2017): 3–10.

19. Studies are already underway at the University of Missouri (https://www .rjionline.org/reporthtml.html) and at the Markkula Center for Applied Ethics (https://thetrustproject.org).

20. See Stephen J. A. Ward, ed., *Global Media Ethics: Problems and Perspectives* (Malden, MA: Wiley-Blackwell, 2013).

Bibliography

Adorno, Theodore, Else Frenkel-Brunswik, Daniel Levinson, and R. Nevitt Sanford. *The Authoritarian Personality*. New York: Harper and Brothers, 1950.

Albertazzi, Daniele, and Duncan McDonnell. *Twenty-First Century Populism: The Spectre of Western European Democracy*. Basingstoke, UK: Palgrave MacMillan, 2008.

Albrecht, James M. *Reconstructing Individualism: A Pragmatic Tradition from Emerson to Ellison*. New York: Fordham University, 2012.

Allen, David S. *Democracy, Inc.* Urbana: University of Illinois Press, 2005.

Alston, Richard. *Rome's Revolution: Death of the Republic and Birth of the Empire*. Oxford: Oxford University Press, 2015.

Arendt, Hannah. *The Origins of Totalitarianism*. New York: Harcourt, 1976.

Aristophanes. *The Knights*. Melbourne, Australia: Scribe Publishing, 2017.

Aristotle. *The Ethics of Aristotle*. Trans. J. A. K. Thomson. London: Penguin Books, 1976.

Aristotle. *Politics*. Trans. Carnes Lord. Chicago: University of Chicago Press, 2013.

Aristotle, "Rhetoric." Ed. Richard McKeon, *The Basic Works of Aristotle*, 1318–1451. New York: Modern Library, 2001.

Augustine. *City of God*. London: Penguin Books, 2003.

Baehr, Peter R. *Caesar and the Fading of the Roman World: A Study in Republicanism and Caesarism.* Piscataway, NJ: Transaction Publishers, 1998.

Bayle, Pierre. *Philosophical Commentary on These Words of the Gospel, Luke 14.23, 'Compel Them to Come In, That My House May Be Full.'* Online Library of Liberty. Liberty Fund, Inc. At: http://oll.libertyfund.org/titles/bayle-a-philosophical-commentary-on-these-words-of-the-gospel.

Bayle, Pierre. *Historical and Critical Dictionary: Selections.* Trans. Richard Popkin. Indianapolis, IN: Hackett Publishing, 1991.

Bentham, Jeremy. "Constitutional Code." In *The Collected Works of Jeremy Bentham.* Vol. I. Eds. Frederick Rosen and James H. Burns. Oxford: Clarendon Press, 1983.

Benton, Wilbourn, ed. *1787: Drafting the U.S. Constitution.* Vol. 1. College Station: Texas A&M University Press, 1986.

Berlin, Isaiah. *The Crooked Timber of Humanity.* London: Fantana Press, 1991.

Berlin, Isaiah. *Political Ideas in the Romantic Age.* Ed. Henry Hardy. Princeton, NJ: Princeton University Press, 2008.

Berlin, Isaiah. "Two Concepts of Liberty." In *Four Essays on Liberty*, 118–172. Oxford: Oxford University Press, 1969.

Biorcio, Roberto. "The Lega Nord and the Italian Media System." In *The Media and Neo-Populism: A Contemporary Comparative Analysis.* Eds. Gianpietro Mazzoleni, Julianne Stewart, and Bruce Horsfield. Westport, CT: Praeger Publishers, 2003.

Boardman, John, Jasper Griffen, and Oswyn Murray, eds. *The Oxford History of Greece and the Hellenistic World.* Oxford: Oxford University Press, 1991.

Bodin, Jean. *Six Books of the Commonwealth.* Cambridge, MA: Harvard University Press, 2014.

Bouwsma, William J. *John Calvin: A Sixteenth Century Portrait.* Oxford: Oxford University Press, 1989.

Boyer, Paul S., et al. *The Enduring Vision: A History of the American People.* Concise edition. Boston: Cengage Learning, 2012.

Bracher, Karl D. *The German Dictatorship: Origins, Structure, and Consequences of National Socialism.* London: Penguin, 1970.

Brinkley, Alan. *Voices of Protest: Huey Long, Father Coughlin & the Great Depression*. New York: Vantage Books, 1983.

Burke, Edmund. *Reflections on the Revolution in France*. Oxford: Oxford University Press, 2009.

Canovan, Margaret. *Populism* Chicago: Houghton Mifflin Harcourt, 1988.

Carey, James. *Communication as Culture: Essays on Media and Society*. London: Routledge, 1989.

Cassirer, Ernst, Paul O. Kristeller, and John H. Randall eds. *The Renaissance Philosophy of Man*. Chicago: University of Chicago Press, 1948.

Cicero. *The Republic and The Laws*. Trans. Niall Rudd. Oxford: Oxford University Press, 2008.

Cohen, Joshua. *The Arc of the Moral Universe and Other Essays*. Cambridge, MA: Harvard University Press, 2010.

Cooper, James Fenimore. "On Demagogues." In *The American Democrat*, 98–104. Cooperstown, NY: H. & E. Phinney, 1838.

Copleston, Frederick. "Aquinas: Political Theory." In *Medieval Philosophy*, Vol. 2, Part II, 132–255. New York: Image Books, 1962.

Dahl, Robert A. *Polyarchy: Participation and Opposition*. New Haven, CT: Yale University Press, 1971.

Darwall, Stephen ed. *Contractarianism/Contractualism*. Malden, MA: Blackwell Publishing, 2003.

Davis, John K. "Athenian Citizenship: The Descent Group and the Alternatives." *Classical Journal*. Vol. 73 (1977/8): 105–121.

de la Torre, Carlos. *The Promise and Perils of Populism*. Lexington: University Press of Kentucky, 2015.

D'Entreves, Alexander P. *The Medieval Contribution to Political Thought*. New York: The Humanities Press, 1959.

Dewey, John. *Democracy and Education*. New York: Createspace Independent Publishing, 2009.

Dewey, John. *Individualism Old and New*. New York: Capricorn Books, 1962.

Diderot, Denis. "Intolerance." In *The Encyclopedia of Diderot and d'Alembert*. Collaborative Translation Project. Trans. Philip Walen, Vol. 8, 843–844. Ann Arbor: University of Michigan Library, 2002.

Dworkin, Ronald. *Is Democracy Possible Here? Principles for a New Political Debate*. Princeton, NJ: Princeton University Press, 2006.

Dworkin, Ronald. *Sovereign Virtue: The Theory and Practice of Equality*. Cambridge, MA: Harvard University Press, 2000.

Engels, Frederick. *The Peasant War in Germany*. 3rd ed. New York: International Publishers, 2006.

Feinberg, Joel. *Offence to Others: The Moral Limits of the Criminal Law*. Oxford: Oxford University Press, 1987.

Fellman, David, "Constitutionalism." In *Dictionary of the History of Ideas: Studies of Selected Pivotal Ideas*. Ed. Philip P. Wiener, Vol. 1, 480–494. New York: Charles Scribner, 1974.

Fichte, Johann. *Addresses to the German Nation*. Whithorn, UK: Anodos Books, 2017.

Fisher, Max, and Amanda Taub. "How Does Populism Turn Authoritarian? Venezuela Is a Case in Point." *The New York Times* (April 1, 2017).

Foot, Michael, and Isaac Kramnic, eds. *The Thomas Paine Reader*. London: Penguin, 1987.

Formisano, Ronald P. *For the People: American Populist Movements from the Revolution to the 1850s*. Chapel Hill: University of North Carolina Press, 2012.

Freeden, Michael. *Ideology: A Very Short Introduction*. Oxford: Oxford University Press, 2003.

Freeden, Michael, Lyman Tower Sargent, and Marc Stears, eds. *The Oxford Handbook of Political Ideologies*. Oxford: Oxford University Press, 2013.

Freeman, Kathleen. *Greek City-States*. New York: Macdonald & Co., 1950.

Freud, Sigmund. "The Disillusionment of the War." In *Civilization, Society, and Religion*. Ed. Albert Dickson, Vol. 12, 61–76. London: Penguin, 1991.

Freud, Sigmund. "The Herd Instinct." In *Civilization, Society, and Religion*. Ed. Albert Dickson, Vol. 12, 148–160. London: Penguin, 1991.

Fritzsche, Peter. *Rehearsals for Fascism: Populism and Political Mobilization in Weimar Germany*. Oxford: Oxford University Press, 1990.

Fromm, Erich. *Escape From Freedom*. New York, Avon Books, 1972.

Fuchs, Christian. *Digital Demagogue: Authoritarian Capitalism in the Age of Trump and Twitter*. London: Pluto Books, 2018.

Gamson, William A. "The 1987 Distinguished Lecture: A Constructionist Approach to Mass Media and Public Opinion." *Symbolic Interaction*. Vol. 11, No. 2 (1988): 161–174.

Gert, Bernard. *Common Morality*. Oxford: Oxford University Press, 2004.

Gewirth, Alan. *Marsilius of Padua: The Defender of Peace*. New York: Columbia University Press, 1964.

Ghosh, Dipayan, and Ben Scott. *Digital Deceit: The Technologies behind Precision Propaganda on the Internet*. Washington: New America, 2018. At: https://www.newamerica.org/documents/2068/digital-deceit-final.pdf.

Glover, Jonathan. *Humanity: A Moral History of the 20th Century*. New Haven, CT: Yale University Press, 2012.

Goldie, Mark. "Introduction." In John Locke, *Two Treatises of Government*. London: J. M. Dent, 1996.

Goodwyn, Lawrence. *Democratic Promise: The Populist Moment in America*. New York: Oxford University Press, 1976.

Greene, Joshua. *Moral Tribes: Emotion, Reason and the Gap Between Us and Them*. New York: Penguin Books, 2014.

Gutmann, Amy, and Dennis Thompson. *Why Deliberative Democracy?* Princeton, NJ: Princeton University Press, 2004.

Habermas, Jürgen. *Between Facts and Norms*. Trans. William Rehg. Cambridge, MA: MIT Press, 1998.

Habermas, Jürgen. *The Structural Transformation of the Public Sphere*. Trans. Thomas Burger. Cambridge, UK: Polity Press, 1992.

Haidt, Jonathan. *The Righteous Mind*. New York: Pantheon, 2012.

Held, David. *Models of Democracy*. 3rd ed. Cambridge, UK: Polity Press, 2006.

Herodotus. *The Histories*. Trans. Robin Waterfield. Oxford: Oxford University Press, 1998.

Hill, Christopher. *The World Turned Upside Down: Radical Ideas During the English Revolution*. London: Penguin Books, 1991.

Hitler, Adolf. *Mein Kampf*. Trans. Ralph Manheim. Boston: Houghton Mifflin, 1943.

Hobbes, Thomas. *Leviathan*. London: Penguin Books, 1968.

Hofstadter, Richard. *The Age of Reform*. New York: Vintage Books, 1955.

Hofstadter, Richard. *The Paranoid Style in American Politics and Other Essays*. New York: Vintage, 1967.

Hooker, Richard. *Of the Laws of Ecclesiastical Polity*. London: Sidgwick and Jackson, 1976.

Howe, Paul, "Eroding Norms and Democratic Deconsolidations." *Journal of Democracy*, Vol. 28, Issue 4 (October 2017), 15–29.

Ignatieff, Michael. *Blood and Belonging: Journeys into the New Nationalism*. New York: Farrar, Straus and Giroux, 1993.

Innis, Harold. *Empire and Communications*. Toronto: Dundurn Press, 2007.

Innocent III. "On the Misery of Man." In *Two Views of Man*. Ed. and trans. Bernard Murchland, 1–60. New York: Gale Ecco, 1966.

Jones, Arnold. *Athenian Democracy*. Oxford: Oxford University Press, 1957.

Kazin, Michael. "How Can Donald Trump and Bernie Sanders Both Be 'Populist'?" *New York Times Magazine* (March 22, 2016).

Kazin, Michael. *The Populist Persuasion: An American History*. Ithaca, NY: Cornell Paperbacks, 1998.

Keen, Maurice. *The Penguin History of Medieval Europe*. London: Penguin Books, 1991.

Kelly, John. *A Short History of Western Legal Theory*. Oxford: Clarendon Press, 1992.

Kingwell, Mark. *Unruly Voices*. Ottawa: Biblioasis, 2012.

Larson, Allan Louis. *Southern Demagogues: A Study in Charismatic Leadership*. Ann Arbor, MI: University Microfilms, 1964.

Lenin, Vladimir. *Where to Begin?* Moscow: Foreign Languages Publishing Series, Vol. 5, 13–34, 1961.

Levitsky, Steven, and Daniel Ziblatt. *How Democracies Die.* New York: Crown Publishing Group, 2018.

Lewis, Anthony. *Freedom for the Thought That We Hate.* New York: Basic Books, 2007.

Lippmann, Walter. *Public Opinion.* New York: Macmillan, 1922.

Lipset, Seymour Martin. *Political Man: The Social Basis of Politics.* Garden City, NY: Doubleday, 1963.

Locke, John. *A Letter Concerning Toleration.* Mineola, NY: Dover Publications, 2002.

Locke, John. *Two Treatises of Government.* Ed. Mark Goldie. London: J. M. Dent, 1996.

Lovejoy, Arthur O. *The Great Chain of Being.* Cambridge, MA: Harvard University Press, 1978.

Lowndes, Joe, and Dorian Warren. "Occupy Wall Street: A Twenty-First Century Populist Movement?" *Dissent* magazine (October 21, 2011).

Lukacs, John. *Democracy and Populism: Fear and Hatred.* New Haven, CT: Yale University Press, 2006.

Luther, Martin. "Against the Murderous, Thieving Hordes of Peasants." In *Luther's Works*, Eds. Jaroslav Pelikan and Hilton C. Oswald. 55 vols. St. Louis and Philadelphia: Concordia Publishing House and Fortress Press, 1955–1986.

Luther, Martin. "On Temporal Authority: To What Extent It Should Be Obeyed." In *Luther's Works.* Ed. Walther Brandt, trans. J. J. Schindel, Vol. 45, 75–129. Philadelphia: Open Court, 1962.

Luthin, Reinhard H. *American Demagogues.* Boston: Beacon Press, 1954.

Mackensen, Heinz F. "Historical Interpretation and Luther's Role in the Peasant Revolt," *Concordia Theological Monthly.* Vol. 35 (1965): 197–209.

Madison, James. *Notes of Debates in the Federal Convention of 1787.* New York: Norton, 1987.

Maiolo, Francesco. *Medieval Sovereignty: Marsilius of Padua and Bartolus of Saxoferrato*. Delft, The Netherlands: Eburon Academic Publishers, 2007.

Maritain, Jacques. *The Angelic Doctor*. Trans. J. F. Scanlan. New York: Sheed and Ward, 1931.

Maritain, Jacques. *Christianity and Democracy*. New York: Arno Press, 1980.

Maritain, Jacques. *Christianity and Democracy and The Rights of Man and Natural Law*. San Francisco: Ignatius Press, 2011.

Marsilius of Padua. *The Defender of the Peace*. Cambridge, UK: Cambridge University Press, 2005.

Marx, Karl. "The Elections in England—Tories and Whigs." *New York Tribune* (August 21, 1852).

Marx, Karl, and Friedrich Engels. *The Communist Manifesto*. Oxford: Oxford University Press, 2008.

May, Rollo. *Man's Search for Himself*. New York, Delta Publishing, 1953.

Mayer, David N. *The Constitutional Thought of Thomas Jefferson*. Charlottesville: University of Virginia Press, 1994.

McMahon, Christopher. *Reasonable Disagreement: A Theory of Political Morality*. Cambridge, UK: Cambridge University Press, 2009.

Michell, Humfrey. *Sparta*. Cambridge, UK: Cambridge University Press, 1964.

Mill, John Stuart. *On Liberty and the Subjection of Women*. London: Penguin Classics, 2006.

Morstein-Marx, Robert. *Mass Oratory and Political Power in the Late Roman Republic*. Cambridge, UK: Cambridge University Press, 2003.

Mossberger, Karen, Caroline Tolbert, and Ramona McNeal. *Digital Citizenship: The Internet, Society and Participation*. Cambridge, MA: MIT Press, 2008.

Mosse, George L. *The Crisis of German Ideology: Intellectual Origins of the Third Reich*. New York: Grosset and Dunlap, 1964.

Mudde, Cas. "The Populist Zeitgeist." *Government and Opposition*. Vol. 39, No. 4 (2004): 542–563.

Mudde, Cas. "The Problem with Populism." *The Guardian* (February 17, 2015).

Mudde, Cas, and Cristóbal R. Kaltwasser. "Populism." In *The Oxford Handbook of Political Ideologies*. Eds. Michael Freeden, Lyman Tower Sargent, and Marc Stears, 493–512. New York: Oxford University Press, 2013.

Müller, Jan-Werner. *What is Populism?* London: Penguin Random House, 2017.

Munro, André. "Populism." In *Encyclopedia Britannica*. At: https://www.britannica .com/topic/populism. Last modified March 15, 2013. Accessed November 13, 2017.

Nathanson, Stephen. *Patriotism, Morality, and Peace*. Lanham, MD: Rowman and Littlefield, 1993.

North, Douglass, John Wallis, and Barry Weingast. *Violence and Social Orders: A Conceptual Framework for Interpreting Recorded Human History*. Cambridge, UK: Cambridge University Press, 2009.

Nugent, Walter. *The Tolerant Populists: Kansas Populism and Nativism*. Chicago: University of Chicago Press, 2013.

Nussbaum, Martha C. "Patriotism and Cosmopolitanism." In *For Love of Country*. Ed. Joshua Cohen, 3–17. Boston: Beacon Press, 1996.

Nussbaum, Martha C. *Political Emotions: Why Love Matters for Justice*. Cambridge, MA: Harvard University Press, 2013.

Nussbaum, Martha C. *Upheavals of Thought: The Intelligence of Emotions*. Cambridge, UK: Cambridge University Press, 2001.

Ober, Josiah. *Mass and Elite in Democratic Athens: Rhetoric, Ideology, and the Power of the People*. Princeton, NJ: Princeton University Press, 1989.

Ober, Josiah. *The Rise and Fall of Classical Greece*. Princeton, NJ: Princeton University Press, 2015.

Ochoa-Espejo, Paulina, "Power to Whom? The People between Procedure and Populism." In *The Promise and Perils of Populism: Global Perspectives*. Ed. Carlos de la Torre, 59–90. Lexington: University of Kentucky Press, 2015.

O'Leary, Kevin. *Saving Democracy: A Plan for Real Representation in America*. Stanford, CA: Stanford University Press, 2006.

Ortega y Gasset, José. *Meditations on Quixote*. Urbana: University of Illinois Press, 2000.

Paine, Thomas. *The Thomas Paine Reader*. London: Penguin Books, 1987.

Pariser, Eli. *The Bubble Filter: What the Internet Is Hiding from You*. New York: Penguin Books, 2012.

Peterson, Merrill, ed. *The Portable Thomas Jefferson*. New York: Penguin Books, 1977.

Petrarch, Francesco. "On His Own Ignorance and That of Many Others." Trans. Hans Nachod. In *The Renaissance Philosophy of Man*. Ed. Ernst Cassirer, Paul Oskar Kristeller, and John Hermann Randall Jr., 47–133. Chicago: University of Chicago Press, 1948.

Pettit, Philip. *Republicanism: A Theory of Freedom and Government*. 2nd ed. Cambridge, UK: Cambridge University Press, 1999.

Philip, Thomas ed. *Thomas Paine: Rights of Man, Common Sense, and Other Political Writings*. New York: Oxford University Press, 1995.

Pinker, Steven. *The Better Angels of Our Nature*. New York: Viking, 2011.

Plato. "The Apology." In *The Complete Works*, 17–36. Ed. John M. Cooper. Indianapolis, IN: Hackett Publishing, 1997.

Plato. "Crito." In *The Complete Works*, 37–48. Ed. John M. Cooper. Indianapolis, IN: Hackett Publishing, 1997.

Plato. "The Laws." In *The Complete Works*, 1318–1616. Ed. John M. Cooper. Indianapolis, IN: Hackett Publishing, 1997.

Plato. *The Republic*. Trans. Francis Cornford. New York: Oxford University Press, 1968.

Polybius. *Histories*. Oxford: Oxford University Press, 2010.

Popkin, Jeremy D. *Revolutionary News: The Press in France, 1789-1799*. Durham, NC: Duke University Press, 1990.

Rawls, John. *Political Liberalism*. New York: Columbia University Press, 1993.

Rawls, John. *A Theory of Justice*. 12th Impression. Oxford: Oxford University Press, 1992.

Rosenstone, Steven J, Roy L. Behr, and Edward H. Lazarus. *Third Parties in America*. Princeton, NJ: Princeton University Press, 1984.

Rousseau, Jean-Jacques. "Discourse on the Sciences and Arts." In *The First and Second Discourses*. Ed. Victor Gourevitch. New York: Harper Torchbooks, 1990.

Rousseau, Jean-Jacques. *The Social Contract*. Trans. Maurice Cranston. London: Penguin Books, 1968.

Ruzza, Carlo. *Re-inventing the Italian Right: Territorial Politics, Populism, and 'Post-Facism.'* London: Routledge, 2009.

Sardoc, Mitja. *Handbook of Patriotism*. Basel, Switzerland: Springer International Publishing. Forthcoming 2019.

Saward, Michael. "The Representative Claim." *Contemporary Political Theory*. Vol. 5, No. 3 (2006): 297–318.

Scanlon, Thomas. *What We Owe to Each Other*. Cambridge, MA: Harvard University Press, 1998.

Schlesinger Jr., Arthur. "An Impressive Mandate and the Meaning of Jacksonianism." In *Andrew Jackson: A Profile*. Ed. Charles Sellers, 44–65. New York: Hill & Wang, 1971.

Sherrill, Robert. "American Demagogues." Review of Alan Brinkley, *Voices of Protest*, in *The New York Times* (July 11, 1982).

Shirer, William. *The Rise and Fall of the Third Reich: A History of Nazi Germany*. New York: Exeter Books, 1987.

Signer, Michael. *Demagogue: The Fight to Save Democracy from Its Worst Enemies*. New York: Palgrave Macmillan, 2009.

Skinner, Quentin. *The Foundations of Modern Political Thought*. Cambridge, UK: Cambridge University Press, 1978.

Skinner, Quentin. *Liberty before Liberalism*. Cambridge, UK: Cambridge University Press, 1998.

Smith, Anthony. *The Newspaper: An International History*. London: Thames & Hudson, 1979.

Southwood, Nicholas. *Contractualism and the Foundations of Morality*. Oxford: Oxford University Press, 2013.

Starkey, Marion L. *A Little Rebellion*. New York: Knopf, 1955.

Stern, Fritz. *The Politics of Cultural Despair: A Study in the Rise of Germanic Ideology*. Berkeley: University of California Press, 1961.

Stockton, David. *The Classical Athenian Democracy*. Oxford: Oxford University Press, 1990.

Strauss, Leo. *Natural Right and History*. Chicago: University of Chicago Press, 1999.

Strauss, Leo. "Plato." In *An Introduction to Political Philosophy: Ten Essays by Leo Strauss*. Detroit, MI: Wayne State University Press, 1975.

Strayer, Joseph. *On the Medieval Origins of the Modern State*. Princeton, NJ: Princeton University Press, 2016.

Szatmary, David P. *Shays' Rebellion: The Making of an Agrarian Insurrection*. Amherst: University of Massachusetts Press, 1980.

Thorley, John. *Athenian Democracy*. 2nd ed. New York: Routledge, 2005.

Thucydides. *The History of the Peloponnesian War*. Trans. Martin Hammond. Oxford: Oxford University Press, 2009.

Tocqueville, Alexis de. *Democracy in America*. New York: Mentor, 1984.

Tolstoy, Leo. *Writings on Civil Disobedience and Nonviolence*. Philadelphia: New Society, 1976.

Tralau, Johan ed. *Thomas Hobbes and Carl Schmitt*. London: Routledge, 2011.

Viroli, Maurizio. *For Love of Country: An Essay on Patriotism and Nationalism*. Oxford: Clarendon Press, 1996.

Volkov, Solomon. *The Magical Chorus: A History of Russian Culture from Tolstoy to Solzhenitsyn*. Trans. Antonina W. Bouis. New York: Vintage Books, 2009.

Waldron, Jeremy. *The Harm in Hate Speech*. Cambridge, MA: Harvard University Press, 2012.

Ward, Stephen J. A. "Digital Reliance: Public Confidence in Media in a Digital Era." *Georgetown Journal of International Affairs*. Vol. 18, No. 3 (Fall 2017): 3–10.

Ward, Stephen J. A. "Epistemologies of Journalism." In *Handbook of Communication Science*. Ed. Tim P. Vos, Vol. 19, 61–77. Berlin: Mouton de Gruyter, 2018.

Ward, Stephen J. A. *Ethics and the Media: An Introduction*. Cambridge, UK: Cambridge University Press, 2011.

Ward, Stephen J. A. *Global Journalism Ethics*. Montreal: McGill-Queen's University Press, 2010.

Ward, Stephen J. A., ed. *Global Media Ethics: Problems and Perspectives*. Malden, MA: Wiley-Blackwell, 2013.

Ward, Stephen J. A. *The Invention of Journalism Ethics*. 2nd ed. Montreal: McGill-Queen's University Press, 2015.

Ward, Stephen J. A. *Objectively Engaged Journalism*. Montreal: McGill-Queen's University Press. Forthcoming.

Ward, Stephen J. A. *Radical Media Ethics*. Malden, MA: Wiley Blackwell, 2015.

Ward, Stephen J. A. "Thomas Hobbes: The Ethics of Social Order." In *Ethical Communication: Moral Stances in Human Dialogue*. Ed. Clifford Christians and John Merrill, 158–164. Columbia: University of Missouri Press, 2009.

Wardle, Claire, and Hossein Derakhshan. *Information Disorder*. Strasbourg, France: Council of Europe Report, 2017. At: https://rm.coe.int/information-disorder -report-november-2017/1680764666.

Warren, Robert Penn. *All the King's Men*. New York: Mariner Books, 2001.

Webb, James. *The Occult Establishment*. La Salle, IL: Open Court, 1976.

Weyland, Kurt. "Why Latin America is becoming Less Democratic." *The Atlantic* (July 15, 2013).

Weyland, Kurt, Carlos de la Torre, and Miriam Kornblith. "Latin America's Authoritarian Drift." *Journal of Democracy*. Vol. 24, No. 3 (July 2013): 18–32.

Wicker, Tom. *Shooting Star: The Brief Arc of Joe McCarthy*. New York: Harcourt, 2006.

Wilentz, Sean. *Andrew Jackson*. New York: Times Book, 2005.

Wiseman, Timothy P. "Roman History and the Ideological Vacuum." In *Remembering the Roman People: Essays on Late-Republican Politics and Literature*. Oxford: Oxford University Press, 2009.

Zoch, Paul A. *Ancient Rome: An Introductory History*. Norman: University of Oklahoma Press, 1998.

Index

Note: Figures and tables are indicated by "f" or "t," respectively, following page numbers.

www.ingramcontent.com/pod-product-compliance
Lightning Source LLC
Chambersburg PA
CBHW030648270326
41929CB00007B/266